ADVANCE PRAISE FOR
CLEARED FOR TAKEOFF

"*Cleared for Takeoff* is a powerful reflection of a young Black woman who dared to claim space where there was none and who, in the face of tragedy and transformation, found her way back to herself. This book moved me deeply. It is a story of purpose, perseverance, and the enduring power of belief."

—KAMILAH FORBES,
former executive producer of the Apollo Theater

"*Cleared for Takeoff* is the deeply personal story of Captain Nia Gilliam, a pilot who navigated both the heights of a glass-ceiling-shattering career and the turbulence of a world in crisis. From the chilling silence of the Newark runway on 9/11 to Gilliam's courageous decision to step away from the pilot's seat for her own battle for survival, her journey defines resilience. A must-read memoir about purpose, identity, and the strength required to soar when the world feels grounded."

—AMY MARINO SPOWART,
president and CEO of the National Aeronautic Association

"For the Black women who followed her as pilots, and for all of us in aviation and beyond who know that competence and passion come in so many different forms, you will be inspired, as am I, by Nia and her story."

—GREG PRINCIPATO,
president of the FAI–World Air Sports Federation

CLEARED FOR TAKEOFF

A PILOT'S MEMOIR OF PURPOSE AND RESILIENCE AFTER 9/11

CAPTAIN NIA GILLIAM

STOREHOUSE VOICES
NEW YORK

Storehouse Voices
An imprint of the Crown Publishing Group
A division of Penguin Random House LLC
1745 Broadway
New York, NY 10019
storehousevoices.com
penguinrandomhouse.com

Library of Congress Cataloging-in-Publication Data is available upon request.

Hardcover ISBN 979-8-217-08746-4
Ebook ISBN 979-8-217-08747-1

Editor: Jennifer Baker
Production editor: Patricia Shaw
Text designer: Aubrey Khan
Production: Heather Williamson
Copy editor: Rob Sternitzky
Proofreaders: Navorn Johnson, Alissa Fitzgerald
Publicist: Jennifer Valentin
Marketer: Mason Eng
Publisher: Tamira Chapman
Associate publisher: Porscha Burke
Editorial director: Jennifer Baker
Publishing associate: Isabela Alcantara
Editorial assistant: Camryn Johnson

Manufactured in the United States of America

1st Printing

First Edition

The authorized representative in the EU for product safety and compliance is Penguin Random House Ireland, Morrison Chambers, 32 Nassau Street, Dublin D02 YH68, Ireland, https://eu-contact.penguin.ie.

For every woman who ever doubted herself but climbed anyway.

For those who lost their lives on September 11, 2001, and for all whose lives were forever changed that day. I carry you with me in every takeoff and every landing.

AUTHOR'S NOTE

This memoir is drawn from my memory and from journal entries, and I've adhered to the emotional truth while doing my best to faithfully represent and honor the people and experiences depicted within. In the interest of narrative clarity and to protect privacy, some names, identifying details, timelines, and locations have been changed.

CLEARED FOR TAKEOFF

ONE

At 5:00 A.M. the shriek of the hotel alarm clock jolted me awake. By 5:30, I needed to be clearheaded, standing up straight, and reporting for work at Boston Logan. That kind of get-up-and-be-ready was no great challenge for me. I knew what it meant to snap awake from a dead sleep, then to pounce into readiness like a soldier. When I was eighteen, I'd enlisted in the Illinois Air National Guard and attended basic military training to help pay for college. Every morning, we woke up to reveille, that undeniable, twenty-one-second military tune, and by the time the bugler hit the last note, I had to be dressed, downstairs, and in formation underneath the barrack. After being tardy once—for which I was reprimanded, then punished with push-ups, planks, and laps around the barrack—I vowed never to be late again. From then on, I showered at night and slipped into bed wearing a bra, panties, and black socks, ready to jump into my uniform and dash downstairs at the first sound of the bugle. This girl forevermore knew the meaning of ready.

Da, da da-da-da

Da, da da-da-da . . .

Now, with that memory blaring in my head, I ran into the hotel bathroom to splash water on my face and brush my teeth. My daily uniform was a perfectly pressed white collared shirt, navy-blue pants and blazer—shoulder epaulets and wings already in place. I glanced at the alarm clock. Five minutes to catch the hotel's five-fifteen shuttle to the airport. After a last check of the room, I snatched my pilot's hat from my luggage handle, then rolled my suitcase out the door and into the elevator.

I dashed across the lobby, out the front door, and into the van, where James, my favorite driver, smiled and said, "Good morning, Captain."

James was a kind-eyed Black man, probably in his late sixties. He was cheery no matter the hour, and he always called me "Captain," knowing perfectly well I was still a first officer. I'd told him I was twenty-five, only a year and a half into my career as an airline pilot, and that I had at least another year to go before I'd be eligible for the training to upgrade me to captain. But James wasn't having it.

"You're the first Black woman pilot I've ever met," he said, his face beaming with the kind of pride I'd seen on my mother's face many times before—when I gave the welcome address at my eighth-grade graduation, when I was elected class president, when I received my high school diploma at the end of my junior year, and when I earned my private pilot's license just six months after my eighteenth birthday. "You're the captain. Captain Nia."

Returning his smile, I said, "*Captain* has a nice ring to it. Good morning."

I was the only Black female pilot at my airline. In the United States, there were only fifteen of us across all airlines, so I graciously accepted James's term of admiration. I loved my job. Every time I stepped into my uniform, I lived the dream I'd had since I was ten. I'd been a laser-focused kid, obsessed with flying machines and the idea of one day being a pilot. Flying wasn't just something I'd wanted to do. It was something I talked about, fantasized about, read about, and wrote about. I breathed it. And in time it became who I was.

I still lived with my parents in a suburb of Chicago because, at the time, regional airline pilots made only $17 per hour. The wage was so low, I didn't know when I'd be able to live on my own, but I worked hard, spent little, and saved every cent I could. When I was scheduled to operate an early flight from my base, I commuted to Boston the night before. It was a regular routine for me. That morning was day one of a four-day trip, and the assigned captain was Shye Gilad. I was always excited to see Shye's name on my schedule. We'd flown together many times, and I used those flights as learning opportunities. He was the type of captain I wanted to emulate: laid-back and easygoing, but also a consummate professional who strictly followed company procedures. During a low-threat environment, or cruise altitude as we call it, it was typical of him to sing a verse from a song he'd written and performed with his rock band. But as soon as we began descent, he would lock into focus with the precision of a surgeon. I couldn't imagine a better captain to observe and support as first officer.

I entered the crew room, a large space enclosed by white walls, except for the storefront windows that faced the ramp area, where aircraft sat parked. I tiptoed past a flight attendant asleep on the sofa and assumed he was a commuter like me. Probably got off duty late the previous night and missed his flight home. Then I strolled over to the industrial table, where ten computer terminals lined the back wall, and logged into the crew tracking system to notify the company I was officially reporting for duty at 0530 hours.

Shye walked in and greeted me with a warm smile, and with that cool, raspy voice of his, he asked, "You want anything from Starbucks?"

Like most pilots, the blood that ran through my veins was Arabica coffee bean, black. "Aw, thanks. I'll have a caramel macchiato, extra caramel."

He grabbed our flight plan paperwork off the table. "I'll get our coffee and meet you on the plane."

I walked out the door of the crew room to the ramp level, where the thirty-two-passenger Dornier 328JET was parked. Its door folded down into a built-in stairway at the forward left side of the fuselage. Affectionately called the "DoJet," we pilots nicknamed it the "SlowJet." It climbed like a rocket—four thousand to five thousand feet per minute, outpacing even the big jets—but once it leveled off, it slowed to a crawl. It was like driving a Porsche in the way it handled curves like a dream, but then it topped out at the speed of a Mini Cooper. Other jets passed us left and right, but for me, the DoJet wasn't about keeping up. It was about the feel of it. On takeoff, the nose lifted with such eagerness it pressed me back in my seat with a force that made me grin. Flying the DoJet always reminded me why I loved to fly. The climb gave me a rush, the handling gave me confidence, and when I set it down smoothly on a short runway, I felt I'd really accomplished something. Passengers on a DoJet probably noticed the plane's smooth ride, but in the flight deck, the experience was much more complex. It was pure joy.

I dropped my suitcase by the nose of the plane. One of my first responsibilities was to make sure the aircraft was airworthy, so I checked around the jet for signs of oil leaks, then examined the tires, wings, and sensors, looking for obstructions or signs of damage. I did a full circle, and when I was satisfied all was in order, I walked up the stairs, stored my luggage in the forward cabin closet, climbed into the flight deck, and sat in the right seat.

As part of his captain duties, Shye initiated a crew briefing with our flight attendant, Deborah, and me to review standard performance expectations and procedures in case of an emergency. Once the crew brief was completed, Deborah gave me the thumbs-up, signaling she was ready for the passengers. I called flight ops over the radio: "Delta Ops, Flight 6413 is ready to board."

As the passengers boarded, I completed my interior preflight check of the instruments and reviewed the flight plan route, while Shye picked up the handheld mic for our welcome: "Good morning, ladies and gentlemen. From the flight deck, this is your captain, Shye Gilad. On behalf of myself and First Officer Nia Gilliam, I'd like to welcome you aboard Delta Connection Flight 6213 from Boston to Newark." He went on, and I finished organizing my navigation charts. Then, as Shye and I discussed our assigned route to Newark, Deborah peeked her head into the flight deck and said, "The cabin is ready" and closed the door. Those words meant the passengers were settled and the flight attendant was ready, so it was time. Soon, we'd be in the air. I took a big breath and let it out slowly. With every flight came the same rush I'd felt my first time flying a plane. It never got old, never became routine. Every time I went up in the air, the exhilaration was the same as in those early days when I'd first experienced taking charge of a plane. And every flight reminded me I'd made it to the place I'd dreamed of.

Logan Airport sits in Boston Harbor just off the Atlantic, and the wind blowing from the ocean can make takeoff and landing challenging, but on this day there was barely a breeze. I looked out the flight deck window and watched the sun rise over the water and into a sky that promised to be bright blue. I was working with a crew I liked and trusted, and taxi and takeoff had gone smoothly. September 11 was already turning out to be a great day to fly.

We landed in Newark, parked at our gate on time at 7:45 A.M., and expected to be on the ground for forty-five minutes before flying back to Boston. With a schedule like that, the captain and first officer usually alternated pilot duties for each leg, but today we were scheduled to fly five legs: two Boston/Newark round trips, followed by a Newark overnight. We agreed Shye would fly the first round trip, while I'd work the radios, then we'd switch roles for the second round trip, and for the Newark overnight, we'd flip a coin.

Newark Airport wasn't a popular destination among fellow crew members. It was nicknamed "Sewerk" because of its close proximity to both LaGuardia and JFK, where the surrounding airspace was usually congested. Ground operations were often just as congested because of the high volume of international and domestic flights, and that often led to delays that made for an extra-long workday. Today, I had the sense there would be no delays.

As we waited for passengers to board, I looked out across the clear, royal-blue Newark sky and spent a few minutes thinking about things I had to be grateful for. I was young and healthy, my parents were alive and well, and I had a career I loved, one that involved doing important work that made it possible for countless people to visit loved ones, conduct important business, and see parts of the world they'd dreamed of. My heart was full.

We welcomed our new passengers onboard Delta Connection Flight 6214, completed our checks, and received our clearance to

Boston. At eight-thirty, we pushed back from the gate on instruction from a ramp tower controller, a critical team member in the air traffic system who directs planes around a busy airport like a traffic cop keeps cars safe and orderly on a busy roadway. Then we heard "Blueridge 6214, due to flow control, contact Ground Metering for taxi instructions."

Our engines were running, and we were ready to go, but we were being delayed for flow control. Flow control is like using an on-ramp traffic light to pace the cars entering a freeway. Traffic jams in the sky are usually caused by bad weather or airport closures, but this was a perfectly clear Tuesday morning. I'd expect a lot of traffic on a busy Friday evening or early Monday morning, but why today?

After several aircraft ahead of us were given taxi instructions, Ground Control gave us clearance. I repeated the instructions back to the ground controller, and we started moving. Then the ground controller continued. "Blueridge 6214, hold short of taxiway November to let a UPS 767 go in front of you, then follow behind the Continental 737 to runway zero-four left. You are number ten in line for departure."

We continued taxiing slowly to the runway, listening to Ground Control on one radio and Newark Tower on the other. That's when I heard the voice of a pilot from another flight waiting to depart. "Do you know anything about the smoke coming out of the World Trade Center?"

Smoke coming out of the World Trade Center?

Air Traffic Control didn't respond immediately. The pause seemed like a long one, but eventually a controller came over the air. "Yeah, we see it. We're looking into it." Then, following standard protocol, the Tower controller handed that pilot's departing flight off to Departure Control, signifying they were officially en route.

I was on the right side of the plane, so I couldn't see Manhattan. Shye looked out his window as we inched closer to the runway. Then in a flat voice he said, "Nia, you should see this."

I unclicked my seat belt and pulled off my shoulder harness. Kneeling on my seat, I leaned over the thrust lever quadrant. "I can't see anything."

Shye adjusted his seat back to give me more room. "Do you see it now?"

I tried to stretch farther, but our high wing created a blind spot. "No." I sat back in my seat, readjusted my seat belt and shoulder harness. "How does it look?"

He answered in a low voice, almost as if he were talking to himself. "Not good." Then, still looking out his window, he said slightly louder, "You'll see when we get on the runway."

Another pilot came over the radio. "Tower, any word on what's happening with the World Trade Center?"

Air traffic controllers are masters of lean speech. There are no communicators I know of who are more efficient or effective, and whenever we heard from Tower, the message was always crisp and clear. But what came next was unlike anything I'd heard on the job since the day I became a pilot. "We know but would rather not say over the radio at this time."

Shye and I looked at each other, and his expression matched my confusion. Controllers *always* told us what was going on. We were all on the same team. For them to withhold information implied they knew something that would be detrimental for us to know. But what?

I said, "Maybe a plane hit one of the towers. Why else would ATC not tell a bunch of pilots about a fire in a building across the river?"

Shye stayed quiet, so I wasn't sure if he hadn't heard me or disagreed with me. I continued to theorize. "You know, those small planes that tour up and down the Hudson? Maybe there was an accident. Maybe one crashed."

Shye thought for several seconds, then said, "It could be another Oklahoma bombing."

I shrugged. We were both just guessing, and sliding down into a dungeon of frightening scenarios wasn't going to get this plane in the air. It was time to shove dark possibilities aside and focus on the job. We were now number two in line for takeoff. I made the PA announcement. "Ladies and gentlemen, we are next in line for departure. Flight attendant, prepare for takeoff."

Newark Tower cleared the Continental aircraft in front of us onto the runway. "Blueridge 6214, hold short of runway zero-four left."

Shye inched the plane even closer to the runway. "Nia, wait till you see this smoke. It's *really* bad."

I thought, *If it's that bad, maybe I don't want to see it.*

We taxied just short of the runway, and that's when all of Lower Manhattan stretched out before my eyes. There it was, thick black smoke flowing from the top of the World Trade Center's North Tower. Shye hadn't exaggerated. It looked like a smokestack.

The Continental Airlines 737 on the runway ahead of us was cleared for takeoff and began to accelerate. Normally, I'd watch a departing flight until it was in the air, but I was distracted by the smoke billowing from the North Tower. The situation in Manhattan looked grim, and we still had no idea what had caused the fire or whether it was even close to being under control.

My pulse throbbed in my neck. I didn't know which was worse, not knowing what had caused that ghastly fire or the fact that nobody from Air Traffic Control was telling us anything.

We were next for takeoff.

I continued to monitor the Ground Control frequency while holding short of the runway, which wasn't standard procedure, but I was hoping to hear an update on the smoke. Instead, a voice came in from Newark Ground. "All departures out of Newark are stopped."

I raised my eyebrows. "Shye, did you hear that?"

His voice was flat. "Yeah."

I wondered if he felt relief. I certainly did. It had to be a serious situation if they were stopping *all* departures. I didn't want to be in the air.

I asked, "Do you want me to tell Deborah?"

"Not until we hear from the Tower."

Technically, we were already under Newark Tower's control, so anything I heard on the Ground frequency wasn't meant for our flight. Still, we were holding short of the runway, and if all departures out of Newark were being stopped, our takeoff should be canceled any second.

A voice from the Tower interrupted my thoughts. "Blueridge 6214, position and hold, runway zero-four left."

"Position and hold" meant we were about to take off. I repeated the instructions, but as I spoke, I thought, *What the hell?* They said they were stopping *all* departures.

Shye and I completed the pre-takeoff checklist and taxied into position, facing north. I checked the white runway markings to verify we were on the correct runway, then mentally locked in for the takeoff sequence that usually follows immediately after. But at least five minutes passed while we remained in position. The radio was silent. No instructions. Just the low hum of the engines idling behind us.

On a normal day, this would be a simple delay, but nothing about this day seemed normal. Sitting there waiting . . . waiting . . . gave me several minutes to watch what was happening across the river. The Manhattan sky was brilliant blue, except for where black smoke continued to gush from near the top of the north WTC tower.

It was very strange to watch something so terrible from all the way across the Hudson River. It was just a distant, quiet, surreal scene of black smoke rising from a skyscraper and up into a blue sky. Being so far away made the situation seem unbelievable, as if at this distance I was far enough away to tell my heart I simply wasn't seeing what my eyes were clearly seeing. Still, I prayed firefighters were getting the situation under control, prayed people were helping each other and getting out of the building quickly. I prayed for the lives of everyone in the building and everyone near it.

Then a plane appeared in the sky. I saw it clearly through the smoke, flying strangely low and headed straight for the towers.

What was that plane doing there? And why was it flying so low?

I looked over at Shye, who was focused on the runway, staring down the centerline, as if he'd had enough of the mystery fire and had decided to put his focus back on the job. His stoicism in the flight deck had always impressed me, but in that moment, I had an urge to snap him awake somehow. Why wasn't he saying anything about that bizarrely low-flying aircraft? "Shye!" I demanded, pointing at the towers. "Look at that plane!"

He glanced at the towers, but didn't say a word.

"What's that plane doing so low?" My mind raced as I tried to reason through the situation. "Maybe it's the media or something, trying to get a closer look?" But wouldn't they use helicopters?

Then Shye spoke. "Could be one of those planes that fight fires."

"Yeah, that makes sense," I said, even though it didn't. The plane looked like a large transport jet, nothing like the turboprop airplanes that fly over California forest fires. Still, Shye's guess was the only logical explanation for why the FAA's minimum obstacle clearance altitude wasn't being complied with. Maybe in the next few seconds we'd see a huge wall of water drop right into the heart of the smoke, and that would be that. Then later, we'd hear about an office fire that got out of control for an hour and was put out.

But the plane flew past the North Tower, right by the smokestack, then headed southbound down the Hudson and past the Statue of Liberty.

Although it looked unusual to see a plane flying so low in the city, it was normal to see one flying down the river. I'd flown many times up the Hudson and past the Statue of Liberty northbound on my arrival into LaGuardia.

I watched the aircraft begin what looked like a well-executed turn back in the direction of the Twin Towers. As it continued to fly toward the buildings, I kept hoping I'd soon see the release of an enormous spray, like water from a giant water gun. The closer the plane got to the tower, the more at ease I felt.

Any second now. Any second now, cascades of water would tumble from the plane and onto the fire.

But there was no water. The plane flew straight into the side of the South Tower.

"Oh my *God*!" I screamed, clapping both hands over my mouth in shock. The plane disappeared into an explosion, and now the side of the building was a fierce inferno of flames and dense smoke.

I turned to Shye for . . . for something, maybe consolation. Maybe I was hoping he'd tell me I hadn't seen what I'd just seen.

But he looked past me and out the right-side window, his mouth wide open. His usually almond-colored skin was pale. No consolation there. No denial on his face. No comfort. Just speechless horror.

We'd both just watched a plane slam into the side of the World Trade Center. And now enormous plumes of smoke rose from both towers.

My eyes filled with tears and blurred my vision. When I'm jolted with fear or something horrible happens, it goes right to my stomach. Anxiety, sadness, trepidation as I anticipate an important exam, wait in the wings before giving a speech, watch the clock as I stand by to hear potentially distressing news—it usually manifests as mild nausea. This wasn't mild. The coffee I'd drunk only a few hours earlier crept up, and I was seconds from vomiting all over the flight deck center console that houses our thrust levers.

Then Newark Tower came over the radio. "Blueridge 6214 cleared for takeoff."

What? Takeoff?

The radio transmission had jerked me out of my fog, and I looked at Shye for a response. It was my job to communicate over the radios, so I needed to speak and speak now. But I wasn't sure what to say because it made no sense that we were actually expected to take off.

My right thumb hovered over the talk switch, and I stayed silent.

"You okay?" Shye asked, but it sounded more like a statement.

"Yeah," I said. That was a huge lie. I was nowhere near okay. My stomach was queasy, and my mind was swirling. I'd never flown with my emotions tossed around like this. I asked, "Are *you* okay?"

Shye took a breath and sat up straight. "Yeah. Let's go. We have a job to do." He pushed the thrust levers forward. "Let's go, let's go."

As the captain, Shye had the final authority to accept or reject the takeoff clearance. Our airplane was mechanically sound, and we had a job to do. That meant *take off.*

I swallowed hard, pushing down the coffee that was trying to climb up my esophagus. Then I cleared my throat with a cough, which stopped the impending vomit but created a lump in my throat. I'm usually clear, smooth, and assertive when I speak, but now my voice was weak, as if I were speaking for the first time after days of silence. But I got the words out. "Cleared for takeoff, Blueridge 6214."

I proceeded as my training had taught me. I said all the required words and adhered to procedure. Although I'd just witnessed a horrific plane crash and explosion, and although every instinct in me said to stay on the ground, *do not take this plane into the air,* like Shye, I chose to follow protocol and do my job. And that choice almost put an end to the career I'd dreamed of for most of my life.

TWO

In 1986, when I was ten years old, I decided I wanted to be the world's first Black female astronaut. Once I'd made the decision, I kept it alive with the fuel of daydreams and what I read in the books I devoured day and night. I was going to be an astronaut, and that was that.

Our family lived in a Chicago suburb called Broadview, which looked a lot like the nice family neighborhoods I saw in reruns of TV shows from the fifties. Kids in Broadview rode bikes down sidewalks that edged manicured lawns. On summer weekends, the singsong of the ice cream truck sent us running to the street, and we played outside until the streetlights came on and our parents called our names across the neighborhood. Hanging out at the Broadview Public Library was my idea of a great way to spend an afternoon. On most Saturdays, I hopped on my banana-seat Huffy, sped the four-minute ride to the library, locked the bike, and dashed past the checkout desk to the youth shelves, which were lined with books about space exploration. I loaded my arms with as many books as I could carry, checked them out, and previewed each one before stuffing them in my backpack to ride home looking like Quasimodo. It was a small library, so it wasn't long before I'd read every book about aviation and aerospace in both the young-adult and adult nonfiction sections. So I read them all again.

Day after day, I barraged my parents with facts about pilots and planes, NASA and space travel. I loved reading and thinking and talking about all of it, and I wanted Mom and Dad to be as excited as I was about my new passion. "I've been reading about female astronauts!" I told my mom one night before dinner, after I'd finished the book *To Space and Back.* "Sally Ride and Kathryn D. Sullivan. But there aren't any Black female astronauts."

"I'm not surprised," she said as she stood at the stove stirring spaghetti sauce. Mom was June Cleaver with the mindset of Angela Davis. She kept a spotless house, and dinner was always hot. My mother also had an active mind and great ambition for herself and her kids. Before Black history was taught in our school, she made sure my older sister, Kamilah, and I knew where we came from. She sat us on either side of her and read books about colonization and how the slave trade affected Black people, handing the book back and forth between us and letting us take turns reading paragraphs. Although I was barely a decade old, I was acutely aware of the history of injustice that Black people, my people, had had to overcome. My mother made sure I knew that women, Black women in particular, had faced unfair obstacles throughout history, and she explained that with every generation came the responsibility to advance the cause of women even more. My mother was the first feminist I knew. Her favorite saying was "I am woman, hear me roar," and although I didn't really understand the feminist movement, I knew that phrase was meant to empower me.

My mother also rotated flash cards of Black inventors, artists, and trailblazers on the kitchen refrigerator, constantly exposing us to information about magnificent Black people like Garrett Morgan, who invented the traffic light and gas mask; Dr. Daniel Hale Williams, who performed the first successful open-heart surgery; and Marian Anderson, the singer who broke barriers by performing at the Lincoln Memorial after being denied the stage at Constitution Hall in Washington, D.C. Every night before bed, Mom called Kamilah and me to the refrigerator and quizzed us on each name, making sure their stories stayed with us. In those trailblazers of the past, she wanted us to see our futures. Eventually, I felt I knew those people on our refrigerator. They gave me pride in my culture during a time when Black people weren't heavily celebrated or even represented in mainstream media. My mother knew the importance of representation and mentorship, so whenever she could, she chose Black female doctors, dentists, dance instructors, and piano teachers for our family. When she couldn't find a Black woman to lead our Girl Scout troop, she stepped in and did the job herself.

Even though my mother was still facing the stove, I sat up straight as I smiled and declared, "I want to become the first Black female astronaut to pilot a shuttle."

"Okay," she said without glancing my way. "Dinner's ready. Go wash your hands." I thought she'd be excited about my space dreams. But she wiped her hands on her apron and pointed to a plate on the counter filled with collard greens, cornbread, pinto beans, and a fried pork chop. "Don't touch that plate," she said. "It's your father's." I sighed and went to wash my hands.

My dad was a reserved man who took his work as an X-ray technician seriously, but made it clear he was also deeply committed to our family unit. While some of my friends' dads took over rooms with their big voices and big opinions, Dad's was a quiet power. He never missed a school event, sometimes slipping in late and sitting in the back because he'd only just gotten off work. I could always find his steady smile in the crowd, and he clapped just as hard for my friends as he did for me, as if every kid belonged to him, too. Watching him throughout my childhood showed me I didn't need to have the loudest voice in the room, that strength took many forms. He taught me that being strong is sometimes a matter of knowing your values and staying true to them because your values will be tested and it is strength that will hold you steadfast to them, to the essence of yourself. He rarely preached or lectured, but instead spoke quick bits of wisdom at just the right time. "Everything has a place" was one he said often, and he lived by that—steady, organized, and dependable.

Whenever I gushed to my father about my space aspirations, he simply nodded and let me talk. I knew Dad didn't know much about space, but he was a listener. Mom also knew little about space travel, but she always reminded me, "If you put your mind to something, you can do it."

For several months after my big career announcement, I continued to read and dream of piloting into space. And I plotted the steps I'd have to take to reach that goal: I'd stay focused in school, study aviation in college, fly for the military, then work for NASA. I knew it was a mountain I'd committed to climbing, but every mountain climb is about taking one step after another. This Chicago girl had her sights set on becoming the world's first Black female astronaut, and to me, a goal like that wasn't unrealistic. I'd grown up free to dream and invent and use my imagination, so even the loftiest goals were within my reach.

From the age of three to eight, I shared a bedroom with Kamilah, and in that room, she and I built things and disappeared into imaginary worlds. One of my favorite in-room creations was the tent we made by draping a large sheet across our twin beds and anchoring the top by tucking the sheet as tightly as we could under the mattresses to create a taut, flat roof. A nightstand sat between the heads of our beds, so at the foot of the bed was the entrance we crawled into, dragging pillows, blankets, and flashlights into our beloved hideaway. Once inside that tent, the outside world disappeared. There were no adults, no homework, no chores—just a dreamy little universe where neither time nor reality existed.

While indoor camping, we sang our favorite songs by Michael Jackson and Prince. We ran through "Thriller" and "Little Red Corvette" so many times that one of us eventually declared, "This is boring," and we turned our attention to TV shows. Kamilah loved *The Facts of Life.* She felt most connected to Tootie because they both liked roller skating. But my favorite show was *Lost in Space,* a sci-fi drama from back in the sixties that was in syndication and aired daily on one of Chicago's local channels. Every weekday, I hurried home from school to watch the adventures of the Robinsons, a family who had planned to spend five years exploring a distant planet but were set adrift in space after the scheming Dr. Smith sabotaged the mission and threw their spaceship off course. In every episode, the Robinson parents and their three kids ventured into the unknown, tried to fix their ship, and managed to survive encounters with aliens. Something about the Robinsons, especially the kids, made me think adventure wasn't just for TV, that maybe even I could venture out into the unknown for real one day, maybe even on my own. I was so invested in the show that on the pale yellow walls inside our bedroom closet, I drew circles and squares to represent the panels of the spacecraft I was going to fly into outer space, where I'd find and rescue all of them. I pressed the circles to start my rocket ship's single engine, then made explosion sounds to signify blastoff, while pretending the squares were the instruments for navigating to a distant planet. Eventually, I moved beyond my fantasy of rescuing that family lost in space, but I continued to think of them fondly as I gazed at the sky and hoped they'd find their own way home.

When I finally got a bedroom to myself, my parents let me choose the room's decor. I was all about purple—the walls and bedding and rugs—and I wanted glow-in-the-dark stars on the ceiling. I spent many hours in my purple paradise, looking out my bedroom window at the clouds floating in the sky, and at night I stared out at the stars and hunted the Big Dipper, the Little Dipper, and other constellations. Before fading off to sleep, I looked up at the stars glowing on my ceiling and dreamed of space, of traveling way out in the magnificent dark sky, where those magical stars flickered through the night.

I was a self-entertaining child. I did homework without being told and in my free time played mom to my beloved Cabbage Patch Kid, who came with his own birth certificate. Sometimes, I set my Cabbage Patch Kid beside me and rested a pencil on his hand, pretending he had homework, too. I would tell him, "School is important. Let's both focus on our assignments until we're all finished." Sometimes, he became my co-pilot, lying next to me on the carpet as we blasted off from my bedroom floor into the glow of the stars on my ceiling. When I wasn't happily occupied by indoor activities, I played outdoors, usually riding my bike around the neighborhood, often carrying my rope and meeting with friends to jump Double Dutch. My books, my bike, and my doll were all I needed to be happy in those days. But in the summer of 1986, I saw a movie that changed me.

SpaceCamp. In the film, a bunch of teenagers go to a camp to learn about NASA and find out what it means to train to be astronauts. During a space shuttle engine test, instructor Andie, a NASA-trained astronaut, and four teenage campers are accidentally launched into space, and with no ground contact, they work together to try to land the shuttle. Earlier in the film, the Kathryn character declares she wants to be the first female shuttle commander, and during the gang's misadventures in space, she serves as the pilot, confronting her doubts during reentry and ultimately guiding the shuttle to a safe touchdown. I watched the movie five times, each time connecting more and more with Kathryn. She was confident and passionate about flying, and I wanted to be just like her. Now I knew more than ever I wanted to pilot the space shuttle. While *Lost in Space* had entertained me for countless hours and had fired up my imagination, *SpaceCamp* etched a sharp edge of reality to the idea of traveling beyond Earth. The movie felt grown-up and real, and it made me more confident than ever that I could, that I *would,* one day explore outer space.

One snowy evening that winter, I was lying across my purple comforter flipping through a photobook of military airplanes when my mom came home from her teaching job later than usual. All the women I knew had jobs outside the home—all the mothers in my extended family and all my friends' moms—and I knew managing both a career and a family took a lot of work, but the way my mom balanced them made it all look like a well-oiled machine.

"Hi, Mom," I said, extending my arms out to greet her. We hugged, and I warmed her cold face against my cheek.

She reached into her tote bag, which was always stuffed with papers to grade, and pulled out a few pieces of printer paper stapled at the top. "I have something to show you."

It felt important, so official, my mother reaching into her work bag to retrieve something for *me*. It was a copy of an article from *The Chicago Defender,* dated 1922. An article from almost seventy years ago? My heart began thumping.

She handed me the papers and said, "I remembered hearing a story about a Black woman who had to go to Europe to learn to fly planes because no one would teach her in the U.S."

A Black woman from seventy years ago who was so determined to become a pilot, she went across the world to make it happen? I wanted to know everything I could about her. "Wow!" I said. "Thank you so much!"

Mom pulled off her hat and set it in the hallway closet. "I thought you'd like that. Her name was Bessie Coleman. I wanted to get you a book about her, so I called several libraries, but only the DuSable Museum had heard of her."

The DuSable Museum of African American History was small but important. It was the only place I knew of that celebrated the history, culture, and achievements of Black people, local and national figures. We visited the museum a few times a year, and I always felt honored to stand amid the art, documents, photos, and artifacts honoring Black people. At the DuSable, I felt connected, a part of something big and important. Each visit reminded me that our history mattered, and that pride showed in how I carried myself, spoke up, and moved with confidence. When teachers talked about history but didn't mention people who looked like me, I didn't feel slighted, nor did I doubt my value. I noted the omission with quiet confidence. I knew there was more to the story, and I walked around every day with a sense that I belonged and mattered as much as everyone else.

"I wish I could find more information about her," Mom said as she walked past me and into the kitchen.

I followed her, clutching the papers. She tied an apron around her waist and stood at the sink washing her hands. I lingered in the middle of the kitchen reading the article. Mom asked, "Are you hungry?"

I didn't look away from the article. "No, no thank you." I didn't care if I ever ate again! I dashed to my room gripping the article, then leaped onto my bed and started reading about this woman the journalist called a "Negro aviatrix."

Bessie Coleman trained at a prestigious French aviation school after being denied entry to American institutions because she was Black. She then returned to the United States and worked as a stunt pilot performing daring aerial flights, but only in front of integrated crowds. I was captivated by this fact, that she insisted on flying for events where everyone was allowed, and where, regardless of race, attendees were free to sit wherever they liked. She went on to use her platform to advocate for racial equality in aviation and aspired to establish a flight school for African Americans.

After reading only the first few sentences of the article, I felt connected to Bessie Coleman. The idea that she'd had the courage to leave her home country, that she'd refused to allow the U.S.

flight school's "No" to stop her from learning to fly hit me hard. It wasn't just about aviation; it was about passion, a focus on goals, and an unwavering belief in her purpose. All the way back in the beginning of the century, Bessie Coleman had carved a path, fought her way to becoming a pilot. That brave woman had become a pilot before women had the right to vote! And even after the success of the women's suffrage movement, some Black women were kept from exercising that right. Wow, I thought, what must she have dealt with day after day—the resistance, the rejections, the barricades. But still, she made it to the sky. The more I thought about her resilience, the more I appreciated how she'd cleared a path for me. Thanks to her, I had no excuses. I was going to reach my dream.

When my mother handed me that article, Bessie Coleman became my mentor. From that day forward, Ms. Coleman's life inspired and motivated me. I thought about her so often, she began to seem like a treasured auntie. Even though I was still a young girl and had lived a relatively sheltered life, I knew that in the story of Bessie Coleman was a big-world lesson I needed to learn from. She'd reached her goal of becoming a pilot even when the social and legal realties of racism and sexism raged against her. In the 1980s, sexism and racism were still alive and well, but at the age of ten, I was a girl already well on her way to knowing her worth. I wasn't going to let anything stop me from reaching for the stars.

On the nightstand next to my bed was a four-by-six wooden picture frame that held a photo of my dad in a royal-blue softball uniform, holding a bat, ready to swing. It was my favorite picture of Dad, taken at one of the many family outings where my mom, sister, and I sat on the bleachers and cheered for him and his coworkers as they played for their hospital's league team. After devouring the Bessie Coleman article several times, I grabbed the picture frame, pulled out the photo of Dad, and used it as a template to cut out the center of the article. I positioned the article in the frame, carefully slid the glass back in place, then returned the frame to my nightstand. Then I tucked the picture of Dad into the edge of the mirror on top of my dresser.

THREE

There's a cadence to the callouts pilots make after being cleared for takeoff. It's a rhythmic, verbal back-and-forth to verify aircraft performance as the plane accelerates down the runway. On the morning of that flight out of Newark, Shye and I were so rattled by what we'd just seen in Manhattan, we were nearly speechless, and by the time I realized we hadn't made any callouts, Shye had already pushed the thrust levers forward. We rolled down the runway approaching our rotation speed, the speed at which the plane is going fast enough for the pilot to pull back on the control and lift the plane off the ground. Shye pulled the flight controls toward his chest. He would usually hand-fly to a flight's cruise altitude, but on that day, he switched right to autopilot. That's when I knew he was as overwhelmed as I was.

We flew the departure procedure as assigned, making a right turn heading east toward Manhattan. In the air, I felt lighter than usual, surreal, almost like having an out-of-body experience. My mind moved fast, as if I were trying to process the situation across the river at hyper speed, but didn't have enough information to make sense of it. I'd had no idea how loud jet engines could be, but with no radio sounds filling the air in the flight deck, the low drumming of the engines was nearly deafening. During the departure and climb-out phase of flight, I was used to hearing a fast-paced sequence of radio calls between air traffic controllers and multiple aircraft, and in all that buzz I rarely noticed engine noise. But now my senses were alight. And I was acutely aware I wasn't hearing any chatter over the radio. We were flying in the country's busiest airspace, but nobody was talking. I wondered if ours was the only plane flying. Glancing out the window, I looked east toward LaGuardia and JFK, then north to Teterboro Airport, scanning for other aircraft in the vicinity. On a normal day, there'd be a sky full of planes, but I saw nothing out the window, and no other aircraft showed on our Traffic Collision Avoidance System (TCAS) radar. There was no indication the TCAS had failed, so I checked to make sure it was switched to ON. It was.

I also should have heard constant communication among New York controllers, but the air was dead. I started to think we might have lost our radios, but then I heard a voice transmission from Newark Tower. "Blueridge 6214. Contact Departure Control."

The communication between pilots and Air Traffic Control has its own choreography, which is normally fast-paced. Instructions are given and acknowledged quickly, but on this day the rhythm was way off, stilted, hesitant. Everything felt anxious and urgent. I switched frequencies, and before I could say a word, the new controller was already calling for us. His voice sounded weak, unsure, as if he needed to hear us, not just for coordination but for confirmation that we were still flying. I gave our position and altitude, trying to keep my voice steady as it quavered. The controller replied with "Roger. I see you on radar," his voice now stronger with relief.

That was when I felt it in my gut: We shouldn't be in the air.

Manhattan now was in clear view, but I tried not to look at the Twin Towers. I kept my eyes on the flight instruments and scanned the sky to the north. But as we flew closer to the New York skyline, the black smoke floated into my peripheral vision and I could no longer resist the need to confirm what I'd witnessed only moments earlier. What I saw was horrifying. And we were only a couple miles from it, so close I could practically count the windows in the towers. Right then, Shye, our passengers, the flight attendant, and I had a bird's-eye view to the gaping hole in the North Tower and a gushing river of gray and black smoke thick as mud.

I couldn't make sense of what I was seeing. Had that crash been an accident? Were we under attack? Was this a declaration of war? If so, war with whom? Was another plane headed our way, maybe targeting our plane at this very moment? Were we about to have a midair collision? *My God,* I thought in a silent shriek, *what's happening?*

At this point in my career, I'd clocked about two thousand hours of flight time, and not once during those flights did I feel unsafe, had never once feared my plane was unsound or doubted the other pilot and I were qualified and prepared to safely fly and land it. But flying past those burning buildings upended my sense of security. I was operating a perfectly good airplane, but I started mentally preparing for worst-case scenarios. Pilots are trained to think defensively in the air, as drivers are taught to anticipate danger on roads. For us pilots, this training addresses such issues as where to land if an engine fails and which way to turn if another aircraft is flying in our path. My eyes swept the sky above and below the horizon for threats of other aircraft, and my gut twisted tight. I feared for my life.

We followed the flight plan and began our left turn northbound toward Boston. I held my gaze on the Twin Towers until the smoking sticks were behind us, no longer in view. Then I tried to focus on my responsibility as the pilot monitoring: to communicate on the radios and back up the pilot flying by confirming and verifying the route and aircraft setup—altitudes, airspeeds, switch positions—so small discrepancies could be addressed early, long before they could affect the flight.

The air was smooth, but my hands were shaking as I conducted my usual flows of turning switches on and off. By now we were at our cruising altitude, twenty-three thousand feet, which meant we'd reached a noncritical phase of flight. Usually at that point, Shye and I chitchatted about our lives as we performed our pilot duties. But since the moment we'd been cleared for takeoff, he and I hadn't said a word, not even the standard challenge and response callouts. And the silence between us only added to my anxiety. It was as if Shye and I were afraid to say our thoughts aloud, as if revealing what we were thinking would make it true and we'd have to accept we'd witnessed a real-world horror show happening in New York City.

About ten minutes into the flight, as I waited for a radio frequency change, my hands shook, and I tried to cover one hand with the other. But then my arms shook, and then my legs. Thousands of tiny vibrations pulsed through my body. I'd never experienced anything like it, not from fear or cold. My body wasn't in my control. I tried to calm myself by wrapping my arms around my torso and rocking, focusing on my breathing . . . in and out . . . in and out, but it didn't help. Tears rolled down my cheeks, and I didn't feel like the professional my uniform conveyed I was.

Back in college, I'd received an unsatisfactory performance evaluation, and I'd cried in front of my evaluator. He'd sneered at me, and I vowed never to let another pilot see me cry. Since then, I'd become very stoic. I'd toughened myself through all the academic coursework that required intense concentration on little sleep, during flight evaluations for which I executed intense in-air maneuvers, and in the midst of the extraordinary stress of training in a flight simulator. I'd been a steady, even-tempered flight instructor and had always remained calm as a pilot. But nothing I'd trained for prepared me for this gutting combination of tragedy and unanswered questions.

Breaking the silence, I blurted, "I'm sorry, Shye, I just can't take this. What's happening? Do you have any ideas? Oh, God." I continued to rock back and forth as I wiped tears from my face.

Shye stared out the window, quiet. I looked at him, confused, waiting for him to speak. How was it possible he wasn't as torn up as I was? Then I thought, maybe as the captain he felt a responsibility not to break, to hold in his emotions. What good would it do any of us on that plane if our captain crumbled in distress?

After several seconds, he shook his head. He didn't look away from the window, didn't look at me, but in a low, monotone voice said, "I almost don't want to say it, but what if they're hijacking airliners?"

I stopped hugging myself and bolted up straight. "We just saw a plane fly into a building." Then my voice rose with irritation. "That's not a hijacking."

Shye kept staring out the window. "What else could it be?"

I didn't answer him. It looked like a horrible accident. Nothing else made sense. Then a distorted voice erupted on the frequency, all the words breaking up.

"What was that?" I pointed to the frequency we were monitoring, then heard another distorted transmission that sounded like a fight, some kind of tussle.

Shye stopped looking out the window and turned toward the radio frequency, then tilted his head. "What *was* that?"

Neither of us would have been surprised by a stuck mic. It happens sometimes—a pilot accidentally holds down the push-to-talk button on the radio and blocks the frequency, which means pilots can hear whatever's going on inside another flight deck. Shye and I strained to hear what sounded like a scuffle and voices, muffled but frantic, cutting in and out. Then the radio went silent.

We waited for another transmission, but none came. After several seconds of silence, Shye shook his head again. "I'm going to call and find out what Deborah saw on the ground at Newark. You have the airplane and the radios." He pushed the autopilot transfer selector to my side, giving me control of steering and leaving the plane on a kind of cruise control.

I took a deep breath and wiped tears from my eyes. Shye pushed the cabin call button to notify Deborah to pick up the phone.

With only thirty-two seats in the cabin, it should have taken Deborah seconds to reach either of the plane's two cabin phones, but after three minutes, she still hadn't picked up. I glanced from the flight instruments to Shye. He said, "She must be doing a beverage service." Then he pressed the cabin call button again. Still no response.

I tapped the heel of my shoe against the floor and waited. *What was taking her so long?*

Finally Deborah answered, and Shye asked her to come to the flight deck. She arrived within seconds, and Shye said, "While we were on the runway at Newark, did you or the passengers see anything?"

"See anything having to do with our plane?"

Shye and I glanced at each other like we had a secret we weren't willing to share. Shye said, "Did you see any smoke?"

"The passengers in the first few rows said they saw smoke across the river. I couldn't see anything."

Shye explained his suspicion that airliners might be getting hijacked. Then he said, "Let us know if anyone seems off or if you notice anything out of the ordinary."

Deborah took a slow breath, then nodded. "Got it," she said, her voice now tighter than before. As she stepped out of the flight deck, she shot us an uneasy look.

With the door closed, Shye turned back to the aircraft instrument panel and said, "My airplane." I transferred the autopilot back to his side and continued to monitor the radios.

Then we heard another transmission over the radio. It came in fast and urgent. "Attention all aircraft. Attention all aircraft. The FAA is requiring all crew members to increase cockpit security procedures at this time."

There it was, near confirmation of Shye's theory. Unless they had reason to believe planes might be hijacked, why would the controllers make a single broadcast that reached hundreds of pilots at once, across dozens of flight decks, telling us to lock our flight deck door, remain inside, and not open the door under any circumstances, not even for a flight attendant?

I turned to look at Shye. His shoulders were slumped, and he stared straight ahead. Then with a tremor in his voice, he said, "I'll relay the message to Deborah."

My heart rate and breathing sped up. My thoughts raced, and it was no longer my imagination making my mind spin but the possible repercussions of what I now knew to be true: That airliner had been hijacked and intentionally flown into the World Trade Center.

My thoughts were a blur of images of the plane and the smoke, but then I started thinking about the crew members and passengers on board that plane. They must have died on impact, but how much terror did they experience before they were killed? And what about the people in the buildings? How many had seen the plane coming? They must have died the minute the plane hit. Or did they? Did they burn to death? It was all unspeakably horrible.

I cried and rubbed my head with both hands, hoping an intense massage would help ease the scorching headache I felt creeping across my skull. The shaking I'd been experiencing escalated until I seemed to be having a seizure, and I pressed myself back farther in the seat to control it.

Several seconds later, I felt a cool breeze against my neck and the sense that someone was standing over me. I gasped and swung my head around expecting to face an intruder, but it was Deborah. She stood with an arm resting on the back of my seat. I snapped, "What are you doing in here?"

She looked confused. "I'm sorry. I knocked twice. No one answered, so I let myself in."

"You're not supposed to be up here," I spat back at her, then glared at Shye. "I thought you gave her the message."

"I was waiting to get feedback on the passengers," Shye replied.

Now she looked even more confused, but said, "I didn't notice anything strange with the passengers. What's the message?"

Shye told her about the FAA security mandate and added, "You can't come in here for the rest of the flight."

Deborah said, "I'm glad it's a short flight. I'll see you on the ground." Then she returned to the cabin, and I locked the door behind her.

With thirty minutes to landing, we prepared for the descent into Boston. For a moment, everything felt routine, then about ten minutes after Deborah left, the Boston controller broadcasted on the radio frequency. "Attention all aircraft: Per FAA directive, you are required to immediately land at the nearest suitable airport. Repeat, immediately land at the nearest suitable airport. Advise intentions."

We were already in the descent phase and only twenty minutes from landing at Boston, so Shye and I agreed to continue our route, and I let the controller know. Then I contacted Boston Tower. "Boston, Blueridge 6214. On the visual, runway two seven left."

"Blueridge 6214. Boston Tower. Cleared to land two-seven left."

I repeated the final instructions, then announced over the PA, "Flight attendant, prepare for landing."

Shye lined up the aircraft with the runway, and as he flew the final approach course, downtown Boston was directly in my view. The skyscrapers against the backdrop of the blue sky looked tall and regal, much as the buildings of New York had only hours earlier.

Shye aimed the nose of the plane toward the large white numbers on the runway. I read the landing checklist aloud, confirmed the gear was down and locked, and continued to call out the altitude as my battered mind spat silent thoughts in between callouts.

"Five hundred."

Boston is going to be targeted next. I have to get away from here.

"Two hundred."

I have to get home. *How* will I get home?

"One hundred."

I'm never getting on a plane again.

We landed and taxied. Logan's ramp area looked like the Wrigley Field parking lot on game day. There must have been thirty other small aircraft lined up right next to each other. Once we were parked, Shye shut down the engines, and I reached for the laminated cardstock checklist to begin the engine shutdown checks. My hands began to shake again. Shye gently touched my hand and said softly, "It's okay. I'll do the shutdown checks. Just relax."

Normally, Shye and I opened the flight deck door and thanked passengers as they deplaned. Not today. From the flight deck, we listened to the usual shuffle sounds of passengers exiting the plane until we heard the last "Thank you, bye-bye" from Deborah.

Then there was a knock on the door. I assumed it was Deborah, but Shye opened the door to the ramp agent who'd just parked us. He was a stocky, kind-faced man, probably in his forties. He said, "I saw your flight attendant leave, but you guys were taking a while in here. I thought I'd check on you."

"Sorry," Shye said. "We're a little shaken up."

"Of course," he said. "This was the Newark flight, right?" He pulled a folded schedule out of his uniform shirt pocket. "You originated out of Boston this morning?"

"Yeah, we were the six-thirty departure. We were having a perfectly good morning, but this last leg . . ." Shye paused, then asked, "Do you know what's going on?"

The ramper looked back and forth between Shye and me. "You guys don't know?"

"We saw a plane fly into the World Trade Center. They cleared us for takeoff, and now we're here."

The agent's eyes flew open wide. "You saw it and then took off? Did you see the first one or the second one?"

Shye and I looked at each other, and our mouths dropped open. Shye rubbed his hand over his short buzz cut as if he were trying to smooth the confusion in his mind. "There was more than one?"

"*What* is happening?" I pleaded.

"It's all over the news. The airport is chaos. An American flight and a United flight left out of here this morning. They were hijacked, and the hijackers flew them into the World Trade Center."

He paused as Shye and I remained speechless. When neither of us spoke, the ramp agent shot us a *brace yourself* look. "They also hijacked an American flight out of Dulles. It hit the Pentagon. The news is reporting there are more."

Shye closed his eyes and whispered, "Jesus."

I could barely see through my tears. And now the absolute turmoil of what was going on shot to my stomach until the coffee I'd managed to keep down during the flight rumbled its way up. I pulled a plastic bag from the center console and vomited into it. Then I started violently shaking again, so I hugged myself tight and rocked back and forth. "No, no, no," I whispered in despair.

Shye reached across the console, pulled me into a hug, and gently said, "It's going to be okay."

But my mind was a violent jumble of terrifying images—screaming, crying, shattered glass, jet fuel and fire, burned bodies, panic, chaos. And hijackers—in my mind they were all men, evil, evil men hiding behind face masks. Nothing was going to be okay. I wept into Shye's shoulder. "I can't do this anymore. I can't fly again."

FOUR

My sister and I had it good. We knew our parents loved us. And though we probably didn't fall asleep thinking about how lucky we were to live in a household run by caring, responsible grown-ups, we sensed it. Because ours was a household of consistency and kindness, Kamilah and I had the freedom to focus on what kids are supposed to: learn, laugh about silly things, and grow into ourselves. There was no chaos, no drama—just love, patience, and wisdom that gave us a solid foundation. And while our parents offered us space to explore, they never let us forget where the lines were. We were expected to be home when the streetlights came on, and if we weren't, we couldn't go outside the next day. On school nights, the rule was no phone after nine o'clock, and when I would get caught sneaking a call after hours, I lost phone privileges for the next day, maybe two. My parents considered "talking back" the worst form of disrespect, so if I ever answered one of my parents with an attitude or sarcasm, I got the big three: the belt, phone privileges revoked, and grounded for a day. Grounded meant no going outside, which meant no wandering around looking up at the sky in all directions, so it was the punishment I most dreaded of the big three. I quickly learned not to talk back.

As I grew up, I saw more and more what other kids' lives looked like, and that perspective gave me great appreciation for my parents and their ways of doing things. In some of my friends' houses, I could tell the parents weren't really listening. Maybe they had so many kids they had only enough energy to keep everybody fed and focused on their homework. But my parents seemed more aware and involved than most, and even when they disciplined us, I knew their choices were about boundaries, not control. Those boundaries gave me the freedom to direct my energy to school, playing with friends, and my ever-growing passion for flying.

After I learned about Bessie Coleman, I spent more time than ever outside looking up. Planes flew out of O'Hare Airport, then over our house and off to faraway places I could only dream of. Day after day, I lay on the grass in our backyard and gazed at the sky, listening for the thrilling hum of a jet. When I spotted one, I watched it move across the sky like a soaring eagle until it was smaller, smaller, smaller. The highest planes left long white trails behind them, like fluffy rivers, until their trails spread wide, then disappeared. If I spent a couple hours out on the lawn, I might see twenty planes, and in my mind, I was piloting every one of them.

Sometimes when I wasn't watching planes, I paid attention to how other things flew. I chased fireflies at night and caught them in jars just to watch them blink like tiny flickering stars. Bumblebees were fascinating, their full, round bulk suspended in air. Dragonflies dazzled me with the way they darted and zipped, quick and sure, then hovered like little helicopters. And I loved to watch birds. My favorites were red cardinals and blue jays, so colorful and vibrant. When I spotted a bird, I followed its course as far as I could, watching its wings flap as the magnificent creature sped up, slowed down, and landed on trees as if it had been through some kind of elite flight training. Flight was my destiny, and any time I could focus on it, I did, including for school assignments.

In fifth grade, I wrote a report about Bessie Coleman. Using articles my mom helped me get from the DuSable Museum, I wrote about Bessie's life in Texas, Chicago, and France, about her work as a stunt pilot, and about her tragic death when she and her mechanic, William Wills, were both killed when their plane crashed during a practice flight. The time I spent immersed in writing my report about Coleman and knowing she'd once lived in Chicago made me feel linked to her, and it hurt that she'd died so young after fighting so hard to become a pilot.

In sixth grade, my entry in our school's science fair was an exhibit on space exploration, which featured NASA astronauts John Glenn and Dr. Mae Jemison. Although Dr. Jemison becoming the first Black female astronaut crushed my dream of being first, I proudly glued her official NASA picture to my display. The photo was proof someone like me belonged in that suit. At the end of the fair, the principal announced the winners over the school's PA system. I sat in social studies, my entire body tense with anticipation. Then I heard "In first place, for her exhibit on space exploration, Nia Gilliam." Everyone in my classroom cheered, and my teacher's face glowed.

In seventh grade, I had to put together materials for a mock job search. In my résumé and letter to American Airlines, I wrote that I'd graduated with honors from the U.S. Air Force Academy with a BA in aeronautical engineering and was a member of the "U.S. Air Force Corps of Aviators" as a test pilot who flew the F-14 Tomcat, A-6 Intruder, A-4 Skyhawk, F-18 Hornet, and P-3C Orion. I also claimed to belong to the Society of Women Engineers, Alpha Kappa Alpha Sorority, and the Federal Aviation Administration. I got an A on the assignment and was sure I deserved it as well as the job with AA.

As the years passed, I continued to earn my mother's nickname for me, "Jabba Jaws"—more so because my growing excitement about aviation made me even chattier. In class, I talked about planes and space shuttles to anyone who would let me, which led to many report cards noting, *Disrupts class with excessive talking*. And heaven help anyone who was nearby when I was outdoors with a clear sky above. One Saturday when I was ten, my dad and I walked home from the Veterans Canteen Service store in the VA hospital where Dad worked. I held his hand as we walked down the tree-lined street, and in my other hand, I carried a bag of Rolos, Twizzlers, and Whatchamacallits, which I'd talked him into buying by promising I wouldn't eat all the candy at once. It was my favorite kind of day: clear blue sky and no school, so I had all day to look for planes, ride my bike, and eat ice cream or candy. Overhead, I saw a white plane with a red, orange, and blue stripe down the body and a tulip-shaped logo on the tail. I pointed and said, "That's a United Airlines Boeing 727."

Dad looked up. "Wow! How can you tell?"

"It's such a cool plane! It has three engines, all in the back, like a jetpack attached to the tail!"

A few minutes later, another plane hummed above us, and I shouted, "There's an MD-80! It looks like a pencil with engines stuck to the back and a tail shaped like a capital *T*."

Dad looked up, then nodded. "That's great. Good eye." Then he looked back to ground level and focused on our walk.

Soon we were in front of our house. I loved that house, so nicely landscaped and cared for. It was a brown-brick, single-story ranch outlined by manicured shrubs and colorful petunias, impatiens, and rosebushes that my mom tended with great care. My chest filled with pride when someone saw me walk in or out of our house.

Once again, the sound of an approaching plane rumbled overhead. I tugged my father's hand. "It's a Boeing 747!" Nothing was more thrilling than spotting a 747, so massive and majestic. "It's *huge*. Dad, do you see that? It's like a whale with four engines."

Dad let go of my hand, then gave my shoulder a soft squeeze. "Is it necessary to point out every plane in the sky?" But I saw his grin. Not even his goatee could hide the deep dimples in his cheeks.

I shrugged, then shaded my eyes as I watched the 747 until it was out of sight. Within a few minutes, another plane hummed overhead, and I almost blurted, "Ooh, a DC-10!" but I glanced at Dad, then stopped myself and watched the aircraft in silence.

One spring day, not long after my eleventh birthday, Dad showed me just how much he'd been listening. I was lying in bed with my Walkman on, belting "Head to Toe" by Lisa Lisa & Cult Jam. Dad, still wearing his white lab coat, knocked on my door and walked in. I stopped singing and yanked the headphones from my ears.

He handed me a gray tote bag with *Jeppesen* printed on it. I reached in and pulled out two textbooks with pictures of generic white airplanes on the covers. One was titled *Private Pilot Manual,* and the other, *Private Pilot Maneuvers.* These were serious books, made for real pilots. The front covers made them look official, like nothing I'd seen in all my trips to the library. I leaped from my bed and hugged my dad. "Where did you get these?"

"I have a co-worker who flies small planes for fun. I told him you want to be a pilot, and he suggested these books."

As Dad left the room, I flopped back onto the bed and opened the *Private Pilot Manual* to the table of contents. Part 1 was "Fundamentals of Flight," and I turned to the chapter on aerodynamic principles and started reading aviation words and their definitions: *Thrust,* the forward-acting force that propels the aircraft through the air. *Drag,* the rearward acting force that opposes thrust and resists the aircraft's motion through the air. The definitions for *lift, weight,* and countless other words sounded just as complex. I could memorize the definitions, but I didn't understand what they had to do with making a plane fly. Thrilled as I was for the gifts, it was like getting a new bike that was just too big for me, so I set the books carefully on my shelf and dreamed about the day my feet would reach the pedals.

Later that year, I began to feel my reach extend. One Saturday, Mom handed me a brochure for Space Camp held at the U.S. Space & Rocket Center in Huntsville, Alabama, near where her sister lived. Mom had taken Kamilah and me to the museum many times, but Space Camp? Like in the movie? Wow. On the front of the brochure was a boy who looked to be my age, a girl who looked like my sister's age, and a man who seemed to be in his thirties, all wearing flight suits and standing at the nose of a space shuttle.

I opened the brochure and read the price for five days of camp, then gasped. "Four hundred and seventy-five dollars! That's so much money."

Mom leaned over my shoulder. "That's the spring session price. Summer is even more."

I looked at her, eyes wide. "Would I even be able to go in the spring?"

She sat back in her chair, and her eyes shifted in thought. "You'd miss a whole week of school. And I'd have to miss a week of work to take you."

I didn't know what to say, but I knew it was a big deal for her to do that. "Will school let me skip a week if I do all my work in advance?"

"If you really want to go, we'll make it work. I'll talk to your principal. We need to show them it's educational. I'll write a letter explaining what the camp is and why it's worth your missing school. You'll have to promise to keep up with your homework."

Now my heart was thundering. I swore, "I will! I'll do whatever it takes."

In a letter to my school's principal, Mom explained that a week of Space Camp would mean a huge step toward my dream of becoming a pilot. Then, in a meeting she and I attended with the principal and the superintendent, I promised to stay on top of my homework, and I watched and listened to my mother explain the value of allowing kids to miss school in favor of an exceptional educational opportunity. She was so poised sitting with fellow educators as they talked about self-discipline and personal responsibility, extracurricular activities, and helping students reach toward their dreams. I left that meeting full of love for how strongly she spoke in favor of something so important to me. This camp opportunity was a very big deal and another piece of evidence that I was the luckiest girl alive to have parents invested in my achieving my greatest dream.

At what point do dreams deserve a new name? When do they change from being stare-out-the-window fantasies into actual goals? Maybe it's when you want it enough to make a plan, when you're so serious about going after the dream you make lists, make calls, research, study, register for exams, save money for classes and camps, and enroll in school programs. And sometimes it's about having a door opened for you. My parents not only indulged and supported my dreams of flight, they sought opportunities for me to take steps toward achieving them. Maybe my parents were actually my partners, the kind who help turn dreams into goals. For me to be able to attend Space Camp, they had to write a big check, Mom had to take time off work and drive a very long way, and Dad stayed back with Kamilah. I knew how lucky I was to have them on my side, and I vowed to make us all proud.

Three days before camp started, Mom and I settled into the family station wagon and headed to Louisville, Kentucky, where we stayed overnight with relatives. Then at 4:00 P.M. on the first day of camp, we pulled up to the U.S. Space & Rocket Center, which looked like an office building. But, oh! That giant Saturn V rocket out front made it very clear I'd arrived! Everywhere I looked, kids were carrying duffel bags and luggage, and at the check-in table, a counselor in a dark blue flight suit greeted us and handed me a camp T-shirt that read GRUMMAN, a lanyard with a name badge, a maroon visor, and a light blue flight suit. As I examined my new uniform, a young Black man with red hair and freckles walked toward us wearing a matching suit. He extended his hand to me and said, "Welcome to Space Camp, Nia. I'm Elliot, Team Grumman lead. We'll be together all week."

My mother scanned the crowd, and I wondered if she noticed that among about a hundred campers and a few dozen counselors, she, Elliot, and I were the only Black people. She turned to Elliot, then smiled and shook his hand. "Hi, Elliot. I'm Nia's mother, Alma."

Elliot smiled back. "After you drop your luggage at the dorm, I'll meet you and the rest of the team back here."

Mom and I followed the signs to the dorm, which was full of plain rooms with metal bunk beds and lockers. Some beds had already been claimed with duffel bags tossed on the top bunks, sleeping bags rolled out, and stuffed animals propped on pillows. I chose an unclaimed lower bunk, and Mom helped me unpack, then we returned to the check-in area to find Elliot surrounded by campers and holding a sign that read GRUMMAN. Mom asked, "Are you excited?"

The twistiness in my stomach made me feel brave and homesick at the same time. I smiled. "Yes."

She reached out to pull me in for a hug. "Okay. I'm going to head out now. I'll see you on Friday. Have fun!"

"I will. See you Friday."

She walked to the building's entrance, then looked back and waved before heading out to the parking lot.

There were ten of us in Elliot's group, five girls and five boys, all fidgeting and glancing around the lobby. I smiled at a brown-haired girl, and she smiled back. "I'm Sarah," she said, tucking a piece of hair behind her ear.

"I'm Nia," I said, already feeling I might have made my first Space Camp friend.

Later that afternoon, more than a hundred people—campers and counselors—crowded into the museum's auditorium. All around us were real rockets and space artifacts, and the air buzzed with chatter. A tall man with gray hair stepped up to the microphone. "Welcome to Space Camp!" he called out, his voice echoing off the walls. "I'm the camp's director. This week, you're going to get a taste of what it's like to train like real astronauts. Listen carefully and follow all the instructions from your counselors. They're not just chaperones, they're trained crew leaders. They're going to guide you through the exhibits, the simulators, and the shuttle missions, and before the week is over, you'll be thinking and talking like astronauts."

After the director dismissed us, Elliot gathered our team and led us to a corner of the room and smiled. "Welcome to Space Camp, guys. Members of a team should know each other, so everybody introduce yourself, and tell the group where you're from, whether you have a favorite planet, and why you wanted to come to Space Camp."

Kids said they'd come to the camp because they wanted to be astronauts. Some wanted to work for NASA. When a sweet-faced blond kid named Mike said, "I really just want to see what it's like to float around without gravity," we all laughed. When it was my turn, I said, "I've wanted to be a pilot since I was little. I think about flying all the time—I'm always looking for planes." A few kids nodded, and it was the first time I didn't feel like the Jabba Jaws who never stopped talking about airplanes. I thought, *This is what it's like to be surrounded by people who think like I do.* It was a wonderful feeling. I looked around at all of them and said, "My favorite planet is Saturn because it has rings around it and rockets named after it." More of the kids nodded and smiled.

After introductions, Elliot said, "Let's have a look through the museum."

We followed Elliot to the exhibit hall, its high ceiling echoing with our footsteps. Rocket engines hung overhead, their black nozzles so enormous I thought I could probably fit inside them.

Elliot pointed to a huge glass case. "There's the Apollo command module."

I got as close to the glass as I could. The actual Apollo capsule, the cone-shaped spacecraft that landed on the moon, was so small!

Astronauts actually rode to the moon and back, packed into a space no bigger than a broom closet. In that moment, all I could think about was how extraordinarily brave they must be.

We passed astronaut suits sealed in cases, their gloves stiff, their helmets reflecting the overhead lights. Elliot said, "Those were worn by the Apollo astronauts during training. And over here is the Skylab trainer."

We stepped inside a replica of Skylab, America's first space station, and Elliot shared some facts about it, but I barely listened. I was daydreaming about floating down its tunnel like a real astronaut, arms stretched out, trying not to bump into the walls. Elliot pointed to a classroom on the far side of the building. "We'll visit that classroom with the shuttle mock-up and Mission Control room later this week. And on the last day, you'll each play a role in a simulated shuttle mission," he said. "Commander, pilot, flight director—just like NASA."

How thrilling! I was going to be just like the kids I'd watched in *SpaceCamp*. I already knew I wanted to be the commander.

We ended the tour in the gift shop, a treasure chest for space fans. Everywhere I looked there were rotating displays full of posters of the shuttle and Saturn V rocket, and postcards of astronauts on the moon. There were caps, notebooks, and bins full of pencils and pens, all with images or logos I wanted to be associated with. Elliot chuckled and said, "Careful, this is the most dangerous room. You'll want everything in here."

He was right. I wanted key chains and mugs, posters and mission patches naming Apollo, Skylab, shuttle flights. I decided I'd buy a space shuttle model, and I found one for $10, half the spending money my parents had given me. I did some math and figured I could leave with a big poster of the space shuttle *Columbia,* a postcard, a few mission patches, and maybe some freeze-dried ice cream, which the package described as a *shelf-stable treat made for astronauts*. That would be a cool thing to take home and share with my friends.

By evening, I was so tired I could barely keep my eyes open. I showered, put on my pajamas, crawled into my bunk, and fell asleep to thoughts of the thrilling training that would begin the next day.

The next morning after breakfast, Elliot walked our group to the museum floor and stopped next to a dark metal chair attached to a giant metal arm. He patted the arm and said, "This is the one-sixth gravity chair. It'll show you what it feels like to walk on the moon. Who wants to go first?"

My hand was up before he finished the question. Elliot laughed and said, "Okay, Nia. You're up!" He helped me into the harness, fastening the straps snug across my shoulders and waist, and clipped me in. It was like being power-strapped into a roller-coaster seat. He said, "Right now, the counterweight is taking most of your body weight. You're only carrying about one-sixth of it, just like an astronaut on the moon." I loved how Elliot spoke to us as if we were adults. It made me think the astronaut life was attainable for me, for all of us.

I tried to stand, and my legs shot up as if I were on springs. The room tilted, and I grabbed the straps to steady myself. "Whoa!"

Elliot laughed. "That's normal. Try taking a small hop, like this." He bounced on his toes.

I shuffled forward and nearly floated. It was like running in slow motion. I took another step, then another, until I was bouncing across the floor. My teammates laughed and cheered.

"Now go for a moon jump," Elliot called.

I bent my knees, pushed up hard, and sailed higher than I'd ever jumped in my life. I floated for two or three seconds before my feet touched the ground again. It was the coolest feeling I'd ever had. I actually felt like an astronaut!

After Elliot unstrapped me, I could barely walk straight, my legs felt so heavy. But I made it back to my spot in the group, grinning the whole way. One small step for a girl, but a giant leap for a girl with space dreams.

The rest of the week was filled with moments like that, exercises that seemed to belong in a different reality, like in someone else's life. The day after my moon walk, I tried the multi-axis trainer, a machine that spun me in every direction until I couldn't tell up from down. Elliot smiled as he buckled me in and said, "Hold on, Nia. You're about to tumble like a real astronaut." The machine started out with a gentle spin, and for the next minute I was tossed around like a sock in a dryer. When the spinning finally stopped, my teammates laughed as I staggered out of the machine, dizzy and laughing with them.

Later that week, we built model rockets and went out to the open field behind the dorms to launch them. We all set our rockets onto their pads, and Elliot moved down the line helping us thread thin ignition wires into place. "Ready?" he said. "Count down!" We all counted down from ten together, our voices tumbling over each other. ". . . three . . . two . . . one . . . Ignition!" Elliot pressed a button, and a sharp *whoosh* split the air, followed by a curl of white smoke and the tangy smell of gunpowder. My heart jumped as my rocket shot upward. For a moment, it looked like a real rocket launch, tiny but fierce, climbing into the sky. Sarah's rocket flew the highest, and we all screamed and clapped for her. We were astronauts, all part of a team.

The evenings were quiet, but just as memorable, as we watched *The Dream Is Alive* and *Hail Columbia!* at the museum's Space Dome IMAX Theater, then listened to Elliot talk about space exploration. Every night, Sarah and I whispered about the evening's movie, like the scene in *The Dream Is Alive* when the shuttle lifts off in slow motion and the flames fill the screen. It was so powerful we felt the seat vibrating. And the scene in *Hail Columbia!* when astronauts float inside space shuttle *Columbia* for the first time, pushing off walls and turning in midair. We talked and dreamed in the dark of our dorm room until one of us finally fell asleep.

March 3 was the fifth day of camp and my twelfth birthday. Had I been in Chicago, I would have taken cupcakes to school, then had a birthday sleepover with a few friends. We would have eaten cheese and sausage pizza from Broadview Como's pizzeria and watched movies from Blockbuster. Not this year. But I was attending a camp for future astronauts, and I couldn't imagine a better birthday present.

On that day, just before lunch, our team was scheduled to taste "real astronaut food." Elliot didn't tell us what that meant, but anything having to do with being an astronaut sounded good to me. On the way to the cafeteria, he stopped our team in front of the gift store and said, "Okay, guys, take a few minutes to look around before we hit the caf." As we wandered the gift shop, Sarah asked me, "Are you going to buy a shuttle?"

I shrugged. "They cost too much. I'll get a poster of space shuttle *Columbia* and some dried ice cream. What are you getting?"

She waved her hand across the shuttle models. "Which one do you think I should get?"

"Depends on how much money you have."

"Twelve dollars. Will you help me pick one?"

I picked up the plastic shuttle I'd admired during my first walk through the gift shop and handed it to Sarah. "I'd go with this one."

"Cool. I like that one, too." As she carried her shuttle model to the register, I watched her with envy.

In the cafeteria, my team sat at our usual table near the window. I loved that we ate every meal with a view of the exhibit area. It meant that three times a day, I got to look at that massive rocket. Every time I looked, it seemed as magnificent as the time before. Shortly after we sat down, a counselor approached our table carrying a milk crate full of square white packages that looked like stuffed envelopes. "You guys ready?" she asked, handing one to each of us. "This is dried ice cream, the same kind astronauts eat in space. See what you think."

I tore open my package, tipped my head back, and poured some of the crumbled ice cream into my mouth. It was hard and dry and tasted like strawberry-flavored air-popped rice cakes. I thought, *How is this stuff supposed to be anything like ice cream?* As the crumbles dissolved in my mouth, I looked around the table. Everyone was grimacing. Maybe I wouldn't buy any of this stuff in the gift shop after all.

On my way to the lunch line, I glanced out the window and saw my mom. What was she doing here? Had something bad happened? And what was that white box in her hand? I dashed out of the line and hustled to the rotunda. Mom's back was facing me as she leaned over a table. I said, "Mom?"

She turned around, set the box and a white bag on the table, stretched her arms toward me, and with a big smile said, "Happy birthday!" We hugged, and she said, "I brought you a cake!" She flipped open the top of the box to reveal a beautiful white and purple cake decorated with balloons, then pressed candles into a delicious-looking buttercream frosting.

I should have known my mother would never let my birthday go by without some kind of celebration. She always made sure to mark the day with something special, maybe a birthday party, but always a tray of cupcakes for me to share with my friends at school. Sometimes both. And now here I was being presented with a birthday cake in front of a giant rocket. This was the best birthday ever! I heard voices behind me and turned to see Elliot and the other Team Grumman members walking toward us. Mom started to sing, "Happy birthday to you . . . ," and they all joined in and clapped. Sarah stepped forward and handed me a bag from the gift shop. "Happy birthday, Nia. Keep reaching for the stars."

I opened the bag and pulled out the plastic space shuttle model I'd guided her to buy. Elliot and all the kids in my group were beaming at me. They'd all been in on it, but I hadn't had a clue. My whole body buzzed with happiness. I'd just turned twelve, a junior astronaut surrounded by a bunch of people who'd seemed like strangers only days earlier, but now felt like my best friends—and not just friends, fellow astronauts!

Mom cut the cake and passed slices around to my teammates, then offered the rest to Elliot to share with the other staff members. While my team ate lunch inside, I sat with Mom outside on the rotunda and told her about all the fun I'd had during the week learning about rocketry and experiencing the one-sixth gravity chair and the multi-axis trainer.

"Sounds like you're having a blast!" Mom said, then she stood up. "I'll let you get back to your team. I promised to keep this visit short."

"I'm surprised they allowed you in at all—and with a cake!"

Mom set her hand on her hip. "Nobody was going to stop me from seeing my daughter on her birthday!" I stood up, and she reached out her arms. "Happy birthday, sweetheart. I love you, and I'll see you tomorrow at graduation."

I let the hug linger. "Thanks, Mom. I love you, too."

That day had offered another example of what a wonderful parent my mother was. She'd arranged with the camp staff to mark my birthday in a way that made me feel special, but that didn't intrude on the immersive experience the people at Space Camp wanted for us. She showed up, showed her love, and then dashed off to leave me to whatever came next. And as far from home as I was, because I knew my mother was just down the road, I was free to fully immerse myself in the camp without having to miss a minute feeling unmoored or homesick. I wished this kind of mom for every kid in the place, for every kid in the universe.

The next morning, my team performed a simulated space shuttle mission. The simulation involved reading from a script as we called out real space flight terminology and procedures. Each of us had clear roles and had to perform our tasks at just the right time. We used real switches and controls, and the video screens in the shuttle and Mission Control glowed with green words and numbers, feeding us mission data. Some screens even displayed black-and-white footage of an actual shuttle mission. What had once been a classroom was now Mission Control. Desks were lined with computers and headsets, and big signs with acronyms like CAPCOM and FIDO made it feel just like Houston. Across a divider stood the shuttle mock-up, its cockpit outfitted with chairs for the commander and pilot, surrounded by panels of blinking lights and switches. Behind them was a small mid-deck area where the payload and mission specialists sat.

The day before the mock mission, we'd taken a test on everything we'd learned at camp, and our scores determined which position we could choose for the mission. I had the third-highest grade, and after Sarah chose the role of commander and Mike chose to be the pilot, I chose to be the boss on the ground, the flight director, which made mine the lead voice on the ground running the countdown. Not being able to be the commander stung for a minute, but I reminded myself we were a team and every member had a crucial role. Other team members chose the roles of payload and mission specialists aboard the shuttle, and guidance and propulsion officers stationed in Mission Control.

I sat at my station, slipped on my headset, and focused on the countdown script in front of me. When Elliot gave me a thumbs-up, I pressed the button on my headset and tried to make my voice sound calm and official. "Shuttle, this is Mission Control. Prepare for launch sequence. Report when ready."

Sarah's voice came back, clear but a little shaky. "Mission Control, Shuttle is go for launch. Crew is strapped in and ready."

I grinned at the sound of the NASA talk, then straightened up and read my next line. "Copy that. All stations, final status check."

One by one, my teammates spoke, some whispering like kids afraid of messing up, others yelling as if they were calling a baseball game.

"Propulsion, go!"

"Communications, go!"

"Payload, go!"

I took a deep breath. This was it, the greatest experience in a week of great experiences. "All systems go. Commencing countdown at T-minus thirty seconds."

Everyone listened quietly as I began the countdown. My voice wobbled at first, but by the time I got halfway down, I sounded strong and confident. ". . . three . . . two . . . one . . . Liftoff!"

Sarah shouted into her mic, "Liftoff confirmed! Roll program initiated!"

All of us on Team Grumman celebrated with cheers and claps as if we'd really sent Sarah and the crew into space. For those few minutes, we were astronauts.

After we completed our space mission and landed back on Earth, Elliot debriefed us, then told us to hustle back to our rooms to pack before graduation. I practically walked on air as I headed to my room.

Graduation felt like a big deal. Even though we knew it was only a weeklong camp we were "graduating" from, all of us seemed to feel the significance of what we'd just experienced. We wanted the acknowledgment that we were now somehow beyond where we'd been on day one, and I felt like the dream was more alive.

The ceremony took place in a large room with a stage at one end and rows of chairs set up for an audience. Parents sat on one side of the audience, and campers sat with our teams in the middle. The camp director called one team up at a time and presented each team member with a certificate and official Space Camp wings. The wings felt solid and heavy in my hand. I looked down at them and thought, *I earned these.* I showed up and paid attention and learned. I was part of a team. In that moment, I was not only proud of myself for taking the program seriously, I was lifted by awareness that the effort and support of my parents and the involvement of every person at this wonderful Space Camp meant my dreams were being taken seriously.

I took pictures with Elliot and said goodbye to my team members, then Sarah and I promised to write to each other. As I watched people hug one another, I felt the weight of goodbye, knowing that some of us would never see each other again. It was the first time I realized people could come into my life, share something meaningful, then move on.

Mom and I left the building, got into the car, and pulled out of the parking lot, and I looked back at the Saturn V rocket standing high above the trees. I watched it as we drove away, not taking my eyes off of it as it grew smaller and smaller.

I'd been at the camp only a week, but it had felt like longer, and as Mom and I rolled down the highway back to Chicago, I sensed I'd changed. I'd had a birthday, and going from eleven to twelve felt like a big jump, but it was a lot more than that. By the time I attended Space Camp, I was already two years into talking about becoming a pilot, writing reports about pilots, and watching the sky, always watching the sky. But Space Camp graduation lifted me to a new place, and I felt it in my gut. Becoming a pilot wasn't a dream anymore, it was a goal. A rocket had just cleared the launchpad. I wasn't up in space yet, but I'd achieved liftoff.

FIVE

Planes crashing into buildings.

Fire and smoke.

The country attacked by terrorists.

Countless people dead.

So many horrible images swirled through my mind, but the only clear thought I had was *I need to get home.*

The ramp agent could see Shye and I were rattled. His eyes were filled with sympathy as he said, "Well, I'll leave you to it," then turned and left the plane. The ramp area was packed with parked airplanes, but there were no trucks fueling them, no baggage cart trains moving luggage, no rampers marshaling airplanes in and out of parking spots. Airport staff was just sitting on picnic tables and benches. It was eerie.

Shye said, "I'm going inside to call Crew Scheduling. We need to be removed from this trip—both of us—and we need to get you home. Do you want to come inside or wait here?"

Seeing how paralyzed I was by the news, Shye hugged me. Wiping my tears, I said, "I don't want anybody to see me like this. And I need to call my mom."

He pulled a box of tissues from the storage compartment and handed it to me. I whispered, "Thank you" and reached into my purse for my phone.

"I won't be long." He stepped into the cabin and closed the flight deck door behind him.

I dabbed my eyes, flipped my phone open, and clicked the power button. As soon as the screen came to life, an alert of twenty voicemails popped up. Before I could check them, my phone rang.

It was Kamilah. "Are you *all right*?"

"I saw it. I saw the second plane hit." I barely recognized my own voice, so low and raspy. "The tower. I saw the plane fly into—"

She gasped, "You're in *New York*?"

"I was. I just landed in Boston."

"Have you talked to Mom?"

"Not yet." I heard my voice go lower, shakier. "I just want to go home and never get on a plane again."

Shye returned to the plane and opened the flight deck door. "The FBI wants to speak to us."

The *FBI*?

I told Kamilah, "I have to call you back."

"Don't worry," she said, "I'll call Mom right now." Then in a delicate voice she asked, "Are you going to be okay?"

"No." And I hung up. Normally, I wasn't blunt, but I blurted that "No" like a cranky gate agent near the end of a long day of hearing "Why is my plane late?" My mind seemed disconnected from my body as I grabbed my flight bag, purse, and luggage, then followed Shye toward the crew room. As I walked, my phone rang again. I took the call. "Hi, Mom."

My mother's voice was quiet. "Oh, Nia. I can't believe what's happened. I am genuinely concerned. You need to talk to someone."

"I'm on my way to talk to the FBI now."

"No, a counselor. The company needs to get someone from a crisis intervention team to talk to you."

"I don't have time right now, Mom. I have to find a way home."

"Wait, who's your supervisor? I'll call the company. But first I'll call your father, tell him you're okay."

That was Mom. Take charge. Do what needs to be done. I gave her the number for my chief pilot, the go-to supervisor for pilots, who handled our scheduling and made sure we were well trained and flew safely.

"Thank you," she said. "I love you. Talk soon." Then she hung up.

I hustled across the ramp toward the crew lounge. As I walked, a young Black man wearing a yellow ramper-in-training vest approached me. He smiled and asked, "When do you think you'll be ready to board?"

Was this guy trying to be funny? "Are you *serious*?"

He pulled a piece of paper from his pocket and glanced at it, then looked up at me. "You're the Newark crew, right? Flight 6217 departing ten forty-five."

I just shook my head.

"They're saying it's only a two-hour delay. I just need to know what time you want to board so I can tell ops."

This was some kind of shocking, confusing screwup. At this point, who in that airport could have been so checked-out they could seriously suggest getting ready to board? I said, "*Ops* will have to find someone else to work this flight. Now excuse me."

I kept walking, but he stayed on my heels. "You're not going to time out, are you? It's only a two-hour delay."

Wait a minute, I thought. *Was it possible this guy hadn't heard the news?* I stopped walking and looked into his eyes. "If you saw what

I saw, you'd know why I'm not flying that plane." Then I turned and walked into the crew room.

The room was full of pilots, flight attendants, and other ground personnel, and they all looked up at me with questions in their eyes. Before I could say a word, someone yelled, "First Officer Nia Gilliam!" It was the ramper who'd told Shye and me the news. He was standing by the admin desk motioning for me to pick up the landline. "The company wants to talk to you."

Great.

I picked up the phone. "Hello, this is First Officer Nia Gilliam."

"Nia, hello. This is Rob Speaks, director of operations. I'm calling to let you know you're released from the rest of your schedule."

Normally, this kind of phone call would come from a crew scheduler, not from upper management. I didn't know how this man knew I'd refused to fly, but I was relieved he was the one to personally release me. "Thank you, sir."

"And First Officer Gilliam, before you leave the airport, the Red Cross is available. I want you to speak with someone."

I said okay, but inside I bristled. I'd never wanted to get away from an airport more than I did in this moment.

Across the room, Shye stood surrounded by police officers. He motioned for me to end my call and mouthed, *FBI.* I thanked the director of ops, hung up, and followed Shye and the Airport Authority Police to a squad car. In a few minutes, we were at the airport's fire station—I didn't ask why—where a man in a black suit introduced himself as FBI Agent Davis and said, "Please follow me," then led us to a room crowded with men and women in all kinds of uniforms—police, fire, airport employees. Shye and I appeared to be the only two pilots. We walked past a room where a group of firefighters and police officers stared at a television. I kept my head down and walked until our escort told us to wait while he looked for a private interview room.

Shye looked back toward the room with the TV and said, "I'm going to see what's on the news." After a few minutes he came back. "You don't want to see it." His voice had the same flat affect as when he'd reported "not good" about what was going on across the river.

The FBI agent returned and led us to a conference room. Shye and I sat next to each other at one end of an enormous table, looking at each other now and then to share a pinched smile. Several minutes later, a middle-aged white woman with wire-rimmed glasses and shoulder-length black hair walked into the room and spoke to an officer, who pointed at me. The woman walked to our end of the table, said, "My name is Holly. I'm with the Red Cross." She pointed to a chair. "May I sit down?" I nodded. "I understand you both witnessed a traumatic event, and I want to help you work through your feelings about what you saw."

Ugh. And so it began. Everybody wanted to talk. Everybody wanted to hear about something I wished I'd never seen. It was too soon for these conversations. Talking about what I saw meant reliving it, and all I wanted was to erase the images and find my way home. I said, "Holly, I know you do important work, and your intentions are good. But I don't want to talk about what I saw. I want to go home. I'm not getting in a plane again. Ever."

The look on Holly's face said, *Wow. This one is a lot.*

Just then, Agent Davis returned and said he needed to talk to me. Holly jumped out of her seat and insisted she speak with me first. Then the two of them shuffled a few feet away and I overheard Holly say she had responsibilities as a crisis counselor. Agent Davis said he was dealing with an issue of national security. The longer they bickered and bartered, the more I became agitated. Eventually, they cut a deal: Holly would get to talk to me again, but not for long. Agent Davis stood nearby waiting his turn as Holly spoke some encouraging words that I tuned out, and when she stood up to leave, she touched my arm. "The terrorists want victory. If they take your career from you, they win. Don't let it happen." She was right, but I simply couldn't imagine ever flying a plane again.

As soon as Holly walked away, Agent Davis sat across from Shye and me. Pad and pen in hand, he was all business. "Captain Gilad, First Officer Gilliam, I understand it's been a difficult day, and I appreciate your time. Your flight was the last to depart from Newark. It would help our investigation to know what you saw."

Shye and I walked him through everything, from pushback in Newark to landing back in Boston. Then Agent Davis leaned forward, pen in hand. "Was there anything en route that was out of the ordinary?"

Shye nodded. "Yes. The command from the FAA to increase cockpit security."

I added, "There was also a transmission that sounded odd. Like a stuck mic. Muffled, scratchy—we couldn't make out the words, but it sounded like there was a struggle. It was very unusual."

Agent Davis jotted on his pad. Then he stood. "Let me quickly check with my supervisor. If there's nothing else, you'll be free to go." And he left the room.

While Shye sat next to me making phone calls, a brown-haired man who looked to be in his early thirties approached me. He wore khaki pants and a light blue button-down shirt. Great. Another interview. Who was *this* guy? His voice was gentle. "Hello, Nia, I'm Ed." He reached out to shake my hand. "I'm with Boston Emergency Services. I'm here to talk about what you saw at the World Trade Center."

I shook his hand and sighed. "I just told the FBI everything I remember."

I glanced past him at the clock on the wall. It was 11:47. Still morning. The morning that hijackers intentionally crashed airliners full of innocent people into skyscrapers full of other innocent people, and I'd seen it. The horror of the experience seemed to be creating a strange numbness in me, all through me. Already it seemed like a surreal, never-ending day, and I was no closer to getting out of this place and getting home.

Ed said, "I'm a grief counselor" and pointed to the empty chair next to me. "May I sit?"

I rolled my eyes. "I already spoke to the Red Cross."

He sat and clasped his hands together. "Boston Emergency Services isn't part of the Red Cross. I'm here to offer counseling." Ed's voice was like a lullaby. "I know you witnessed a tragic event, and I want to help you process it."

"If you want to help, help me get home."

Before he could continue, Agent Davis returned to the table and handed Shye and me business cards. He said, "Thank you again. You're free to go. Please call if you think of anything else."

Shye and I sprang from our chairs and headed toward the hallway with Ed following like an emotional support Labrador.

Once we were away from the FBI, Shye stopped and shook his head. "I called around for rental cars, but there are none—not at this airport or anywhere near Boston."

"*Every* rental car is gone?" I gasped. "How are we supposed to get home?"

Shye let out a heavy breath. "One of the flight attendants lives in Burlington and offered me a ride."

I pressed my hand to my chest. I was happy for Shye, but the idea of his taking off for the comfort of his home life and leaving me behind sent a stab into my stomach. I didn't want him to see me upset, so I said, "Maybe I can take a bus to Chicago. I need to get the schedule. . . . Where's a phone? I'm getting home if I have to walk."

Shye said, "I'll find a computer and check the bus schedule online." Then he dashed down the hall.

I walked toward a bench along the edge of the hall, and Ed stayed close by. We watched the chaos in the building—people walking or running in every direction. A clergy member wearing all black with a white collar wandered in circles, then stopped and clasped his hands and lowered his head to pray. He must have felt me watching because after he opened his eyes, he walked toward us. With his hands still clasped, he said, "I'm praying for you both." I nodded and forced a smile. Ed said, "Thank you. We appreciate your prayers."

The clergyman walked off, and I turned my attention to Ed, who was now leaning against the wall with his arms crossed. He looked like the new kid who's afraid to talk to anyone at the school dance. I asked, "What did you say your name is?"

He uncrossed his arms and stood straight. "Ed Henrichs."

I slid over on the bench to give him room to sit. "Were you assigned to me or something?"

Ed sat on the opposite end of the bench and turned to face me. "I was one of the first people dispatched to help the Red Cross, and when I got to the terminal, the supervisor said they needed a counselor to talk to a pilot at the fire station. I volunteered."

Mom. She'd made that call just as she'd said she would. And now

I had Ed hovering and caring. I appreciated that he cared, but was in no mood for hovering. I knew Mom meant well, but her help was slowing my escape. I managed to smile. "Ed, I really appreciate what you're trying to do here, but I'm in no mood to talk. I need to get home."

He leaned forward. "Where's home?"

"Chicago."

Before he could ask anything else, Shye marched back up the hall, waving me to him. Ed and I stood and walked toward Shye, who said, "There's a computer in one of the offices upstairs. Follow me." The three of us made our way through the chaos, and Shye talked as we walked. "I checked online. The bus schedule is bad. The next available bus isn't until tomorrow night, and it doesn't get to Chicago for three days."

A tear rolled down my cheek.

"You could take the train?" Shye said with hope in his voice.

"I don't think I can afford that."

We finally reached a large office with a window looking out toward the dormant airfield. Shye sat in the black leather chair behind the desk and logged on to the computer. I sat across the desk from him in a cloth office chair and picked at the fabric. I crossed my legs at the ankles and tried to stop them from shaking. Ed walked around the office looking at the books on the shelves and certificates on the wall.

"Okay," Shye said, looking up from the computer. "I made your reservation. The train leaves at one forty-five P.M. You'll be home by tomorrow."

"Really? Tomorrow?"

Shye's smile beamed. "There was only one seat left. It's in business class. You should be able to relax on the trip home."

"Do I pay at the station?"

"I bought the ticket. You're all set."

I cleared my throat. "How much do I owe you?"

He flicked his hand in a dismissive wave. "That's the least of my concerns. Right now, we have to get you to the train station."

"Thank you so much! I'll pay you back as soon as I can."

He said, "Your train leaves in less than forty-five minutes." Then he snatched the paper from the office printer and handed it to me.

I read my reservation confirmation with the ticket number and price: $161. More than half what I had in my bank account.

Shye said, "Listen, I really want to make sure you get to the train, but Sherri said I'm not the only one catching a ride with her, and they're leaving in twenty minutes with or without me. It's my only way to get to Burlington."

Another knot twisted in my gut. Shye and I already had a great working relationship, but now, bonded through trauma, I wasn't ready to detach. I forced a smile and said, "I'm fine! Go, go! You've done so much already. I'm so grateful."

He didn't look convinced. "I really want to go to the train station with you, but—"

Ed interrupted. "I'll ride with her."

Shye reached out to shake Ed's hand. "I really appreciate it. I don't think Nia should be alone right now."

Shye and I hugged like loved ones at a funeral, and he said, "Call me as soon as you get home."

"I will."

He pulled away and looked at me. "You'll get through this."

I thanked God I had an escape from the confusion at the airport, stranded passengers who stared nowhere, and people asking me what I'd seen. Most important, I didn't have to get on a plane.

I was running out of time to get to the train station, so Ed called for an Airport Authority Police escort. I grabbed my luggage from the crew lounge and yanked the epaulettes and wings from my uniform, then pulled my crew badge lanyard over my head and stuffed it all in the pocket of my suitcase. I usually liked standing out as a pilot, but today I wanted to blend in.

An airline employee walked into the crew lounge and said, "You have a room at the Marriott. The company is putting up all crew members who are stuck in Boston."

"Thanks, but you can give my room away. I'm going home." I ran outside and jumped into the police SUV next to Ed, and we took off with sirens wailing. We screeched through intersections, then pulled up at the train station, and Ed and I hopped out and ran inside.

All around, crowds of people gathered in front of televisions, silent but for occasional gasps and moans of distress. I glanced at a screen and saw a plane flying toward one of the Twin Towers, so I looked away.

Then I scanned the departures board. My train had been delayed an hour. Not too bad. I stepped up to an agent at the ticket counter and slipped my reservation under the window. Now all I needed was a paper ticket, then I'd wait for my train and be on my way home. The agent glanced at my reservation, then up at me. "This train is delayed."

"Yeah, I know. By an hour."

"No, ma'am. It's not clear when this train will be departing." He turned away from me to look at the computer.

"*In an hour,*" I said. My voice was higher than usual. "I read it on the board."

The agent said, "Do you know about the planes in New York?"

Do I know about the planes in New York? Hot, red lava oozed through my veins. "What does that have to do with anything?" I yelled. "I'm *trying* to take a train to Chicago!"

The agent peered over his glasses and said softly, "Ma'am, all the trains going to Chicago run right through New York. With everything going on, they're not letting trains in or out of there."

What he said made sense, but I couldn't bear it to be true. I'd given up my hotel room. I couldn't get a car. *No train* would mean I was now genuinely stranded.

A voice boomed over the PA. "Attention in the terminal. Due to recent events in the New York and Washington, D.C., areas, all operations are suspended indefinitely."

I closed my eyes and stood frozen. The agent waited several seconds. Then he said, "Ma'am, I'm sorry. I have to close this window."

I rolled my luggage to where Ed stood in a crowd watching the news. Again, I refused to look at the screen. I'd watched it happen in real time, and I knew as long as I lived, I wouldn't be able to unsee it. All day I'd been living a slow-motion nightmare. And everything I'd worked for, everything I thought was solid, was coming apart.

Ed turned to me and said, "Let's get you to the Marriott. Maybe you still have a room."

At the hotel's reception desk, I stood in line behind a white man in a business suit, who slid a room key card across the counter. He said, "I'm checking out early."

What a lucky guy, I thought. Going home. I smiled across the lobby at Ed, who sat in a big comfy chair—still nearby for support, but giving me the space I needed to check in alone. Finally, a clerk gestured me to the counter.

I said, "I work for Atlantic Coast Airlines. They reserved a room for me."

"May I have your last name?"

I placed my crew ID badge on the counter and glanced at the man who was checking out. The clerk looked at my ID and said, "May I ask what you do for the airlines?"

"I'm a pilot."

Just then, a wave of something came over me—inspiration? Desperation? Determination? I said to the reception agent, "Could you give me just a minute?" Then I took a step toward the man in the business suit and cleared my throat. "Excuse me, sir. I overheard you say you're checking out early?"

He smiled. "Yes. My wife and I were supposed to fly home on Thursday, but with what's happened in New York, we decided to leave early."

After a long, awkward silence, I said, "Do you mind if I ask how you're getting out of town? I hear there are no rental cars left in or around Boston."

"Fortunately, we already had a rental and were able to extend it."

Could he feel my desperation? The awkwardness surging through my body? I had to get home. I had to try. "Sir, I work for the airlines, and I've had a very difficult day. I know this is going to sound crazy. . . ." I took a deep breath. "I really need to get home, to Chicago, but there are no rental cars. Could I please just ride with you somewhere? Anywhere, it doesn't matter where you're going. I just need to get someplace where I can rent a car."

His smile faded. "Well, we're headed to Memphis."

"I'll gladly ride with you toward Memphis. All I need is to get someplace where I can rent a car. I'll pay you whatever."

The East Coast felt like a war zone. The airport and train station had been chaos, and here everyone in the hotel lobby was scrambling as news reports blared from televisions. I needed out, *today,* and this man was my last hope. I started to cry, and through my tears I saw his face soften. He said, "Let me talk to my wife."

As he walked away, I said, "Thank you. Thank you so much."

I turned back to the desk clerk. He said, "Ms. Gilliam, if you could just sign here. Your room number is—"

"Cancel that." I yanked my ID badge from the desk and turned to see the Memphis-bound man talking to a blond woman, who held her arms tightly crossed against her chest.

Ed approached me. "What were you saying to that guy?"

"He's giving me a ride!"

Ed's eyebrows shot up. "Do you know him?"

"No, but I'm going home."

"Did you tell him what happened to you?"

"No, just that I work for the airlines."

"So he doesn't know?"

"He knows I need to get home."

"I'd better talk to him. Where is he?"

I could tell from Ed's tone he was most definitely going to talk to the Memphis man, and it warmed me that he felt protective of me in light of my willingness to jump into the car of these strangers I'd just met in a hotel lobby. For a moment, I thought about how much care I'd been shown in the past few hours. My mother's jumping into action to check on me and insist I receive counseling. Shye's hustle to help find me a way home. Ed's determination to stick around until he felt confident I was safe and going in the right direction. And maybe this couple headed to Memphis would be another source of help on a day I needed help so much. The attacks had created a strange, unstable, frightened atmosphere all around us, and in the midst of the chaos and darkness, I was grateful for the support of relatives, friends, and even strangers.

I walked Ed over to the couple and said to the man, "Hi again. This is Ed. I told him you were giving me a ride, and he wanted to meet you. I'm sorry, I didn't get your name."

The man extended his hand. "Rick." Ed shook his hand first, then I extended my hand and said, "Nia, Nia Gilliam."

His wife's face was a big blank stare. Rick touched her elbow affectionately. "This is my wife, Karen." Ed and I took turns shaking her hand.

I turned to Ed. "Could you keep an eye on my bag? I need to call my parents." Cell service was so spotty, I walked around the hotel until I found a pay phone at the side entrance. I dialed my father's cell number, and he answered after one ring. I took a deep breath. "Hey, Dad. I assume Mom caught you up on everything. I'm trying to get out of Boston. I met this couple from Memphis, and they're giving me a ride to . . . Well, to somewhere. Not sure where yet."

"Wait, I thought you were on a train."

"They shut the trains down." Then I told him about meeting Rick.

"Who are these people?" he asked. "Do you feel comfortable with them?"

"Rick seems nice. Not sure about his wife."

He paused. "Women usually aren't crazy about their husbands inviting strange women into their cars."

We both laughed, and I realized I couldn't remember the last time I'd found something funny. "I need to run, Dad. Just wanted to let you know."

"Okay, be safe, and thank them for me. And call in a few hours to let us know where you are. I love you."

"I will. Love you, too, Dad."

I hurried back to the lobby, where Ed was standing with Karen. Ed said, "Rick went to get the car."

By this time, Karen's energy had shifted. She seemed welcoming. Maybe this ride would be okay. "Were you able to get in touch with your parents?" she asked.

"Yes. My dad said to tell you and Rick thank you."

Karen smiled. "If you're ready, we can head out."

Ed said, "Just need to run to the restroom. I'll meet you out front."

Rick pulled up in a green minivan, and I sighed with gratitude at the size of it. I opened the back passenger door and placed my luggage inside. Then Ed came out of the hotel, smiling as he walked toward me. "I was hoping you hadn't left!" He handed me a business card and looked deep into my eyes. "Let me know when you make it home."

I took the card, then wrapped my arms around him. I'd known him for less than five hours, but he'd stood by me like a loving brother. When I got into the van and closed the door, I felt lonely to be leaving him. I rolled down the window, and he reached for my hand and wrapped it in both of his. "Have a safe trip, Nia. I'll be sending you very positive thoughts." Then Rick pulled away from the hotel, and I waved to Ed until he was out of sight.

It was then I realized this was the worst day of my life, I was in a vehicle with strangers, and I had no idea what was going to happen next.

SIX

After Space Camp, I was more convinced than ever I was meant to fly, and I looked for ways to feel involved with aviation. After building a model rocket at camp, I wanted to make a hobby of it, and my dad was happy to share that with me, so most Saturday mornings, he and I went to the local hobby shop and bought a rocket kit. One Saturday, we bought an Estes Alpha III, assembled it in the basement, then folded the orange and white parachute and clipped it to the nose cone, packing it carefully inside. We set the launchpad and rocket into a cardboard box about the size of a milk crate, gently positioned it in the back of the station wagon, and drove a mile and a half down the street to Pioneer Park.

I pointed toward the open center of the field. "What about there?"

"Looks like a good choice," Dad said. In the middle of the field, he placed the launchpad in the grass and knelt next to it. Two wires were clipped to a tiny igniter tucked into the rocket's motor, and they stretched across the grass, where their other ends connected to a handheld controller sitting about fifteen feet away. I stood beside my dad and held the rocket steady while he looked at me over his glasses. "You sure you packed the engine right?"

"Positive. I checked three times."

He smiled. "All right. Set it on the pad."

I slid the rocket down the base's silver rod until it rested perfectly on the red pad. Dad stood up. "Looks good. Ready for countdown."

We walked to the controller and slid the safety key into it, then I wrapped my thumb around the red launch button. My heart was thundering. It was like being back in Mission Control. "Five . . . four . . . three . . . two . . . one . . . Go for launch!" I pressed the button.

With a sharp hiss, the rocket shot off the pad and straight up. I gasped as it climbed higher and higher, until the parachute popped and the rocket drifted about two hundred feet into a cluster of oak trees along the perimeter of the park, getting stuck in branches. I looked at Dad and laughed. "First launch, partial success!"

The following weekend, we chose the wide-open softball field at Hines VA Hospital, where we'd have no interference from trees. I slid the rocket onto the pad. We hustled to the controller, and Dad said, "You ready? Five . . . four . . . three . . . two . . . one . . . Ignition!" The rocket climbed fast and straight into the air, and after a few seconds, the parachute opened perfectly, then the rocket drifted gently to the grass. Dad smiled with satisfaction. "Mission accomplished."

When I wasn't out riding my bike, jumping Double Dutch with friends, or launching rockets with my dad, I was usually reading, and I often chose my books based on the recommendations I'd heard on *Reading Rainbow,* a show hosted by LeVar Burton, whom I adored. *Reading Rainbow* was a PBS series that celebrated story-telling and encouraged kids to explore the world through books. Every episode felt like stepping into a new adventure, and I imagined someday I'd fly to the places I learned about.

My passion for flying kept growing. Over the next three years I returned to Space Camp two more times, but those later camps didn't offer near the thrill of my first. The more academic, lecture-heavy environment of Space Academy I was a drag, and when they told us that after astronauts return to Earth they undergo a crazy amount of physical testing, I thought, *No way do I want to be a lab experiment!* So I lost interest in space travel. Dr. Mae Jemison had already become the first Black woman in space anyway, so I no longer had that goal to reach for. But I was as excited as ever about one day becoming a pilot, and I convinced my parents to let me go back to Huntsville for Aviation Challenge. While Space Camp was about rockets and NASA missions, Aviation Challenge was Space Camp's cousin, focused on fighter jets and military-style training. It was like a teen version of *Top Gun*. We wore flight suits, sat through mission briefings, and spent long days built around teamwork and discipline. We trained in fighter jet simulators, practiced takeoffs, landings, and dogfights, and flew mock combat missions as a squadron. Outside the planes, we tackled obstacle courses and endured survival training on land and in water, using call signs and working as a team. It was rough and exhausting and thrilling.

Aviation Challenge gave me my first real look into the life of a military pilot. Strapping into a simulator, gripping the throttle and stick, I got to feel what it meant to be a pilot in command of a jet, which hooked me more than ever.

When I was back at school, one of my teachers told me about a real-life flying class offered at a nearby high school. I was desperate to take the class, but how was I going to do that if it was offered only in a different school district? I dashed home, called the high school, and asked a counselor about their aviation class. She said, "Yes, we do offer one, but only for juniors and seniors."

I could wait! "Do you take out-of-district students?"

"No, you'd have to live in the district to enroll. No exceptions."

I hung up disappointed, but determined. I had to take that class. That night during dinner, I blurted, "Mom, Dad, if you're already planning to pay tuition for me to attend a private high school, what do you think about using that money to live in Oak Park instead? The neighborhood and the schools are better, and did you know Oak Park and River Forest High School offers an aviation class? I could start learning how to fly a plane *in high school.*"

They exchanged the kind of look that said, *Here she goes again.* But I kept pushing. I told them everything the counselor had said about the aviation elective and ended my speech with "It would be a jump start on my flying career!"

Dad set down his fork. "Aviation class? In high school?"

I leaned forward. "The counselor said they have a real aviation elective—an actual course where you learn about flying, and then you go to the airport and fly."

Mom sat back in her chair. "Fly? At your age?"

"Not by myself. With an instructor."

Dad frowned. "That's a huge move for one class. What if you change your mind and don't want to become a pilot?"

I looked at him and tilted my head. "Me? Change my mind about becoming a pilot?"

Mom folded her napkin. "Oak Park is expensive."

"I know. But if you're already planning on private school tuition, moving to Oak Park makes sense. No tuition bill."

The table fell quiet. Dad glanced at Mom. They weren't convinced, but I could see the idea approaching the runway.

Then, in 1990, my parents made an extraordinary sacrifice: They sold the ranch home they'd loved for eleven years, and we moved six miles into a townhouse across the street from Oak Park and River Forest High School. The new home was much smaller than the one we'd left. We no longer had a finished basement, and because the new house was only a two-bedroom, my parents transformed the small den into their bedroom, so they'd gone from a master with en suite bath to a tiny makeshift bedroom with a bathroom across the hall. And we were so close to the tracks of the L, the constant rumble of the trains kept us all awake. Also, my father could no longer walk to work, so he became a driving commuter. They said goodbye to their beautiful garden and now were surrounded by cement. All so that I could be a pilot.

The next three years sped by, and I was on track to graduate as a junior. I took the aviation class, which was disappointing because, although the instructor was a private pilot, he didn't teach with passion. I'd imagined trips to airports and hands-on experience, but most of the class was just him at the front of the room reading from the Jeppesen *Private Pilot Manual* my father had given me when I was in fifth grade. I'd already been accepted at Lewis University, where I planned to study aviation, so during my last year of high school I focused on keeping my grades up and dreaming of the day I could pilot a plane. Then, when I was a couple months away from graduating high school, my history teacher made a suggestion that changed my life.

One spring day, a few minutes before the start of my AP World History class, my teacher, Mrs. Marques, called my name, held up a newspaper, and motioned for me to come to the front of the room. Mrs. Marques knew all about my aviation dreams. Why wouldn't she? I told everyone I met. When I reached her desk, she said, "Do you read the obituary section?"

"Um, no."

She looked down at the newspaper. "Yesterday, I came across this one for a pilot." She slid the paper toward me. "A female pilot. Chicago native. African American woman."

I grabbed the newspaper.

Mrs. Marques smiled. "Janet Harmon Bragg. Ever heard of her?"

"No, never."

"Seems like a very interesting woman. Maybe you should go to her funeral."

I looked at her. "But I didn't know her."

"Sounds like someone you would have liked to have known. She broke barriers. Who knows what you might learn?"

I looked down at the newspaper. She was eighty-six when she died and had been the first Black woman to earn a commercial pilot's license. *Wow,* I thought, mesmerized by those words. *The first.* I could only imagine the barriers she'd fought through. And she'd even bought her own plane! I kept reading and saw her service was the next day. I'd attended my aunt Modest's funeral when I was six, but that was all I'd ever known of death. I had certainly never expected to attend the funeral of someone I'd never heard of. It seemed like such an odd idea, but it was kind of cool that Mrs. Marques suggested it. And that she was encouraging me to do something so grown up. I looked up from the newspaper. "It's tomorrow. I can't go to that."

I thought I saw a twinkle in her eyes. "Do you have someplace else to be?"

Was she kidding me? "Well, there is school."

She looked at me without blinking.

"I'd have to *skip school*."

"And?"

Mrs. Marques was definitely one of my cooler teachers, but I didn't know she was this cool. I leaned forward and lowered my voice. "Are you telling me to ditch school?"

She peered over her glasses and spoke slowly. "I can't tell you what to do." Then she whispered, "But I think you should go."

For the rest of the morning, I thought, *Could I do this? Should I? Attend the funeral of a woman I hadn't heard of before today? What if I get in trouble for ditching school?* But my instincts were screaming at me to go. For the past seven years, I'd held on to thoughts of Bessie Coleman as the only Black woman who'd ever piloted a plane, but now I'd found out that Janet Bragg had been right in my backyard.

At lunchtime, I scrambled to find Kami in the cafeteria. She was just the person to tell about this crazy "skip school, go to a stranger's funeral" idea.

I'd met Kami in a summer school pre-algebra class three years earlier. She'd slid into the chair next to mine and said, "Hi, I'm Kamilah."

"Really? My sister's name is Kamilah."

She laughed. "Then you'll never forget mine, but everyone calls me Kami."

We compared birthdays and realized ours were two days apart. She nudged me with her elbow. "So basically, we're twins." Kami was funny, smart, warm, and easy to be around. From that day on, she was my best friend.

During our sophomore year, as a member of student council,

Kami had organized an assembly involving some of the original Tuskegee Airmen. They were scheduled to give speeches, then stay for a private gathering with student council members and school administrators. Kami, a great champion of my flying dreams, pulled off a thrilling surprise for me: She showed up at my chemistry class, told the teacher I had student council business, and escorted me to the event. Those former World War II pilots shared their heroic stories of battling racism while fighting fascism, and they talked about how, after the war, though highly trained pilots who had proven themselves in combat, they still couldn't get commercial pilot jobs because they were Black. They proudly called themselves "the DODO chapter" as a nod to the extinct dodo bird, which in its own way had also been grounded. I was fascinated by those pilots' stories. One of them, Captain Robert W. "Bob" Martin, was a Chicago native who flew P-51 Mustangs with the 332nd Fighter Group's 100th Squadron during the war. I approached him during the reception and asked, "Mr. Martin, what was it like flying the P-51?"

He smiled softly. "Like freedom. But it wasn't. We had to prove every day that we belonged in that cockpit."

"Were you ever afraid?"

"Of course. Every pilot is. Courage is flying anyway." Then he looked deeply into my eyes. "You're the reason we did it. Don't let anyone say you can't."

In the cafeteria after Mrs. Marques's class, I plopped myself down at the table, where Kami was about to bite into a hamburger. "I have to ditch school tomorrow for a funeral."

She looked up. "Oh, I'm so sorry. Who died? Wait, why would you have to ditch to go to a relative's funeral? It's an excused absence."

"It's not a relative. I never met the lady."

Her hamburger dropped onto her plate. "What?"

"Mrs. Marques showed me an obituary for a pilot, the first Black woman to earn a commercial pilot's license. Can you imagine? And she thinks I should attend the funeral."

"That's kind of weird. Isn't it?" She drummed her fingers on the table. "But no, maybe it's cool. Why not, right? And this pilot lived in Chicago?"

"Yep. Makes me sad I'd never heard of her. Didn't get a chance to meet her."

"Where's the funeral?"

"A church on Michigan Ave. I'll take the L."

She pushed her plate away. "Do your parents know you're going?"

"You think my parents would let me miss school for something like this? They *can't* know about it."

Kami looked up, as if into her thoughts. "You could say you're sick and need to stay home. Then when they leave for work, you leave for the funeral."

I shook my head. "It's at ten a.m. I'd have to get out of the house *before* my parents leave for work. It only works if my parents think I'm going to school and school thinks I'm home sick."

Kami leaned back. "Okay, how about this? You leave for school at the regular time, then go to the L stop on Lake Street and use the pay phone to call the dean's office pretending to be your mom. You're not sick, though—your mother is excusing you because you have to *actually* go to a funeral. Then hop on the L." She crossed her arms and smiled.

I smiled back. What would I do without Kami?

After school, I dashed home, called the Chicago Transit Authority, and asked for directions to the church. The agent explained a route I could take and sorted out the timing so I'd arrive in time for the visitation at ten o'clock. Then I could be back in school by twelve-thirty in time for lunch. Was I really going to do this?

April 15, 1993, felt like a day for mourning. The air was cool, the sky gray and dreary. As I sifted through my closet looking for clothes appropriate for both school and a funeral, I thought back to Mom's advice about riding the train. "When you ride the L, know who's nearby and what's going on all around you. All kinds of people ride the L, and some of them are crazy. Just mind your own business, keep your bags close to your body, and don't wear anything flashy."

No worries about not wearing anything flashy. I never wore flashy clothes. But I got the point: Don't draw attention to yourself.

I dressed in blue jeans, a long-sleeved navy-blue turtleneck, blue plaid flannel jacket, and white K-Swiss tennis shoes. Not great for a funeral, but it was the best I could do. I grabbed my book bag, ran into the kitchen, and almost crashed into my mother, who was dressed for work, holding a cup of coffee. "You're leaving for school already?"

I fidgeted with the straps on my book bag. "I'm going in early for help with a history assignment."

"Great," she said. Then she hugged me and headed out of the room. "Have a good day."

It surprised me how easy it was to lie. I'd always been honest with my parents, but this lie felt justified. I grabbed an apple from the counter and hurried downstairs, then out the door, calling, "Bye, Mom! Bye, Dad!"

On the way to the L station, I put Kami's plan into effect. I felt a little guilty calling school and lying, but was also impressed with my ability to impersonate an adult. The secretary actually believed me. Then I rode the L train and later a bus, following the steps the agent had given me. As I rode, I thought about how close Ms. Bragg had lived to me and what an opportunity I'd missed to reach out to and learn from a legend. But at least I'd be able to pay tribute to her now. About fifteen minutes before the funeral was to start, I arrived in front of St. Edmund's Episcopal Church, a tall redbrick building with bright red doors propped wide open.

My hands shook as I walked up the front steps. What was I trying to pull? I didn't know anything about funeral etiquette or even how these people might react to my not knowing anyone here.

At the top of the steps, I paused and caught my breath. *Nia,* I thought, *you need to see this through.*

At the entrance, a middle-aged Black woman in a dark skirt suit greeted me. "Good morning, young lady." She handed me a program. "Thank you for coming."

I peeked past her and looked inside the church. "Thank you. Can you tell me where I should sit?"

"Are you a member of the family?"

Ugh. Busted already. "No, ma'am."

The lady smiled. "Well, we're glad you're here." Then she pointed to the left. "Please sit on this side of the church."

I sighed with relief and took a few steps up the aisle. There were several people seated to the right and only a few on the left. At first, I worried about standing out, but then I thought, considering who Ms. Bragg was and what she'd accomplished, maybe it wouldn't be strange for Ms. Bragg's family members to see a bunch of unfamiliar faces over there. I also noticed there was no casket at the front of the church, just an easel with what appeared to be a fairly recent picture of Ms. Bragg. It was framed, and beautiful bouquets of flowers surrounded the photo.

I turned back to the woman who had greeted me. "Excuse me, I don't see, um, Ms. Bragg."

"It was the family's request to host more of a memorial service."

Disappointment flushed through me. I'd so wanted to see this magnificent pilot in person, even if I'd been too late to meet her in life. "Oh, okay. I think I should leave."

The greeter touched my arm and asked, "Are you okay?"

"I came here to . . . I was hoping . . ." I couldn't tell this lady why I was here, that I'd come just to see Ms. Bragg, that for the past twenty-four hours I'd been obsessed with a woman whose life had embodied everything I dreamed of and that I'd skipped school for the first time in my life so I could see her. I couldn't tell her I wanted desperately to see if I felt something magical in Janet Bragg's presence. I said, "I'm not really dressed for a church service. I just wanted to make a quick appearance, and—"

"Please don't leave," she interrupted. "I'm sure the family will appreciate it if you stay."

I glanced all around at the people gathering for the funeral in their lovely dresses and suits. "But the family doesn't know me."

"What I've learned is, when someone passes, loved ones appreciate who shows up. You're genuinely welcome to stay and pay your respects."

My *respects*. Interesting choice of words. To be here today, I'd been completely disrespectful to the most important people in my life. And to the school secretary. Add to that, I'd involved my best friend in my deceit. I sighed and took a seat in a pew on the left side.

It was almost ten o'clock, and the church was about half full. From where I sat, I could see past the greeter and into the outer lobby, where people were just arriving. A small crowd entered and thinned, then two people walked in who made me gasp.

Pilots. Two *Black* pilots! A man and a woman. She was light skinned, about thirty-five. She stood straight like a soldier and wore a suit of navy blue with three thin gold stripes on each sleeve cuff. Her relaxed black hair made me think of Dionne Warwick's: softly curled, feathered just right, and gently tapered at the sides. She looked so confident and put together—she was extraordinary. The man she was with also wore a pilot's uniform, and the two of them walked into the church, then headed up the aisle to the picture of Janet Bragg.

I thought, *Oh my God! Who is this woman? Could she be a relative of Ms. Bragg's?* I couldn't believe I was seeing two Black airline pilots in uniform, but I was fixated on the woman. Seeing her in front of me made all my piloting dreams seem even more possible. I couldn't have been more excited if I'd just bumped into Prince. Or Michael Jackson. Or LeVar Burton!

The service was scheduled to start at ten o'clock, which meant I had about ten minutes to meet that pilot. I had to talk to her now. What if she'd only come to pay her respects and was going to turn around and leave?

I edged up the aisle toward the duo, never taking my eyes off the lady pilot. When I reached them, I sensed I was standing in front of something sacred, as if Mother Teresa were in the room. I couldn't smile, couldn't speak. I just stood there, frozen in the moment.

The guy pilot noticed me first. "Hello," he said politely.

"Hi," I said and quickly turned my attention to the woman.

Then she spoke. "Hello, I'm Stayce Harris."

I gently shook her hand. "You're a pilot," I said, my voice quavering.

She smiled. "I am."

I swallowed and said, "What airline do you work for, and what plane do you fly?"

She and the other pilot exchanged smiles. "United Airlines. B747. What's your name?"

My joy spilled out in heavy tears that slid down my cheeks, and I fumbled over my words as I cried. "Nia. I'm . . . I'm an aspiring airline pilot . . . and I've wanted to . . . for half my life I've dreamed of meeting a Black female pilot."

Stayce pulled me into a warm hug. I wiped my eyes as fast as I could so she wouldn't see, and I couldn't bear to stain her sharp uniform. She gently patted my back. "Your name is Nia?"

"Yes," I said through sniffles.

She pushed back from the hug, but kept her hands on my arms and looked into my eyes. "Purpose."

She knew the Swahili meaning of my name! I nodded, which was all I could do as I tried to hold it together despite the emotions thundering through every part of me.

Stayce asked in a soft voice, "Are you staying until the end of service, or do you have to get back to school?"

I was an honor roll student who loved school, and I was only two months from graduating early. But in that moment, school felt irrelevant. I managed to whisper, "I'm staying."

"Great. Find me after the service."

The rest of the funeral passed in a blur. I heard speeches and tears. Someone told stories about Ms. Bragg's heroism and determination. Somebody said she'd had the dream of being a pilot since she was a girl and eventually owned her own plane. Another speaker said she'd bought her own plane and co-founded the first flight school owned and operated by African Americans at the Black-owned airport in Robbins, Illinois. It was a deeply moving morning, listening to people speak of such a brave, admirable woman. And the more I heard about Ms. Bragg, the more I wished I could turn back time and find her in Chicago, become her friend. Throughout the service, I stole glances at Stayce, sitting several pews ahead, and my stomach fluttered with anticipation.

When the service ended, I took deep breaths to gather the courage to talk to her again. She'd invited me to, but I still felt like an imposition, an interruption, a kid. She was standing in the aisle chatting to a few people, and I crept toward her, hoping I wouldn't have to speak first.

She spotted me and flashed a smile. "Hey, Nia," she said, stepping close to me. "What did you think about the service?"

"I'm glad I stayed."

Stayce laughed and nodded. "I'm glad, too." Then she reached into her purse, wrote something on the back of a business card, and handed it to me. "This is the hotel where I'm staying tonight. I fly out tomorrow morning, so can you call me tonight at eight? We'll talk about you becoming a pilot."

It was as if someone had just handed me a lottery ticket with six winning numbers.

On the train back to the suburbs every part of me lit up and tingled with joy. I'd just met the most fascinating person in the universe. She was smart and beautiful and kind. She was a real-life airline pilot. And she wanted to keep in touch with me!

Elated and confident about my path, I decided to come clean

with my parents that night. I'd been home for about an hour when I felt the rumble of the garage door opening. That meant Dad was home from work and Mom would arrive soon.

I looked into my bedroom mirror and practiced my opening line. "Mom, Dad—I have something important to tell you."

I'd just have to be honest. I'd tell them everything, starting with Mrs. Marques and the obituary. They'd be upset about my lying, but I'd try to breeze past that and focus on the life-changing event that had me floating on air.

I walked into the living room and said hi to my dad. Then I leaned into the kitchen. "Hi, Mom, can you come in here? I have something important to tell you both."

My mother hurried into the living room and stood near my father. Both of my parents were expressionless.

I took a deep breath. "I have some good news and some bad news. Which do you want first?"

Mom spat, "You're pregnant!"

"What? No!"

My mother's entire body seemed to relax, and she sat on the couch next to Dad. "Then you can tell us whatever you want, doesn't matter the order."

My dad half smiled toward Mom, then asked, "What's the bad news?"

"I ditched school today."

His face dropped. "You ditched school, and you're smiling?"

Mom said, "Shall we assume the good news has something to do with your skipping school?"

I rattled off the story in less than a minute, then, almost in unison, my parents said, "*What?*"

Dad said, “Slow down. Your *teacher* suggested you go to a funeral? And you decided—”

Mom interrupted. “Your teacher told you to skip school?!”

I decided to shift the attention away from Mrs. Marques. And I didn’t want to drag Kami into it, either. I looked at my mother. “No, it was my idea. I called myself in sick, pretending to be you. Sorry, Mom, really—so sorry.”

Dad said, “Why on earth did you feel the need to attend the funeral of—”

“I met a Black female pilot!” By now my voice had reached a crazy pitch. “Her name is Stayce Harris. She was there to pay her respects to Janet Harmon Bragg, the first Black woman to earn a commercial pilot’s license, who I’d never even heard of, by the way, even though she was from Chicago. I thought it would be an honor to go pay my respects to her. Stayce lives in California, and she flies Boeing 747s for United Airlines!”

They sat silent, apparently waiting for me to keep rambling.

“Aren’t you happy for me? I’ve wanted to meet a Black woman pilot almost all my life! She’s living the life I want! And I met her, and she wants to keep in touch. I’ve just met the mentor I’ve been wishing for all my life!”

My dad glanced at my mom, then looked at me. “Number one, you skipped school, and we’ll talk about that in a minute. But yes, I’m excited you met a Black woman pilot to be your mentor.”

Mom’s face softened. “And how do you know she wants this mentoring job?”

I handed her the business card. “We didn’t have long to talk today, but she told me to call her tonight at eight. That’s her hotel. Am I going to be punished for ditching school?”

My parents smiled at each other. Then Dad said, "You get a pass. This time."

That was just like my parents. I'm sure they thought they should punish me for being dishonest, but more important was that, on this day, I'd just met someone who we all knew would be a positive force in my life, and they wanted to let me fully experience the joy of what that meant.

I finished my homework and picked over my dinner. Then at 7:45 P.M., I announced I was going to call Stayce, and I ran up to my room, where I sat on my bed with the cordless phone in my hand and looked at the clock, then practiced what I'd say first. "Hi, Stayce Harris, this is Nia Gilliam. I don't know if you remember me, but . . ." That was ridiculous. We'd met ten hours earlier. "We met at the funeral today. I'm the aspiring airline pilot and . . ." Ugh, this was worse than asking a guy to homecoming. I wiped my hands on my lap, dialed 411, and got the number for the hotel. Then I dialed and asked for Stayce Harris's room. The hotel operator said, "One moment please."

I held my breath and tapped my feet on the floor.

The phone rang a few times. Then, "Hello?"

"Hi, Stayce, it's Nia Gilliam—"

"Nia, hey! Great to hear from you."

What a relief.

From there, our conversation flowed naturally. "I've wanted to fly since I was little," I told her. Then I went on to describe how I'd grown up watching planes take off from O'Hare, that I'd gone to Space Camp in Huntsville three times, that I'd spent weekends launching model rockets with my dad, all of it.

"That's amazing. Honestly, I didn't even consider flying until college."

"Wait, seriously?"

"Yep. I was a military brat, moved around a lot. Flying wasn't really on my mind growing up. But I was in ROTC, and one day I signed up for an intro flight lesson."

"And that's what did it?"

"Hooked me instantly. I ended up majoring in engineering, got commissioned in the Air Force, and later found my way to United."

I was quiet for a second. "Wow. I always thought every pilot was like me—dreaming about it since forever."

"Not always," she said gently.

I asked several questions about training and flying and listened carefully to everything she said. Then I asked, "Are you married?"

She hesitated a second. "Mmm, no." Then, with a little smile in her voice, she added, "But I did own a dog once."

I laughed. "I guess that's close enough."

How independent she seemed. I was mesmerized. I'd never met a woman who carried that kind of confidence and who didn't seem to need to prove anything to anybody. I could have stayed on the phone with Stayce all night, but after an hour she said, "Well, Nia, my flight leaves early tomorrow, so I have to get going. We'll talk again soon, but let me leave you with this: There's a two-week flight academy at Tuskegee University, where teenagers get ten hours of flight training with the goal of flying solo at the end of the two weeks. The students come from all across the U.S. to attend. There's an application fee and tuition fee, but there's also scholarship help." She paused. "Is this something you'd be interested in?"

I couldn't believe what I was hearing. Had God lined this day up just for me so I could meet Stayce Harris, who would guide me straight to a program like this? I silently screamed, then gathered myself. "Yes! That sounds awesome. I'd love to attend!"

"Great! I think you'll be perfect for the program. I'll send you the application as soon as I'm back in Los Angeles. Have a good night, Nia."

After she hung up, I sat there holding the phone. I was afraid hanging up might dull the joy surging through my entire body.

SEVEN

Stayce did send me that application. Four days after our conversation, the envelope dropped through our mail slot, I grabbed it, ripped it open, and within twenty-five minutes had applied to the Negro Airmen International (NAI) Summer Flight Academy on the campus of Tuskegee University and placed the application into the outgoing mail. Then I waited. One week later, I received a letter congratulating me on being selected to attend the two-week session. And the news got even better: The Organization of Black Airline Pilots would cover the $1,800 cost of the program. All I had to do was get there.

All my life I'd been uncomfortable saying the word *Negro*, but after I was accepted into the Tuskegee program, I told everyone I knew that's where I was headed. I was seventeen years old and a month away from becoming a first-year aviation student at Lewis University, a predominately white college, so I was eager to attend two weeks at one of the country's oldest institutions serving African Americans.

In the Montgomery Airport, I spotted a Black kid wearing a baseball cap and holding what looked like a walkie-talkie. He was lanky, about average height, with high cheekbones and a long, narrow face. I walked toward him. "Excuse me. Are you here for the NAI Summer Flight Academy?"

His voice was nasal but warm. "Yeah, hi. I'm Charles."

I shook his hand. "I'm Nia. What's this walkie-talkie thing you have?"

He held it up. "It's a transceiver so you can listen to pilots talk to air traffic controllers."

I'd never known a kid my age to own anything so professional or official. I said, "Wow! That's pretty cool." We sat on a bench together holding the transceiver close to our ears. All I heard was a steady squeal of radio noise, interrupted by male voices rattling off phrases so obscure, they could have been in some kind of spy language.

I liked Charles right away. He was an airplane geek like me. An hour passed, then we saw another Black teenager walking around, rolling a suitcase behind him. He gave a quick head nod, the kind of silent "What's up" Black folks everywhere recognize as a sign of kinship. I smiled and waved. He walked over to us and said his name was Freddie. Charles and I nodded and introduced ourselves, and Freddie joined us on the bench. Then a tall, slender Black man wearing a baseball cap that read NAI approached us. He said, "NAI Summer Flight Academy?"

We said a collective "Yes."

"I'm Al Glenn. Welcome to Montgomery." He opened his folder and confirmed we were on his list. "You three stay here while I look for the fourth."

About twenty minutes later Al returned with a short, skinny, brown-skinned kid with braces who looked about twelve years old. He said, "This is Andre." We all said hi, then walked to a van parked just outside the airport terminal and piled in. At first, the ride was quiet except for the hum of the highway and the low sounds of R&B on the radio. Then we told each other how we found out about the flight academy, and before long, the van passed through the gates of Tuskegee University. I sat pressed against the window admiring the brick buildings and wrought-iron fence with the big seal on the front. The place looked part university, part military, and being there felt like stepping into a history book. The air outside shimmered with heat, and the trees stood tall, their branches arching like a canopy over the road. The buildings weren't just brick and glass. They were a reminder of everything important that had been built here, by students who'd come long before us. I spotted the bronze statue of Booker T. Washington lifting a veil from a young man's eyes. It rose from the lawn like a symbol carved straight from the past.

Al stopped at a standard-looking student residence, shaped like a rectangle and about three stories high. He glanced back and said, "Freddie, Charles, and Andre, this is your dorm. Nia, I'll walk them inside and be back in a minute."

When Al returned, he drove me to a building that looked more like a historic mansion with its red bricks and rows of white-framed windows. It appeared to have been there for generations. In front of the building, a sign read SAGE HALL. Al walked me into the lobby entrance, which smelled of old wood and polished floors, then dropped me off at my room and headed out.

When I stepped into the room, two girls about my age were already settled in, beds claimed, bags unpacked. Carla, Monique, and I introduced ourselves, and Monique said, "We're gonna walk around campus. Do you want to come?"

I said, "Oh, thanks. But I'm going to stay back and unpack."

The door closed behind them, and the room felt huge. I unzipped my bag, arranged my clothes in the dresser, and stacked my notebooks on the desk. Soon I was laughing and dancing between the beds. I'd be here for two full weeks of learning to fly, and I couldn't wait to start.

AT SEVEN-THIRTY THE NEXT MORNING, we were on the bus to Moton Field, the very airfield where the Tuskegee Airman had trained during World War II—Captain Robert W. "Bob" Martin had taken off from here decades earlier—and now I was on my way to walk in all their footsteps. Seven years of passionate study and dreaming and talking about flying had led me here, and it wouldn't be long before I was at the controls of a plane for the very first time.

The twenty-four of us were divided into two groups. Half of us were to fly in the morning and attend ground school in the afternoon—vice versa for the other half—then we'd switch, which would allow us to experience both smooth, calm morning flying conditions and the rougher conditions usually present in the afternoon. During the first week, my group flew in the afternoons, and while I was antsy to fly, I was grateful to spend the morning hours studying aerodynamics, weather, and FAA regulations in the cool of the school's double-wide, mobile home-turned-office building. Our instructor, Mr. Spicer, explained that we'd "start with the basics of how a plane stays in the air: lift, weight, thrust, and drag." And he added, "By the time I'm through with you, you'll be explaining this stuff at the dinner table, and your mama will look at you sideways, wondering when you got so smart."

A few of us laughed, and I thought of how often I'd explained aerodynamics to my parents at the dinner table.

By eleven-thirty, the students in the morning flying session had logged their first hour of flight, while my group had completed an entire textbook chapter on aerodynamics. We broke for lunch, and by noon the cafeteria was buzzing with excitement. Monique and Charles had flown that morning, and they could hardly sit still.

After lunch, my group went to Moton Field, and Al directed me to a man waiting inside the trailer by the water station. He was broad shouldered and towered over me at about six feet four. He said, "I'm Sal, pilot for United Airlines. I know this is our first lesson, but today you'll be flying the plane."

I had known this was coming, but I felt my eyes grow wide.

He said, "Don't worry, we'll take our time, and you can ask me as many questions as you want. Grab a headset, and I'll meet you on the ramp at the plane."

I stepped into a room of the trailer, where several gray headsets hung neatly on hooks, and reached for one, my hand trembling. I stepped out of the trailer, scanned the ramp, and saw Sal standing with a few other men near the Cessna 172 I'd been assigned to fly. Two of them were flight instructors, but I didn't recognize the man who I guessed was in his eighties. He was dressed in khaki slacks and a white, short-sleeved button-down. He had the younger men in some kind of trance.

I walked over to them and stood next to Sal. When the older man stopped talking, Sal said, "Chief Anderson, this is my student, Nia. Nia, Chief Anderson was the chief flight instructor at Tuskegee during World War Two. He taught the Tuskegee Airmen how to fly."

The Chief Anderson? In aviation circles, everybody knew that name. I extended my hand and said, "It's an honor to meet you, sir."

He shook my hand and said a few words, probably encouraging

me to study hard and listen to my instructor, but I was in a trance. I snapped out of it when he clapped his hands once, like a signal, and said, "Okay, everyone, back to it. There's a car waiting to take me to my plane."

As Chief Anderson walked away, Sal said, "Do you realize who you just met?"

"Chief Anderson. A Tuskegee Airmen instructor."

Sal leaned back against the nose of the plane and crossed his arms. "Not just any instructor. He taught himself how to fly and with another aviator was the first African American to complete a round-trip, transcontinental flight between Atlantic City and Los Angeles. But he's most famous for flying Eleanor Roosevelt right here at Moton Field! That flight changed everything, because she went back to D.C. and convinced President Roosevelt that the Tuskegee program was worth backing. That's what opened the door for the Tuskegee Airmen."

Sal was right, I'd had no idea who I'd been standing in front of. Because of the doors that man had opened, I now had the chance to fly.

I climbed into the Cessna 172 and settled into the left seat, tightened the lap belt, and slipped on the headset. Sal folded himself into the right seat, his long legs bending awkwardly as his knees rose high. He pulled on his headset and grinned. "Ready?"

"Ready."

Sal talked me through the checklist, his voice steady and reassuring, like a guide on a trail he knew by heart. The engine started with a whine and a cough, then settled into the steady four-cylinder thrum Mr. Spicer had described in ground school. When the gauges came alive, Sal eased the power in to move the plane forward. I mirrored his every move on the controls as he taxied to the runway. My pulse drummed in my ears.

When we were lined up on the centerline, Sal said, "Your airplane."

I repeated, "My airplane."

I pushed the throttle forward and pulled back on the yoke, then the wheels lifted, and we climbed into the sky. I felt weightless—not like in the gravity chair at Space Camp, but something bigger. This time my hands were on the controls, and houses and trees shrank to tiny toys, cars crawled like ants, and the horizon stretched so wide it felt like the sky went on forever. All I could think was *I'm really flying. I am the one flying this plane!*

At altitude, Sal pointed to the horizon out the front window. "That line out there that divides the ground and the sky—that's your guide. Straight and level is about keeping the nose steady against it."

I tried to keep the nose steady, but it dipped, and Sal said, "Increase back pressure." I pulled gently on the control yoke and leveled the plane. A moment later, the sky filled the windshield, and Sal said, "Decrease back pressure."

I eased forward on the control yoke, and the horizon returned. Each correction sent a thrill through me. I was making the airplane do as I wanted.

After an hour of Sal's instructing me how to perform climbs, descents, and turns, he guided us back to the field. The airport seemed to grow larger, my pulse quickening with every second. Then he lowered the flaps to slow the plane and pulled back the power to let us descend, explaining each as he did them. "Eyes outside. Keep the centerline under your nose."

I tightened my grip on the yoke. From the right seat, Sal placed his hands on his own yoke so he could steady my movements if I drifted.

Together we guided the plane down, the hum of the engine softening as he reduced power and we sank toward the pavement. Then came the last step of the landing. He said, "Now the flare . . . Hold it off . . Hold it." I pulled gently, and the plane's nose rose, the sink of the plane slowed, and the wheels brushed the runway with a soft bump. Then the airplane settled, rolling straight, humming along the asphalt.

I'd done it! I hadn't done it alone, but I'd flown and landed a plane! It was the most extraordinary feeling I'd ever experienced. I'd felt the plane respond to my adjustments, my controls. I'd felt the landing through my own fingertips. My first time *controlling* an airplane. It was something I'd dreamed of for as long as I could remember, and it had been as thrilling as I'd imagined it would be. I exhaled for the first time in what felt like minutes. Sal glanced over and grinned. "Not bad for your first one."

I laughed, a little shaky, but I couldn't stop smiling.

For the next two weeks, I spent an hour a day with Sal, learning how to fly straight and level, turn the airplane, recognize and recover from a stall, follow engine failure procedures, and safely land the plane. Then there was only one more day left in the program, and everyone wanted to know if they were going to solo. Sal would decide that, based on how we flew with him on this second to last day. If I flew well, he might sign my logbook right then, then hop out of the plane, and send me back up *alone*.

That day, Charles, Monique, and Freddy were all chosen to solo, and when each of them was airborne, all of us on the ground erupted with cheers. During all three flights, it made me dizzy to think each of them was the only one in that plane. And after each flight, the instructor doused the pilot with a bucket of water, then cut a large square from the back of their T-shirt, and with a marker wrote the date and aircraft's tail number across the fabric and handed it back to them. I clapped and cheered with the others, but inside I was all tangled up. I was desperate to solo. I wanted the dousing, the cheers—all of it.

As the laughter and celebration carried on across the ramp, I felt a tap on my shoulder.

It was Sal. He nodded toward the Cessna 172 Freddie had just soloed in. "Our plane's back. You ready to fly?"

My heart leaped—this was it. I was going to handle the plane so expertly with Sal next to me, he'd sign me off, and I'd be up again in minutes, all by myself in the air.

I strapped into the left seat beside Sal, my palms already damp on the yoke. He gave me a steady look. "Just fly the airplane like you've been doing, Nia. You can do this."

I nodded, but my chest was tight, and as we taxied to the runway, then took off and began our climb, my thoughts ran wild. *Don't mess this up. Hold your airspeed. Not too high. Not too low. Keep it steady*. Sal watched every move. By the time we came in for the first landing, I was gripping the yoke so tightly my knuckles ached. I flared too high and felt the airplane sink, then I landed *thud* on the runway, harder than I should have. Sal's voice was calm. "All right, let's try another."

We tried twice more, and both times, instead of making small, steady corrections, I reacted late and did too much. I was overcorrecting, second-guessing myself, and pulling back on the control yoke too soon. Both landings came down hard and rough. After we taxied clear, Sal let the silence hang for a while, then his voice was gentle but firm. "I know you want this badly. And you're close—really close. But today you're in your head, and I can't sign you off like this. I'd be doing you a disservice."

My throat tightened. "I know. I was overthinking everything. I cracked under the pressure."

He nodded. "It happens to every pilot. What matters is that you keep flying. You'll get there."

After sunset, all the students and staff gathered in a campus meeting room to celebrate the new solo pilots and close out two weeks we'd never forget. I hadn't soloed, but I'd flown, and I'd completed ten hours of flight time. I'd also shared the same skies, the same runways, and the same spirit of determination that launched the Tuskegee Airmen into legends. That night, I felt a quiet strength.

BY OCTOBER OF MY FRESHMAN YEAR at Lewis University, I was deep into my studies as an airway science major. The program blended classroom courses in navigation, weather, and aircraft systems with the hands-on training required by the FAA—forty hours of flying, written exams, and a flight test—so I could earn my license while working toward a degree. In the last five weeks of training at Lewis, I'd logged another ten hours of flight time with Nancy, my flight instructor, and I expected I'd solo any day, so every day before heading to the airport, I dressed in a beat-up T-shirt, hoping that would be the day Nancy would finally cut the back off. But as the weeks passed, I tired of waiting, so one morning I gave up the ratty-shirt routine and just pulled on my favorite T-shirt with the Looney Tunes Tasmanian Devil stamped across the front and headed to the airport.

Nancy met me at her cubicle in the flight instructor's office. We went through our briefing as usual, talking through the maneuvers and her expectations of the day. I walked around the airplane to check everything—the fuel, the oil, the wings, and control surfaces—before climbing into the little Cessna 152, a smaller version of the Cessna 172, with only two seats instead of four. Nancy climbed into the right seat beside me. After takeoff, we headed to the practice area, a stretch of open sky used for training, and I practiced a stall, a steep turn, and "touch-and-go," which involved landing, then taking right off again without stopping. In the air after the touch-and-go, she said, "This time, make it a full stop, and taxi back to the runway."

I landed the plane, and Nancy turned to me. "You ready to solo?"

I blinked fast. "*What?*"

She smiled. "It's time. Where's your logbook?"

My hand shook as I dug in my flight bag and handed her my logbook. She scribbled in the book and said, "Do three takeoffs and landings to a full stop. I'll be listening on the radio. Have fun."

Oh my God, my first time flying alone. Could it be fun?

Then she stepped out of the plane, and it was just me. Alone. In an airplane. And before long, it would be just me alone in an airplane in the air.

The time had finally come, and my stomach twisted and twisted. I took a big breath, held it, then blew it out and thought, *You can do this.*

I pushed the throttle forward and eased onto the runway. At Lewis Airport there was no control tower, so it was up to each pilot to call their own takeoffs and landings over the radio. My voice shook as I announced, "Lewis Traffic, November seven-one-four-Yankee-echo, taking off runway two-seven . . ."

I pushed the throttles to full power and began rolling down the runway. Then I pressed the rudder pedals to keep the airplane straight on the centerline, my focus jumping between the instruments inside and the runway stretching ahead.

The speed built quickly, my heartbeat racing to match it. I could feel the airplane wanting to lift off, eager to fly, but this time there was no instructor beside me. The decision to leave the ground was mine alone. I wasn't sure I was ready.

Then I thought, *Too bad if you're not ready. What are you going to do, chicken out now? Fly!*

I scanned the airspeed indicator and said, "Sixty knots, rotate," then gently pulled back on the yoke and lifted the plane into the air. I was flying.

As the plane climbed, the altimeter needles moved clockwise in sync with my ascent to a thousand feet above the airport. "Lewis Traffic, November-seven-one-four-Yankee-echo, right traffic runway two-seven." My voice sounded stronger now.

I turned to the right, entering the traffic pattern like the solo students did at Tuskegee, and the airplane hummed along, light and eager without the weight of an instructor beside me.

I forced myself to breathe, scanning outside and then inside at the gauges. Airspeed, stable. Altitude, good. My palms were damp on the yoke, but the airplane felt steady in my hands.

Another right turn, and it was time to land. My heart boomed. Now it was just me, the airplane, and the strip of asphalt ahead. No voice in my ear to correct me. No steady hand on the controls to back me up.

But I'd come in too high. The plane wasn't sinking fast enough to land safely, and I was about to sail right over the runway, so I pushed the power back in and climbed back up for another try.

I brought the airplane back into the pattern, taking my time to set it up again—slowing down, lowering the flaps, lining up just right. This time, everything felt smoother, and the runway seemed to rise to the plane, the way it should. I eased back on the yoke, the nose lifted, and the wheels touched down with a gentle bump.

I'd done it—my first flight, my first landing. Alone. But there was no time to celebrate. I had to push the power in and get right back in the air for two more.

As the wheels touched down on the final landing and I slowed to exit the runway, relief washed over me. I parked on the ramp and shut down the airplane, the cockpit suddenly quiet except for the ticking of cooling metal.

It was late in the day, and the campus felt empty. There was no crowd waiting, no classmates cheering. Even Nancy wasn't outside waiting for me. She was inside at her desk. I walked in, and she said, "Congratulations." Then she outlined the next day's lesson, grabbed her bag, and said, "I've got to hurry home and make dinner."

That was it. No water bucket, no T-shirt cutting, no ceremony. Just me and the echo of what I'd accomplished. With no celebration in sight, I called home. Both parents answered. "I did it! I soloed today!"

My mother said, "You flew a plane all by yourself?"

I laughed, nearly shouting with excitement. "Yes! Three takeoffs and landings!"

My dad's voice boomed with pride as he sang out, "Well, allll right!" and my mom chimed in, cheering, "Go Niaaa! Go Niaaa!"

Later, I painted the details of my solo across the back of my Tasmanian Devil shirt, cut my artwork out in a large square, and framed it myself. I had *soloed.* I had a long road ahead—maneuvers, cross-countries, and the FAA exam still waiting before I'd become a pilot—but on that day, I'd flown a plane, with no one sitting next to me.

THROUGH THE END OF FALL and into winter, Chicago's skies were often covered in low gray clouds. As a student pilot, I was limited to flying only under visual flight rules, which meant the weather had to be clear enough for me to see and avoid other airplanes, airports, and obstacles. When the clouds sank low, my practice flights were canceled. Each cancellation pushed my training back, and the long gaps meant I spent more time reviewing old lessons instead of moving forward. Progress felt painfully slow. And I never clicked with Nancy. She was often terse, impatient, rushed. She showed no understanding of why an instructor should offer not only guidance but compassion. I was never sure she was on my side.

By spring semester, with the end of my freshman year approaching, I still hadn't finished the last training requirements for my private pilot's license, without which I couldn't enroll for my sophomore year. I hadn't yet done my cross-country flight, which usually meant flying far enough from the home airport to practice navigating and landing somewhere new. After that, I'd have to prove myself while flying with an FAA examiner.

Finally the weather cleared, and the day came for my cross-country flight. From my dorm room, I checked the morning weather, mapped my route, and made a detailed plan to track my flight from start to finish. Then I drove to the campus airport.

I didn't see Nancy in the briefing room, so I walked on the ramp toward the two-seater Cessna 152 I'd be flying that day. We were scheduled to fly 230 nautical miles from the Lewis University Airport to Whiteside County Airport in Rock Falls, Illinois, then to Peoria International Airport, then back to Lewis.

I hummed a happy tune while I completed the exterior preflight. I'd already spent forty hours flying C152s, so this was going to be a great day. All I needed was a successful flight, then I'd get Nancy's endorsement in my logbook—the final stage before taking my FAA exam and becoming a licensed pilot.

I climbed into the plane, latched my seat belt, and waited. Still no sign of Nancy.

Ten minutes passed, and with every minute I waited, I feared my flight was going to be canceled. Then, five minutes after we were scheduled to depart, Nancy burst into the plane. "Ready to go?"

Her frenetic entrance shook me up, but I kept my voice steady. "Preflight checks are complete. Before start checklist . . ."

I ran through the checklist items, started the engine, and taxied us out. Within minutes we were lined up on the runway, and I pushed the throttle forward, the airplane surged, and we lifted into the air. My grip on the yoke was tighter than usual, my pulse still racing from her hurried energy, but as the Cessna climbed and leveled off, the steady hum of the engine calmed me.

Ten minutes into the flight, I glanced at the altimeter, which read approximately 4,500 feet, my planned cruise altitude for the first leg of the flight. I looked at my sectional chart and noticed we were approaching the first checkpoint, a railroad track—right on time. I glanced at my watch, then down at the railroad tracks stretching across the ground. The checkpoint was right where I'd planned it, based on my aircraft speed and distance after departure. I cross-checked with the VOR—a ground-based radio beacon. By tuning into its signal, I could confirm exactly where we were in the sky. Everything lined up.

"Checkpoint confirmed," I said, proud of my precision. This flight was going beautifully.

Just then, Nancy leaned in, her voice sharp. "You're taking too long!"

"Too long? We're exactly where I calculated we'd be."

She shook her head. "You should have already figured out what time you'll cross your next checkpoint. And that railroad isn't the best choice. You need a major highway intersection."

My grip tightened on the yoke. "You approved my landmark choice."

"*I'm telling you* a major highway intersection is what you should have chosen!"

I fired back, "*Don't* yell at me!"

Nancy slid to the right, as if trying to distance herself from my anger, then bumped into the right passenger door. She yelled, "We're done here! We're going back to Lewis!"

She tried to reach for the controls, but I pushed her hand away and yelled, "We are *not* going back. You're going to shut up and sit there! I know what I'm doing. Be quiet and let me show you!"

For the rest of the trip—during which I successfully navigated to Whiteside Airport, where we landed, refueled, and continued to Peoria, then back to Lewis Airport—Nancy kept her mouth mostly shut, speaking only when I asked flight-related questions. After I landed and parked the plane, she said coldly, "Your flight was well planned and well executed."

I thought, *Of course it was. You just needed to give me a chance to show you.* Out loud, I said, "Thank you. I'm sorry I yelled. I just wanted to get through the lesson."

Nancy unclicked her seat belt. "I'll let the chief pilot know I will no longer be your instructor." Then she got out of the plane and walked away.

Her words hit me like a punch. I'd thought she'd accept my apology, maybe grumble about it, and then we'd move on to finish my training. I sat stunned.

What if I didn't get another instructor? What if I was kicked out of the program?

Before long, Nancy resigned from the flight department, stopped flying altogether, and enrolled in culinary school. I thought it great that no other flight student would be subjected to her lousy attitude.

There were now only three weeks left in the spring semester, and without a flight instructor assigned to me, there was no way I was going to finish my training before the term ended. Despite many calls, I wasn't getting answers from the program coordinator, academic adviser, or chief flight instructor. Then, thirteen days after Nancy quit on me, the chief flight instructor called and said I'd been assigned to instructor Andy Collins. What a relief. He had a reputation for being great with students and very easy to talk to. Working with Andy, I practiced takeoffs, landings, and engine failure procedures. He and I reviewed the test standards and completed my final cross-country flights. Working with an instructor so kind made it easy.

I kept training with Andy through the summer, and one day he ran me through a full mock check ride—an oral quiz and flight test where he played the role of an FAA examiner, carefully evaluating my performance. When we finished, he said, "You're ready to be tested by the FAA," and wrote the endorsement in my logbook. When he handed the book back to me, I nearly cried. I was one exam away from becoming a licensed pilot.

A few weeks later was the day of my FAA exam. That summer I'd been staying at my parents' home, about a forty-five-minute drive from campus, and my mom drove us to Lewis Airport, where I was to meet Bob Flynn, the FAA examiner who would conduct my oral and flight exam for my pilot's license. I looked out the window at the ramp, where a Cessna 152 sat waiting, its white wings gleaming in the morning light. Without looking away from the plane, I said to my mother, "If I pass . . . when I pass . . . I'll take you up. You'll be my first passenger."

She reached over and squeezed my hand. "You can do this. I'll be right here waiting."

I took a deep breath, got out of the car, and walked toward the building, where Bob Flynn was waiting.

Bob wore glasses and had curly gray hair. I thought he looked like a short, round Tony Bennett. I thought it odd that for such an important meeting he was so casually dressed in a T-shirt, jeans, and sneakers. But he had a reputation for being a fair evaluator, so I told myself, *Just breathe, Nia. Breathe and do your best.*

Bob greeted me with a quick handshake and a smile, then he got right to business. "If you're safe and follow the FAA practical test standards, if you stay inside those tolerances and use good judgment, you'll pass. Step outside of them or show me you can't stay ahead of the airplane, and you won't. Simple as that. Okay, let's start with the oral exam."

I nodded and tried to take clearing breaths without letting Bob know what I was doing. He sat across from me at a small table, thumbing through his notes. Then he looked up and said, "Walk me through how you'd recover from a stall."

I said, "First, reduce the angle of attack—smooth forward pressure on the yoke. Then add full power, keep the wings level with coordinated rudder and aileron, and climb back out once we're flying again."

He nodded, jotting something down, then moved to the next question. After an hour and a half of questions, Bob must have seen doubt on my face. He said, "You're doing fine. Keep going." Finally, he closed his folder. "All right. Let's see what you can do in the air."

I ran through the maneuvers, but Bob kept me moving faster than I expected. With Nancy and Andy, there was always time to pause—recover, breathe, reset for the next maneuver. Not with Bob. The second I recovered from the stall, he said, "Okay, steep turns."

I tightened my grip, rolled the wings, and tried to keep the horizon level. Then, before I even leveled off, he launched the next command. "Show me slow flight."

After he pushed me through several more maneuvers, he said, "Okay, let's head back to Lewis."

I banked the airplane toward the field, relieved to have only a simple landing ahead. But then Bob snapped the throttle back, and the engine wound down to a whisper. "You've lost power," he said. "What do you do?"

My heart jumped, but my training kicked in. I eased the plane into a steady glide and kept my eyes moving, checking both the view outside and the gauges inside. At the same time, I scanned for a field and set up for an emergency landing. Then I pointed to an area of grass below, just off the wing, and ran through the checklist, calling out each step.

"Nice job," Bob said. He pushed the throttle forward and the engine roared back to life. "Take me back to Lewis."

I exhaled and flew us back into the pattern at Lewis, lined up with the runway, and eased the Cessna down for a smooth landing. As I taxied clear of the runway, my pulse finally slowed.

I'd done it. I'd kept up with Bob's quick pace and gotten us safely back on the ground. But everything had happened so fast, I feared I'd missed something.

I parked on the ramp and ran the shutdown checklist as the engine ticked to silence, and we both pulled off our headsets. Then Bob stuck out his hand, a big smile spreading across his face. "Congratulations, Nia. You passed."

For a moment, I couldn't move. The weight I'd been carrying all flight lifted so suddenly, I almost couldn't breathe. My chest expanded, my eyes stung, and I felt a rush of joy so sharp, I wasn't sure it was real. I reached out and gripped his hand, still stunned. "Thank you," I said with a smile. "Thank you, thank you so much."

"I'll meet you inside to finish up the paperwork. You did great."

My hands, still tingling from the yoke, finally unclenched. I'd earned my first license. I was on my way.

I met Bob in the briefing room, expecting to go over the flight and fill out paperwork, but he rubbed his stomach and grinned. "Mind if we debrief in the cafeteria? I'm starving."

The campus cafeteria was nearly empty, the food line was closed and workers were wiping down tables and stacking chairs. "Looks like we missed lunch," he said. "This won't take long—we'll finish up here and get you on your way." Bob and I sat, and he spread my logbook and papers across the table.

A gray-haired Black woman in an apron walked over. She looked from Bob to me and smiled at Bob. "Is this your granddaughter?"

He was white, I was Black, and we'd only met a few hours earlier. Bob chuckled softly and said, "No, she's a student here at Lewis, and she just earned her private pilot's license. Just now, in fact."

"Oh, how nice!" she said before walking away.

Bob and I chuckled, then he finished signing my logbook, closed it, and extended his hand. "Congratulations again," he said warmly. "Here's your temporary license. You'll get the permanent one in the mail within a month."

I shook his hand and thanked him again for a terrific experience. I met Mom back at the car, where she was still parked reading a book. I was too tired to take her flying, but I held up the piece of paper stating that I was now allowed to do just that.

My mother isn't a crier, but I could always see in her eyes when something had hit deep. "Your father and I are so proud of you! Let's get you home."

As she pulled out of the parking lot, I opened my logbook. Next to the line that read *Private Pilot Flight Satisfactory,* Bob had written, *(Nice job, Granddaughter!).* I laughed out loud. What a day. What a nice guy. What a journey. After years of dreaming, training, and sometimes doubting, I was now a pilot. Like Bessie Coleman. Like Janet Bragg. Like Stayce Harris. *I* was a pilot.

EIGHT

Since landing in Boston, all I could think about was leaving. Now, four hours later, I was finally in the back seat of a minivan heading west, but uneasiness crept across my skin. I was deeply grateful to be on my way home, but only now that I was heading out of Boston did I have a chance to wonder how safe I really was. I knew nothing about these people. I realized I was the one who'd asked for their help, who'd nearly pleaded for them to allow me into their vehicle so I could get away from the chaos. They'd graciously agreed to let me ride with them for part of the way home. But were they genuinely good people, ethical people? Were they responsible, competent drivers?

I glanced toward the front seat and wondered if they were thinking similar thoughts. Did they wonder if it had been a safe choice to let me into their rental? Rick and Karen hadn't gone through the trauma I just had, but surely they were rattled and distraught, as most people throughout the United States must have been by this point. Did having a stranger in their back seat increase their stress? This was going to be a trust exercise for all of us.

We'd left Boston on the Mass Pike, then followed a chain of highways I didn't know well. I was too tired to pay close attention to Rick's turns and exits, but the longer we drove, the more signs I saw pointing toward New York City, the last place in the world we should be headed to. I wanted to speak up, but I didn't want to do anything to make him regret letting me ride with them. I just had to trust that Rick would eventually head in a different direction.

Exhausted, I wished I could rest my head against the window of the van, close my eyes, quiet my mind, and drift off into merciful sleep. But my phone was ringing and buzzing. Friends and relatives from all around the country wanted to know, *Are you okay?* Each time I answered, I added, "I was on the runway when it happened," after which the caller usually paused, as if to process what I'd just said. If the caller was someone I considered pretty tough, I'd follow with "It was horrible. I'm still in shock." But if the person was someone I thought to be more sensitive or delicate, I'd say, "Don't worry. I'm safe. I'm on my way home now and will be with my parents soon." No matter the nature of the caller, I tried to end the call quickly. All the rehashing was wearing me down.

For the first hour, Rick and Karen barely spoke, but I could feel them listening up there, their eyes flashing toward each other when they heard me say things like "My flight originated in Boston. Yes, where two of the hijacked planes flew out of," "I was on the runway when United hit the first tower," and "We were cleared to take off after the second tower was hit." The more I spoke, the more I feared I might be starting to freak Rick and Karen out. On the other hand, I thought, maybe the more they heard, the more comfortable they might become with who I was: a pilot, one who hopefully sounded professional and articulate; a patient person, despite the trauma I'd just undergone; and, at the least, someone cared for by a great many people.

During a break in the calls, Karen turned to me, her voice careful. "So you . . . you saw it happen?"

I looked up, sighed, and said, "Yes." In that moment, I had no other words.

Karen pressed her lips in a tight, understanding smile as she nodded and turned back around in her seat. I was grateful for her astuteness, grateful there were no follow-up questions.

After about two hours, we seemed to have gotten fairly far into the countryside, and my phone reception died off. With racing thoughts, I knew there would be no sleep for me in the near future, so I pulled my journal from my black tote. It was a small, light blue book about half the size of a sheet of printer paper. On the cover was a design of two young girls with brown faces, both wearing dresses and holding flowers, standing inside a white rectangle as if framed within the blue cover. The little girls made me think of my sister and me. The image was sweet and simple, and in that moment it offered comfort to try to get lost in it. Kanika, one of my favorite flight attendants, had given me the journal several months earlier for my birthday, and ever since, I'd been making a practice of filling its pages with everyday experiences, private thoughts, and expressions of gratitude. I'd grown to love the ritual of journal writing. It was a relaxing practice that helped quiet the noise and clear my mind of whatever I wanted to release from that day.

At the top of the page, I wrote *A DAY OF TERROR 911,* and began writing everything I could remember, including waking up in Boston, greeting Shye, the beautiful blue sky, and watching from Newark as the plane struck the tower. In a world that now felt unrecognizable, unsure, and entirely unsafe, writing offered a kind of soft security, even though I was writing about some of the most horrific events imaginable. The process of moving my pen across the page gave me a sense of control over my thoughts and a place to let out what felt too heavy to carry. On the page, I could step back from the moment, as though I were observing someone else's life instead of standing inside my own. After I wrote a few pages, my eyes grew heavy. I stretched out across the back seat and drifted off to sleep.

When I woke, it was because the van had slowed. I sat up, and for a moment, I couldn't place where we were. To my right was a giant Costco store. It was the only thing that felt familiar, but even that felt strangely out of place on the day the entire world had been knocked around.

A few minutes later we rolled up to a toll plaza, and Rick leaned out the window toward the attendant. "Can you tell me how to get to the George Washington Bridge?"

I couldn't believe what I'd just heard. I leaned forward. "Did you just say the GW Bridge?"

Rick looked at me in the rearview mirror. With a calm, sure voice, he said, "Yes. I'm trying to avoid New York City."

Trying to avoid New York, but getting directions to the George Washington Bridge? *Oh no,* I thought. *He has no idea what he's doing.* This was a guy from Tennessee who might have no sense of the Northeast at all. Would now be a good time for me to tell him I'd used the GW Bridge as a visual checkpoint hundreds of times while approaching LaGuardia Airport? I didn't want to press Rick in front of his wife, but I also didn't want to go anywhere near the site of the horror I'd witnessed only hours earlier. I said, "If I can help . . . that's exactly where we don't want to be. That'll take us right into the city."

Rick's face dropped. Karen looked at him with a pinched forehead. "We definitely don't want to be anywhere near Manhattan," Rick said, though his tone had lost its certainty. "Hopefully this route will keep us away from there."

We pulled out of the toll plaza and within five minutes merged the van into a line of slow-moving cars. The farther we crept forward, the heavier the air seemed, as sirens wailed in the distance, traffic thickened in every lane, and endless glowing brake lights flowed out ahead of us. Then we stopped. All the cars around us were just stopped, no longer even creeping ahead by inches. We were sitting in the middle of an apocalyptic scene right out of *Independence Day*. The I-87 freeway had essentially become an enormous parking lot in some kind of dystopian movie, with hundreds of people sitting on car hoods and roofs, staring at the massive gray cloud that stretched across the horizon. We could hear reporters blaring from car radios, describing the now-collapsed towers and asking for help finding people who were unaccounted for.

Tension seared through my chest as we inched toward New York City, and all the while the horrible cloud made it impossible to forget the reality we were now living in. I looked at my watch. We'd been on the road for four hours. Our goal was to get back to our homes, and all we'd managed to do was end up within clear view of the smoke cloud of death. I'd been cleared for takeoff and had flown away from the atrocities, and now I was sitting in a vehicle headed right for it.

Eventually, the cars began to move again, and we had no choice but to just follow the conga line of slow-moving vehicles toward the nearest exit, only a mile and a half past the toll plaza. We were now just north of the Bronx, and for the next hour, Rick took us through wrong turns, missed exits, and detours before Manhattan was finally in the rearview mirror. I closed my eyes and breathed deeply, picturing home, conjuring images of the oak trees that lined the street of my parents' house. I ached for the Midwest, thinking there would be some kind of safety there, that I'd reach the Illinois border and somehow feel normal again.

For the next two hours, all I heard was the rumble of the tires on the freeway. The radio was off, and all three of us were quiet. I couldn't remember ever feeling so tired. It was the deepest kind of exhaustion; much more punishing than physical fatigue, it was weariness born of emotional devastation. The kind that comes not from effort but from grief and that empties you out. My eyelids felt heavy, but I kept forcing them back up. I wanted to keep watching our progress. Then, after about six hours on the road, Rick said, "It's probably a good idea if we find a hotel soon and stop for the night."

At this point we weren't even into the western half of Pennsylvania, and I wanted desperately to keep going, to drive straight through the night. But it wouldn't have been appropriate for me to say so. My spot in this vehicle had been a stroke of timing and luck. I was like a standby passenger who'd heard her name over the airport PA system, then breathed relief as she hustled to the gate counter to claim her seat. I'd been allowed in, but that didn't make me a co-pilot. I tried to be gracious and patient, though inside I was a beehive of agitated energy.

Karen said, "That sounds good. I'm exhausted."

And now I'd have to pay for a hotel room with a credit card that might be rejected. I couldn't bear the embarrassment of Karen and Rick knowing about my financial struggles, so I planned to make sure they didn't find out. As we all checked in, I'd speak in a near whisper to the hotel receptionist helping me. If my card didn't go through, I'd quietly step away from the counter and tell Karen and Rick I needed some air, needed to take a walk, and that I'd meet them out front the next morning at whatever time they wanted. Then I'd find a chair in the lobby to sleep in and hope I wouldn't be kicked out as a vagrant.

The sun had set by the time we pulled into a generic motel in Drums, Pennsylvania. One look at the reception desk and my heart nearly plunged into my stomach. The lobby was tiny and intimate, and there was only one young woman working the desk. Rick gestured for me to check in ahead of him. I forced a smile and said, "Thanks, you go ahead. I need to dig my ID out of this bag." Then I pretended to rummage around in my purse.

Rick and Karen grabbed their room key cards and picked up their little suitcases. Rick said, "Have a good night, Nia. Let's plan to leave at eight A.M." I smiled, wished them good night, and watched them walk down the hallway to their room. Once they were out of sight, I stepped up to the reception desk, slid my credit card across the counter to the young woman, and said, "Just a single room for tonight." Then I prayed the card wouldn't be rejected.

"One night it is," the woman said as she slid the card through the track of the credit card machine.

I held my breath and waited for results from the slowest credit card machine in the history of technology.

Then the reception clerk smiled and said, "Okay, perfect" as the machine crackled and hummed what appeared to be approval. I nearly cried from relief. She handed me a key card. "You're just here to the right and down the hall."

I thanked her and rolled my travel bag and purse down the hall toward what was sure to be the most glorious bed I'd ever collapsed onto. The motel's gray carpet muffled each step I took down the eerily silent hallway. I felt like some kind of stealth detective trying to move along undetected as I read the numbers on all the doors preceding mine. In my room, I shut the door behind me, flipped on all the lights, and fell onto the bed, still in the clothes I'd been wearing since I'd dressed that morning in my Boston hotel. How long ago that now seemed. I left every light in the room and bathroom on, as if brightness could chase away the dark images that burned in my mind, and I lay there, utterly spent but not really resting, just waiting for the night to pass.

When I opened my eyes again, the room was ablaze with sunshine and the lights I'd left on all night. I showered and changed into my staple overnight outfit: jeans, T-shirt, and gym shoes, which I always carried in my luggage for layovers. Then I checked out of my room and met Rick and Karen in the lobby at eight o'clock. The hotel offered a continental breakfast, so I grabbed some juice and ate a piece of toast, while Rick and Karen grabbed coffee and bagels. Then we climbed into the minivan. It was a relief to be even one day past September 11. In just a few hours, I'd be home with my parents. Maybe then I could catch my breath, regroup, and start to put myself back together again.

The morning sky was clear, but the air carried a heavy stillness, like the silence that lingers after a massive windstorm, like the uncertainty that looms until you've investigated whether there's been damage to the family home, to the neighborhood, the community's old churches and beloved trees. Rick kept his eyes on the road as we headed toward Ohio, where my parents were set to meet us around two o'clock in Strongsville, a Cleveland suburb that was roughly as far from Chicago as it was from the hotel we'd just left.

The hum of the tires filled the space between us until Karen turned in her seat, her voice breaking the silence. "Is your family from Chicago?"

It was a simple question, and I could tell she wasn't trying to pry. She was just trying to connect.

"My dad's from Mississippi and my mom's from Alabama. They both moved to Chicago when they were kids. And I was born in Chicago." I thought about my grandparents, who'd gotten the family out of the Jim Crow South during the Great Migration, how they'd escaped oppression as they reached for opportunity. They'd been extraordinarily strong people, determined to give their children a better life in the North. Because my parents had witnessed that kind of determination, they raised me to believe I could dream big. And because of that, I had the chance to chase my dream to fly. I could practically feel the strength of all of them, beside me in the van.

I would have been happy to end the conversation right there, but I was ever conscious of how I was presenting myself to my gracious drivers. I couldn't bear for them to think me difficult or ungrateful or anything but pleasant to have along for the ride. Karen was still looking back at me, so I asked, "Are you and Rick from Memphis?"

Karen nodded. "We both are. We met at Memphis State, and we've been married ten years now." She pulled pictures out of her purse. "This is our son, Rick Jr. He's eight, and our six-year-old daughter, Bethany."

I glanced at the wallet-size school pictures of her kids. Her son was dressed in a polo shirt with slacks and loafers, and her daughter in a pink cotton dress and Mary Jane shoes. On the clothes of both kids, the Ralph Lauren polo player on horseback stood out prominently. What was I supposed to say about these kids? All that came to me was "They're cute."

Her face softened. Then came the question I knew was coming. "What about you? Married? Kids?"

I did want to be married. Only three months ago, I'd broken up with a boyfriend for that very reason. For four years, I'd dated Devon, a fellow pilot, but we wanted different things: I wanted marriage, and he wanted the freedom to travel the world. He also wanted to be able to focus on building his aviation education consulting business. For Devon, settling down was something that wasn't going to happen until he was "down the road," and he could never say just how far down the road. I was heartbroken, and before long I slipped back into seeing Theo, my high school sweetheart, not because I wanted a future with him but because it dulled the sting of heartbreak.

"I'm not married," I said, and I paused as I considered whether to say my next thought to a woman who was clearly proud of her motherhood. Then I decided, *Why not? She asked.* "I don't want kids."

Her forehead creased into the expression of a woman who'd just been asked to decode some alien transmission. But then her face brightened, as if she'd come to some realization. "I understand that. You'd have to stop flying."

That irritated me. I'd been raised to believe I could do anything I put my mind to. Every woman I knew worked and raised children, so the idea that motherhood automatically meant giving up your career felt misguided. Maybe it was my battered state of mind at the time, but I found her perspective offensive. "Why would I have to stop flying if I had kids?"

Karen's eyes opened wide. "Who would take care of them while you're at work?"

I shot back, "Who takes care of your kids when you go to work?" I'd meant it as a genuine question, but judging by the pause that followed, it must have landed sharper than I'd intended.

She let out a little burst of breath. "I'm a stay-at-home mom. That's my work." Then she rested her hand on Rick's leg, almost like a quiet nod of gratitude. "Rick takes care of us."

Rick glanced at his wife with a look that said he liked being the one she depended on.

"That's nice for you." I felt my face in a tight smile that I knew stopped at my mouth, didn't reach my eyes. It was the kind of smile you make when you're finished with a conversation but too polite to say so.

Her words had triggered something in me, sparked my independence and made me feel defiant in the name of freethinking women everywhere. To me, Karen represented tradition and a predictable walk down the road more traveled. I barely knew this woman, and already I'd decided what she was all about. There in my exhausted, stressed, irritated psyche, I'd concluded Karen had somehow sold out, that she'd taken the easy road of tradition and subservience and dependence on Rick to keep her fed and sheltered. That sounded awful. All the women I'd grown up around had been working women; they had jobs or careers, and many of them also had kids. I couldn't think of one woman who didn't work outside her home, not a neighbor, not a relative, not the mothers of my friends. My mom had always told me not to rely on anybody, to never set myself up to need taking care of, and I'd run with that. I was going to be entirely independent and free to make decisions that were best for me. Karen and I couldn't have been more different, and somehow her questions felt like an indictment.

It was the first conversation during the ride that had gone beyond the surface, and I sensed that as long as I was in this minivan, I might be better off keeping it light. Rick cleared his throat and shifted in his seat, catching my eye in the rearview mirror, then focusing back on the road. These were nice people. What they were doing for me was an extraordinary gesture of generosity and trust. I appreciated their kindness. But Karen had a position on a woman's options that simply rubbed me the wrong way. That was supposed to be *it* for a woman? Career or motherhood? If that were the case, you could keep the motherhood. That said, for most of my life I'd carved my identity as a pilot, and after what had happened today across the Hudson River, I was pretty sure I didn't want that anymore, either. Good Lord, who was I now?

MIDDAY, SEPTEMBER 12, WE PULLED INTO the Macaroni Grill parking lot in Strongsville, Ohio, and when I spotted my parents' Ford F150, my body finally unclenched. My shoulders dropped. My breath deepened. For the first time since yesterday morning, I felt grounded, as if my nervous system finally recognized familiar territory. My mom was already out of the truck, standing with her hands tucked in her jeans pockets, scanning the lot. My dad stood beside her, stoic and alert, as if he'd been tracking every car that pulled into the lot.

Rick parked in a spot not far from the truck. I opened the van door and stepped out, stiff from the five-hour ride across the rest of Pennsylvania and into Ohio. My mother didn't rush over or cry, she just held her arms open, and when I fell into them, she wrapped me in a long, tight hug. After all the tension and fear and uncertainty my mind and body had been bound by for the past day and a half, my mother's arms were a tender balm.

My dad reached for my bag, then wrapped his other arm around me. For a moment, the three of us stood there hugging between the minivan that had gotten me out of Boston and the truck that would take me the rest of the way home. Rick and Karen stood close together, with Rick's arm around his wife, waiting for us to finish our family embrace. Then they walked over to meet my parents, and my dad extended his hand to Rick. Dad's voice was steady and filled with gratitude. "Thank you for bringing Nia all the way here to us."

Rick shook his hand firmly and gave a modest nod. "I'm glad we could help."

Karen offered a soft smile. "You have a lovely daughter. We were happy to get her here safely."

My dad said, "We can't thank you enough for what you did. Without your help, Nia might still be in Boston." Then he reached into his wallet, pulled out a few bills, and extended them to Rick. "Please take this for gas."

Rick held up his hands. "You really don't have to—"

Mom cut in. "It's the least we can do. Please take it."

Karen glanced at Rick, then nodded slightly, and Rick accepted the money with a quiet, respectful nod. "Thank you," he said simply.

I hugged Karen, then Rick, and looked back and forth between them while shaking my head, as if to say, *We've been through quite a lot together, haven't we?* With my eyes welling up, I said, "I'll never forget this. Thank you so much for saying yes back in Boston. For helping me get home."

Rick gave a small nod. "I'm glad we were able to help."

"Have a safe drive back to Memphis."

Karen smiled. "We will. I can't wait to get home and see my babies. Please stay in touch."

After Rick and Karen drove off, I stood and watched the van disappear. In the years that followed, I checked in with them once or twice, and eventually we lost touch. But I knew I'd never forget them, as I'd never forget Ed from Boston Emergency Services. The three of them had shown great humanity on the day the world came down around us.

In my parents' truck, the silence offered a lovely stillness. Dad kept his hands easy on the wheel, his attention focused on the road. My mom sat turned slightly toward me, and now and then she glanced back at me, as if to reassure herself I was really there. Eventually she said, "We're so glad you're here and safe," and turned to face the front. Then they gave me quiet space, grounding me with their steady presence.

I leaned back against the seat and listened to the familiar hum of tires on pavement. I was back in the Midwest, and before the end of the day, I'd be back in the city I'd known all my life, a city where nothing horrible had happened overhead, where no smoke billowed from skyscrapers, and buildings didn't tumble to rubble. But then what?

Thirty-six hours earlier, I'd said I never wanted to fly again, and I'd meant it. My world up in the sky no longer felt predictable because terrorists had rewritten the rules. My trusted airspace and all systems and structures that defined aviation for me had been shockingly, horrifically violated. The idea of going up there now left me feeling exposed and defenseless. Somewhere along the long-stretching road, another feeling began to rise beneath the fear. Flying wasn't just my job; it was an enormous part of my identity, and to walk away from it would mean much more than making a career change. It would mean letting go of a critical part of myself. And then what? If I never flew again what would I do? And how would I define myself? I closed my eyes and tried to think about anything but planes.

NINE

I was very proud to have earned my private pilot's license at the age of eighteen, but that was only the first big step on what would be a long road to becoming an airline pilot. The second step, as I saw it, was figuring out how to pay for all the expenses, and there were many. In addition to using what I'd earned for my service with the Illinois Air National Guard, I'd pay for school with student loans and scholarship money from the Organization of Black Airline Pilots. The Guard would help cover tuition, but only if I attended a state school. That meant transferring out of Lewis University, which was private. Lewis was a good school, and aside from my distressing experience with Nancy the instructor, I valued the training I received there. But flying was an expensive pursuit, and transferring to a state school was going to be a necessary trade-off. Nothing was going to stand between me and the sky.

After my freshman year at Lewis, I endured six weeks of basic military training at Lackland Air Force Base in San Antonio, which I thought was a good step toward becoming a military pilot. I liked the regimentation and the discipline, and I appreciated that the training was about sharpening our edges rather than breaking us down, but it was rough. Reveille announced the start of the day before sunrise, the bugle cutting through sleep like a command. Then, on weary legs, I ran in formation with my squadron, stood at attention while instructors scrutinized every detail of our dress down to our boot shine, and endured drills designed to expose weakness. Within all that exhaustion and pressure, I learned about mental control and how to keep showing up even when all I wanted was the relief of quitting.

Technical school was next. Basic training taught me how to be in the military, and technical school would teach me the job I'd do while serving. While others in my squadron moved on to other bases for their tech school, I stayed in San Antonio and studied supply logistics at Lackland. There were other job fields I qualified for, but my goal was to return to college as soon as possible, so I chose a job that required the least amount of training time. After eight weeks of tech school, where I learned to read requisition forms, track serial numbers, and manage inventory, I headed back to college to focus on flight training, the only thing I really cared about. Then, in January 1995, I transferred from Lewis University to Southern Illinois University Carbondale, where I used my military education benefits as a new student in the Aviation Management and Flight program.

My first class at SIUC was Electronics for Aviators, and after being out of school for four months, it felt great to be back to focusing on the subject I was passionate about. The classroom was tucked inside an old aircraft maintenance building, and the air in the room carried a faint smell of cool metal and machinery. Fluorescent bulbs hummed overhead, casting a harsh light that made the room feel more sterile than inviting. Five neat rows of desks filled the space, their metal legs scraping against the tile as students shifted and settled.

Most of the seats were already taken by white males, who clustered in small groups, leaning in to talk and laugh among themselves. Their voices rose and fell with easy familiarity, but none of them offered me so much as a gesture or smile of welcome as I walked in.

Out of habit, I slipped into the first desk by the door, the vinyl seat cool and hard. As more students trickled in, they found their friends and filled the back rows, hovering near one another. The seats to my right and left remained conspicuously empty, as if my presence designated an invisible boundary. I'd always been comfortable in my own company, so being alone, even in a crowd, wasn't something I dreaded. Still, in that classroom, the air was heavy with camaraderie, and sitting alone at the front, I felt like an outsider.

About five minutes before class was to start, I saw a familiar face. A brown face, and my heart soared. "Charles!" I called out, forgetting the reserve I usually carried in white spaces. I hadn't seen him in the two years since we'd trained together at Tuskegee.

His face lit up, and he flashed an enormous smile. "Nia!"

I stood up and we hugged like the long-lost friends we were. For a moment, the classroom faded away, and it was just the two of us, laughing and catching up. But soon, I sensed the curious stares from around the room. Even the instructor wanted to know what was going on here. He stepped toward us and smiled. "What a happy scene. Are you two related?"

Charles smirked. "No."

I said, "We're friends. Haven't seen each other in years."

"Ah," the instructor said, "well, have a seat. You can resume the reunion after class."

Charles chose a desk behind mine, and just like that, I wasn't alone anymore.

He and I grew close over the next couple of years. We were two of only three Black students in the aviation program when I arrived on campus, and we found in each other a sense of safety in an environment that often felt foreign and isolating. Each semester, when another Black student enrolled, we celebrated it. It signified progress. It meant we weren't quite so alone. Slowly, the flight program began to feel like something we might be able to belong to.

Recognizing how isolating the experience could be for underrepresented flight students, I started an organization I called the Minority Aviation Council (MAC). When we launched in the fall of 1995, our membership consisted of only five students and two instructors. And though our numbers were small, our purpose was clear: to share our love of aviation and to help each other navigate the road to graduation. Our meetings were simple, sometimes just a few of us sitting around a table with notebooks and pizza boxes, trading study tips and encouragement. Other times, we hung out at the airport for an informal social hour, talking about flying and sharing our dreams. Two of us wanted to become airline pilots. Another hoped to manage an airport. Someone else planned to become a mechanic. We weren't just passing time—we were naming futures out loud. And we felt like we were part of a team. There was a camaraderie that existed within the white aviation community in our school, and no matter how we minorities tried to assimilate, there was always some sign we weren't included. Maybe we weren't invited into a conversation. Maybe we weren't asked to be part of a study group. But within MAC, we all belonged.

One evening, Charles burst into a MAC meeting about ten minutes late and breathlessly announced, "I just heard Captain Bill Norwood is retiring, and to honor him, they're painting his name on the side of a Boeing 727 at the Museum of Science and Industry! There's also going to be a big retirement party. Both things are happening in three months. We have to go!"

For a second, we all just stared at him. Then the air exploded into a tangled cloud of questions and thoughts exclaimed all at once.

I looked around the table and saw it on every face, the same thing I felt in my body. Hope and excitement. We all knew about Captain William "Bill" Norwood. He was a trailblazer, and his name was often mentioned within the Black aviation community. He was more than just United Airlines' first Black pilot and an SIUC alumnus, he was also one of the founders of the Organization of Black Airline Pilots, the very group that had given me scholarships, support, and a sense of belonging simply because they existed. Captain Norwood had broken barriers at thirty-one thousand feet and built pathways for us to follow. He was a living legend.

Two of the seven Minority Aviation Council members had scheduling conflicts, but the rest of us were fired up to attend the events in Chicago, five hours north of campus. The party itself was going to be a formal gala, and the ticket to attend was pricey. The event at the Museum of Science and Industry would be more affordable, but it was scheduled for almost a week before the gala. Most of us were from Chicago, so we didn't have to worry about where to stay overnight near the city, but to attend both events meant we'd have to figure out transportation and raise enough money for all those tickets, which was no small task for college students stretching every dollar.

I said, "We're not missing this. We'll find a way."

Later that week in the library study room, all seven council members brainstormed ways to fund both trips for five of us. "What about a bake sale or raffle?" one member said. Another suggested, "What about a car wash?" We discussed the pros and cons of those grassroots fundraisers, and decided we should try them all. Within a week, we'd hosted our first bake sale at the airport. Using funds from our student organization budget, we bought cupcakes and a variety of cookies and pastries, then sold them individually with a small markup. We didn't raise much, but it was a start. Later, we organized a few weekend car washes and held a raffle featuring a $75 gift certificate donated by the university's bookstore. By February, just two weeks before the museum ceremony, we'd raised enough money for all five of us to attend both events. Charles and I were the only two with cars, so we decided we'd carpool, which meant our only shared expense would be gas. We'd done it. It was on. We were going to be part of an event to honor one of the most historically significant pilots any of us had heard of.

The event at the Museum of Science and Industry was centered on the unveiling of a retrofitted, suspended Boeing 727 in the *Take Flight* exhibit. On the side of the plane, Captain William R. Norwood's name was painted in big bold letters. There were about four hundred attendees—pilots, students from local schools, aviation enthusiasts, and friends and relatives of Mr. Norwood, along with media—all gathered along a balcony and marveling at the enormous aircraft that honored the great man. Seeing the captain's name displayed there sent electricity through me, but standing in the same room as Captain Norwood himself, watching him being honored for his groundbreaking career and contribution to aviation, made me practically overflow with hope.

The five of us stood among the crowd of admirers and supporters, witnesses to history. At the center was Captain Norwood himself, a distinguished light-skinned Black man, nearly sixty, with dark hair, a clean-shaven face, and a mustache. He wore a navy-blue uniform, just like the one Stayce had worn the day I met her at Janet Bragg's funeral. And standing by his side was his wife, Molly, the other half of one of aviation's most inspiring couples. Representatives from United Airlines and the museum said a few words, then a local politician introduced Captain Norwood himself. The room was silent and rapt as he spoke in a steady, clear voice. Now and then he glanced at Molly, who listened adoringly to his every word. He ended his speech with words I knew I'd always remember: "Dream big, set your goals, work hard, and make the right choices. Nobody does it alone, but with help and effort, you can go farther than you ever imagined."

For us, as college flight students and members of the MAC group, the event turned out to be much more than a great trip and an honor to celebrate Captain Norwood; it was a message to all young Black pilots. It was proof we weren't invisible in aviation, that someone had already broken through and helped carve out space in a sky that hadn't always welcomed us. I felt the weight of that moment, equal parts pride and challenge. His legacy seemed to whisper: *If I can do it, you can.*

The following week, the five of us carpooled again to Chicago, this time to attend Captain Norwood's retirement gala. Before the event, we all met at my house for photos, dressed in formal attire. I wore a deep purple A-line halter dress with a black shimmer overlay that fell just below my knees and black satin heels. I'd pinned my hair up to show off my dangling sparkly earrings. Charles and the three other members wore black suits and ties. Dressed up like that and surrounded by the guys in nice suits, I felt like a real adult, a proper member of the aviation community. We carpooled the twenty-five-minute drive from my parents' house in Oak Park to the Hyatt Regency O'Hare, and after we dropped the cars at the hotel parking lot, we hustled to the Hyatt's ballroom. More than eight hundred people were in attendance, including Captain Norwood's friends, family, co-workers, and dignitaries, all dressed in formal elegance. The five of us MAC members grabbed seats at a round table toward the back of the enormous ballroom, which didn't offer a great view of the stage, but it gave us a clear line of sight to the ballroom's entrance. I kept my eyes glued to the ballroom doors because I was hoping Stayce might walk through them. I'd seen Stayce only a handful of times since our first meeting at the funeral—at OBAP conferences in 1994 and 1995, at Women in Aviation in 1995, and again at the 1995 First Day of Issue ceremony for the U.S. Postal Service's Bessie Coleman stamp. Outside of events, we spoke occasionally by phone. I'd call to tell her I'd finished another course or earned another flight certificate. Every so often, she'd send me postcards from exotic places like Istanbul and Tokyo, and I'd study them like sacred artifacts.

I'd been scanning the ballroom entrance for so long I began to accept that this wasn't my night, that I wasn't going to see the pilot I admired so much, the mighty, mighty Stayce Harris.

Then my heart skipped. She appeared in the doorway, unmistakable. Poised. With the kind of effortless presence that shifted a room. A smile spread across her face as someone called out to her and reached for her arm, already pulling her toward the crowd. I jumped from my chair and wove between tables, murmuring, "Excuse me" as I passed, hoping I could reach her before she disappeared into the crowd. She wore a striking, Asian-inspired dress in rich tones of red, gold, and black, paired with delicate black-and-gold jewelry. Everything about her felt intentional, regal. Stayce didn't just enter rooms, she commanded them.

For a moment, I lost sight of her, but then she emerged again, and our eyes met. Her face lit up. "Nia!" She pulled me into a warm embrace, the kind that made everyone else in the room fade for a moment, and said, "How are you, darling?" I wanted her to say it louder. I wanted everyone in the room to know that I personally knew this extraordinary Air Force major and B747 pilot for United Airlines.

"I'm good, Stayce. Really good. And I'm so happy to see you."

"And you! Where are you sitting?"

I gestured toward the back. "Over there with guys from school."

"Well, come walk with me for a moment."

And that's how it always went. Every time we were together, she made the encounter feel personal, genuine, and intentional, but everybody was drawn to Stayce, so within seconds, someone else approached. Then another.

"Major Harris, may I introduce—"

"Stayce, could I get just a moment?"

"Ma'am, it's such an honor—"

I stood there politely, but inside I felt the familiar combination of gratitude that Stayce was so loved and respected and the quiet ache of always having to share her. Still, no matter how many people pulled at her, Stayce always came back to me, always found a way to circle back. To ask how I was doing. To listen. She never made me feel like I was just another face in the crowd.

The ballroom shimmered with soft lighting, and every table was crowned with a stunning centerpiece, a model of a DC-10 mounted on a silver spiral, soaring upward through tufts of cotton clouds. Gazing at the decoration, I thought about how just hearing of an aviation-themed table embellishment so beautiful would have made me dizzy with joy as a little girl. And here I was, now all grown up and part of the aviation community. I was living my dreams.

The evening included speeches by Captain Norwood's friends, former colleagues, and other airline leaders, each one acknowledging that the captain had opened doors for the rest of us. Every time the room rose in applause, I jumped up in gratitude. And when the speeches were finished, nobody rushed to leave. People lingered in clusters, exchanging stories, hugs, handshakes. When the crowd finally began to thin, I scanned the room again, determined not to leave without finding Stayce one more time. I spotted her near the edge of the ballroom, mid-conversation. I waited patiently until there was a break, then stepped forward.

"Stayce," I said softly.

She turned and smiled. "There you are."

"I didn't want to leave without a picture," I said. "If you don't mind."

"Of course, darling."

Someone nearby offered to take the photo. I stood beside her, still in awe of how natural it felt to be close to her, how familiar and grounding her presence had become in my life. After the picture, she held my hands. "I'm so proud of you. You're doing exactly what you're supposed to be doing. Keep going. And keep me posted."

"I will," I promised.

She hugged me once more, and this time I let myself hold on to the moment a little longer before stepping away.

What a glorious night it was. All five of us left the hotel smiling, and I was sure the guys felt the magic as I had.

BY THE SPRING OF 1997, I was in my final semester at SIUC, and I'd logged over two hundred flight hours. Now there was only one check ride standing between me and my graduating with a degree in aviation flight, which would mean I would qualify for a job flying airplanes with one or more engines. The flight instructor who had trained me in the multi-engine airplane signed me off for a multi-engine flight evaluation with Tom, a retired airline captain with silver hair and a sharp eye. I needed to pass an oral and then an in-flight evaluation with him, then I'd face another evaluation with a different FAA examiner. Once I passed that, I could be hired in the industry.

I passed the oral exam, but once Tom and I were in the air, everything unraveled. The maneuver I struggled with was a holding pattern using an NDB, a type of navigation from before GPS and moving maps. Back then, you didn't see your airplane on a screen; you followed a single needle that swung back and forth. You had to interpret what it meant, anticipate where the airplane actually was, and make the correct turn at exactly the right moment. I misread it. One wrong turn. That's all it took.

I felt it immediately, the sick drop in my stomach, the quiet realization that I'd blown it. All the preparation, all the effort, undone by a moment of misjudgment.

"Let's head back," Tom said evenly. No frustration in his voice. No second chance, either.

By the time I parked the Cessna 310, my tears blurred my vision. It wasn't as much embarrassment as disappointment, the quiet sting of knowing exactly where I'd gone wrong. I tried to hide my tears from him, but he saw my distress, and he offered no comfort. His face, lined by years of experience, looked disgusted. He said, "If you think you're going to make it in this business, you'd better develop a thick skin."

He was right. In that moment, I felt small and exposed. So I made a decision that would follow me for years: No one in aviation would ever see me cry again. I knew there would be harder flights, tougher training, and sharper criticism ahead, but I'd fly with composure and absorb pressure without showing fracture. I vowed to never again show vulnerability on an airplane.

A week later, I was back in the left seat. Same airplane. Same airport. Same knot in my stomach. This time, with a different evaluator. Flight training policy required that any retraining event be conducted by someone new. No familiar voice. No familiarity to lean on. This time when I was asked to perform that hold, I didn't misread it. This time, everything seemed to have slowed down. Not because the task was easier but because I was no longer rushing ahead of myself. I tracked the needle and visualized the entry. When the needle swung, I interpreted it correctly, and when it was time to turn, I turned. No second-guessing. No scrambling. Just execution. When we landed, I parked the Cessna 310. The evaluator finished his notes, looked up, and said simply, "Congratulations."

A few days later, I held my multi-engine certificate in my hands, the final requirement needed for me to graduate with a degree in aviation management and flight from the SIUC flight program. I hadn't ended my SIUC experience with perfection, but with resilience and some solid lessons for the future. I took it all as a victory.

The day before graduation I took my parents up in a Cessna 172 and let them see my campus from the air. Like an aerial tour guide I flew them over my old dorm, the football field, and the arena where I'd be graduating the next day. My parents were so comfortable with the idea of me as a pilot, it was as if I were taking them out on a nice drive in a car I wanted to show off. The next day, I walked across the graduation stage while my parents and sister cheered from somewhere in the audience of thousands. After the ceremony, we found each other on the edge of the crowd, hugged, took photos, and then headed back to the townhouse, where we sat around the dining room table and celebrated with cake, chicken wings, spaghetti, and salad. My parents and sister were there, along with my flight instructor, Ken, and my classroom professor, Mr. Hunt, who'd been especially helpful carrying me through my journey. Charles was due to graduate the following semester, and he joined us with Tammy, another student in her first year in the aviation program. I had invited Stayce, but she was flying that day and couldn't attend. That night she called me. "Nia, I'm sorry I couldn't be there, but I promise you this: When you finish USAF undergraduate pilot training, I'll be there to pin on your wings." Stayce knew I wanted to follow in her footsteps, to fly for the military and then the airlines, and her promise meant everything to me. It was her way of saying she believed in me, that she expected me to get there.

Graduation was an extremely satisfying milestone, but I knew I still had a long way to go. By graduation, I'd logged just over 250 flight hours, but to even begin applying to regional airlines, I'd need closer to 1,000. So now it was time to go after my dream of flying for the Air Force.

A few months after graduation, in May 1997, I interviewed to be a pilot with 126th Air Refueling Wing, the unit of the Illinois Air National Guard I was already working for in a logistics role. I passed the exam to become an officer, then appeared before a board of officers. They selected me to advance, which meant I had one more hurdle to scale before I could become a pilot with the United States Air Force.

In the nineties, the Air Force didn't just measure your determination or your test scores. They measured your body, down to the inch. To be a pilot, you had to stand between sixty-four and seventy-seven inches tall. That meant pilots were between five foot four and six foot five. Those requirements were created based on how well a person would fit inside and be able to operate a T-37, the little jet trainer every flight student had to fly. That airplane set the standard. Too short, and you might not reach the rudder pedals. Too tall, and your knees could jam against the cockpit and your head risked missing the ejection seat clearance. Both scenarios were unsafe, and with anything in aviation, unsafe could be fatal. It didn't matter how strong your passion was—if your body didn't fit that cockpit, the dream of being a military pilot would end right there in the medical exam room.

I knew going into the exam that I was under the minimum height requirement. I stood at sixty-two and a half inches tall, but I arrived at the medical clinic determined to stand taller. The air in the building smelled faintly of disinfectant and old linoleum, sharp and sterile, like every doctor's office I'd ever known. All my life, that kind of atmosphere had made me anxious, but in this clinic, the stakes felt much higher, so my heartbeat raced. When I approached the counter to check in, the medical tech wasted no time and no words. She directed me to the exam area and started immediately.

"Shoes off. Back against the bar. Look straight ahead." Her voice was clipped and efficient, like this was the hundredth body she'd measured that day.

I did as I was told, except I stood slightly on the balls of my feet, trying to eke out any extra height I could. The cold metal measuring device pressed between my shoulders, and she slid the headpiece down until it touched the crown of my head with a sharp metal snap. For her, it was just another measurement. For me, it was a verdict, military flight school or not.

"Five three," she said flatly, jotting it down.

My stomach sank. Too short. I couldn't let her record that number. I had to get her to remeasure me.

She began to walk away and said, "Follow me to the next room."

I said, "That can't be right. I know I'm taller than that. Can you remeasure me?"

She sighed, clearly annoyed, but walked back and reset the slider. I rose slowly, balancing on the edge of my tiptoes, hoping she wouldn't notice what I was up to. My back stayed rigid against the bar as I stretched my neck tall, begging my body to give me just one more inch. I tried not to sway, holding my breath, as if sheer determination could change the number she was about to call out.

"You're right," she said. "You are taller."

This was fantastic! What a relief. I asked, "How tall?"

"Five three and three-quarters."

No. No, no, *no*! A quarter of an inch too short. The room seemed to tilt, and I knew I couldn't beg for another chance. This no-nonsense woman was done with me. She said, "You should hear the results of your medical in a few weeks."

Until then I could only wait. I told myself the measurement was so close, there was a chance they might make an exception and let me into the program. I had hope.

I waited almost a month for the call. Then it came. "This is Captain Robinson from medical standards." His voice was professional and measured. No warmth.

"Yes, sir," I replied.

There was a brief pause, papers shifting on the other end. "I'm calling regarding your medical."

I sat on the edge of my bed and held my breath.

"It's been reviewed and denied. Your standing height doesn't meet the minimum, and as a result, you're medically disqualified for pilot training."

The words hit like the slam of a heavy door.

"Is there . . . any appeal process?" I asked, though I already knew the answer.

"No, ma'am."

That was it. No explanation. No advice about how to move forward. Just a declaration of policy. After the call, I sat there and buried my face in my hands. I hadn't missed my chance because of lack of effort or skill or preparation. I was disqualified from pilot training by a quarter of an inch. Okay, so I'd just have to take the civilian route. That meant becoming a flight instructor and building experience hour by hour. It would be a slower, more circuitous path. But it was the one available to me.

IN MID-NOVEMBER OF 1998, I arrived in Scottsdale, Arizona, at CRM Flight School as a newly certified flight instructor (CFI). Through word of mouth, I'd learned of the opening for a CFI position, faxed my résumé, followed up with a call, and was interviewed, then hired. The flight school was a modest operation. The owner, Kevin, who had hired me, was a pilot, and his wife, Mia, ran the front desk. Kevin introduced me around, and I immediately felt a connection with one of the instructors, Dan, who was newly hired as well. Dan was twenty-one, with blond hair, a quick smile, confident posture, and what I interpreted to be "playboy energy." After Kevin introduced us, Dan offered his hand and said, "You're the new flight instructor."

We shook hands, and I smiled. "Is it that obvious?"

"Only because everyone's been talking about you," he said with a grin. "You're the one we've been waiting for."

I laughed. "That sounds like pressure."

"You wouldn't be here if you couldn't handle it." Then he winked. "Besides, this whole place runs on pressure and coffee."

Right away, I was assigned two students of my own, a student at Arizona State University, who showed up to every lesson with a spiral notebook full of handwritten questions, and a high school senior who talked nonstop about types of planes and often pointed to the sky before saying, "That's where I'm headed." Both of them dreamed of becoming professional pilots, and in their nervous energy, their questions, their eagerness to learn, I recognized pieces of myself.

On my third day with CRM, I was in my apartment working on lesson plans when the phone rang. It was Mia. Her voice was strained. "Your lesson tonight is canceled," she said. "There's been an accident."

Her words hung in the air. My throat tightened. "What happened?"

There was a pause and she exhaled deeply. "It was Dan. He and his student went down."

"Are they . . . ?" I couldn't finish the question.

"A midair. Dan was the only survivor," she said softly. "It's on the news. We're closed for now. Kevin will call you later."

She hung up, and the phone felt heavy in my hand. I couldn't move. All I could hear was that one word, echoing in my head. *Midair.* Just three days in, and I was already staring at the cost of the dream, the risk none of us ever wanted to name.

It was all over the news. Two airplanes from our school had collided in midair over Scottsdale. One was flown by a solo student, the other by Dan with a student on board. Both students were killed, and Dan had somehow survived, but with serious injuries. The news sent me reeling. I didn't know how long the school would be closed or how the accident would affect the flying schedule, but until I received word, I hung around the apartment and tried to focus on lessons plans.

Two days later, Kevin called. "Hi, Nia," he said, his voice steady but softer than usual. "Just wanted to check on you. How are you holding up?"

"I'm okay," I answered, though the words felt thin. "It's been a lot to take in."

"I know. It's shaken all of us. But I do have something for you. We have an Air Force guy, F-16 pilot, who wants to get back into small planes, just for fun. I'd like you to take him up for an aircraft familiarization flight this evening."

I weighed the words, and the thought of climbing back into a plane so soon sent a chill through me. Not panic, but the kind of fear that sits quietly and doesn't announce itself, just presses heavier the longer you stay still.

An accident can happen to anyone. Every pilot knows that. We're trained with that truth ingrained in us. From day one, we're taught the risks of mechanical failures, weather, other aircraft, birds. But this wasn't theoretical. This wasn't just a story on the news. I didn't have all the details of the accident yet, but I felt the weight of knowing something had gone wrong up there, that lives had been lost.

"Okay," I said finally.

"Good," Kevin replied. "I think it'll be a good one for you. Eases you back in."

My car was in the shop, so about an hour and a half before my lesson, I called a cab. The driver was a middle-aged man who wore glasses, a baseball cap, and a big smile. "Heading to the airport?" he asked, glancing at me in the rearview mirror.

"Yes," I said. "I'm a pilot."

He said, "Oh, that's cool!" Then his tone turned serious. "I heard about that plane crash on the news. You must know about it."

"Yes. That was my school. And to be honest, it has me a little scared."

He looked at me again. "Makes sense. Something like that'll shake anybody. But fear doesn't just disappear. It always rides along."

I let out a nervous laugh because that was exactly how it felt, as if fear had taken the front seat and left me in the back. He kept talking, his words sounding more like wisdom than small talk. "Resilience isn't about erasing fear. It's about carrying the fear with you and not letting it be the one calling the shots. You feel it, but you fly anyway. That's how you take its power away. You don't let it have the last word."

His words landed hard. They were so perfectly timed, and almost mystical because they'd come from a stranger. I didn't have the impression he was trying to say anything profound. He was just speaking honestly, offering insight. And it reminded me how sometimes the right words arrive from unexpected places, and sometimes clarity comes not from the people closest to us, but from someone who has no idea they're offering just what we need to hear. By the time he dropped me off, I felt calmer, almost as if I'd been prayed over.

The student was already inside the flight school building. He looked to be classic military, neatly groomed, his gray-flecked brown hair cut short and tight. As I walked in, he stood up perfectly straight.

"You must be my instructor," he said, offering his hand.

"I am. I'm Nia."

He smiled easily. "I'm Mike. Air Force. F-16s, but I'm here for a familiarization flight in a Cessna 172."

Mike caught me off guard with his calm friendliness. No apparent ego, no bravado. He wasn't some kind of arrogant *Top Gun* type, and if the fact that I was only twenty-two years old bothered him, he showed no sign of it. I led him to the classroom and reviewed the cockpit layout, speeds for climb, cruise, and landing, and went over the plan. Then I said, "Any questions?"

Mike, already a professional pilot, said with a smile, "No questions."

"Okay," I said, smiling back. "Let's go fly."

I demonstrated the first takeoff and climbed to two thousand feet to get him warmed up to flying a plane much slower than the F-16s he was used to. When we were straight and level, I said, "You want the aircraft?"

"I've got it," he said.

Something about the rhythm of the flight—the checklist calls, the coordination, Mike's quiet competence—settled me. It reminded me why I loved the work, why I trusted the process, why I trusted the airplane. I let Mike fly around the area, and when he was ready, we returned to the airport, where he completed a few takeoffs and landings. After two hours in the plane, we wrapped it up, then shut down, and Mike pulled off his headset and grinned. "That was a great flight."

"It was," I agreed. I signed his logbook. He shook my hand, thanked me, and walked to his car.

Kevin was waiting for me inside the CRM building. "So?" he asked, leaning back in his chair.

"He was solid. Calm. Professional. It reminded me that the training works. That the systems work. That I still trust this."

Kevin nodded slowly. "That's why I gave you that student."

I tilted my head.

"You didn't need chaos today," he said. "You needed confidence."

Kevin drove me home, and when I was back in the solitude of my apartment, I realized that in the past few hours something small but significant had shifted. My fear hadn't vanished, but it no longer felt like the loudest voice in the room.

YEARS LATER, I LEARNED SOMETHING about my connection to CRM that chilled me. Hani Hanjour, the hijacker who flew American Airlines Flight 77 into the Pentagon, had trained at CRM just eight months before I started working there. That news served as yet another reminder that aviation, the very thing that had given my life purpose, could be the setting of unimaginable harm. The midair collision at CRM and the terrorist attacks on 9/11 offered two painfully vivid examples of the hard, unavoidable truth about the pursuit I loved: Air travel isn't safe just because you want it to be. Life isn't, either. But what's the solution? To stay put? I let both tragedies serve as ever-present teachers to always prepare, always stay aware. And to keep going.

TEN

After the accident at CRM, business dropped way off, but I needed more flight hours, so I left the school for another flight instructing job in Atlanta, where I lived with relatives to save money. After leaving that job, I took a position as a traffic patrol pilot in St. Louis, and when a flight instruction job opened in Chicago, I grabbed that. I chased every opportunity I could to fly, and by the year 2000, I'd accrued enough hours to be a regional airline pilot. I applied to Atlantic Coast Airlines (ACA), and they called me in for an interview. At the time, ACA was one of the largest regional carriers in the country, flying under the United Express banner out of Washington Dulles. For many new pilots, ACA was a gateway into the jet age, the first real step from instructing and time-building into a career as a pilot. Landing a position with ACA would be the break I needed. My hope was they'd base me at O'Hare because first-year pay was only $17 an hour for regional pilots, so I was going to have to live with my parents. At this point I not only had life expenses, I still had college debt.

Eight days after the interview, I took the day off from flight instructing to celebrate my twenty-fourth birthday. I planned to start the day with a visit to my sister at the Village, a West Side group home for teenage boys who'd experienced instability in their family homes or in foster care and needed a safe place to live. I'd never been to the Village, and I was excited to see my sister in the place where she did such important work. As a counselor at the group home, she was in charge of four teenage boys, acting as teacher, coach, and even big sister. She supervised daily routines, helped with homework, de-escalated conflicts, and generally offered support and encouragement whenever she could. The career choice suited her so well, I thought. She'd always had a calm, caring way about her. Kamilah was the kind of person who noticed when someone needed help and stepped in without being asked. A few years earlier, she and I had been in a grocery store line, and the cashier had become visibly flustered, her hands shaking as the line grew and customers became impatient. My sister leaned toward the cashier and said gently, "You're doing fine. Take your time." It was just a simple sentiment, but the girl's shoulders dropped and her breathing appeared to slow. If one of Kamilah's friends was spiraling over a breakup or problem at school, Kamilah just listened and offered calming support with thoughts like "I'm here. You don't have to figure it out tonight." That was her way, just making people feel safe without grand gestures or words.

That day, my idea was to invite her to join me and a few friends that night at a local sports bar to celebrate my birthday, but my other motivation for visiting was to check out the guy she had a crush on, a fellow counselor. It was mid-morning when I pulled up and parked in front of the Village, which sat on a quiet block of brick bungalows. From the outside, it looked like any other residential Chicago house with a small front lawn, concrete steps, and metal railing worn smooth by years of hands running along it.

Kamilah was waiting for me with a smile. "Hey, sissy," she said, reaching toward me. "Come on in." I followed her and glanced all around the first group home I'd ever been in. The air in the house carried the faint scent of disinfectant and whatever someone had cooked for breakfast, maybe bacon and toast. The walls were painted a neutral beige and decorated with motivational posters about choices and second chances. A bulletin board near the entryway held chore charts, weekly schedules, therapy appointments, and handwritten reminders: *Laundry Day, Group Meeting at 6 pm, Respect Each Other*. The mismatched living room furniture consisted of a couch and a few chairs, a scuffed coffee table, and a TV on top of a sturdy entertainment stand. Something about the atmosphere in the house made it seem supervised even when staff wasn't in the room.

Kamilah said, "Come on in here. The boys are working on school assignments." I followed her into what looked like a dining area, where teenage boys were gathered around a big rectangular table. One slouched deep in his chair, another tapped a pencil impatiently, and another tried to get attention by talking too loudly. Schoolwork was spread across the table in uneven piles—worksheets, spiral notebooks, battered textbooks. There was an underlying tension all around, the kind that comes from kids who have been through too much too young.

A twentysomething man about six foot three with dark skin and braids stepped into the room. This had to be Jamal, the guy Kamilah was so excited about. Before she could speak, I extended my hand and said, "I'm Kamilah's sister, Nia."

He smiled and said, "Aha, so you're the sister. I'm Jamal."

I looked at Kamilah, then back to Jamal. "So you're the Jamal."

Kamilah seemed to try to shrink into herself.

He laughed. "The very one."

Kamilah crossed the room and started checking the boys' homework, while I dove right in with a barrage of questions for Jamal: "Where are you from?" "How long have you done this kind of work?" "Where do you see yourself in five years?" Then I said, "Take your time. I have all day."

Jamal laughed again, an easy relaxed chuckle. Then he started telling me about himself. I liked this guy. He wasn't trying too hard, and I had deep respect for the work he'd chosen.

My cell phone rang. "Excuse me," I said as I grabbed it from my purse. The call was coming from Atlantic Coast Airlines. I looked over at Kamilah with wide eyes, pointed to my phone, and mouthed, *The airline!* My hands were shaking. Into the phone, I said, "Hello, this is Nia."

"Hi, Nia. This is Diana from Atlantic Coast Airlines." Diana was the HR representative who had sat on the pilot hiring panel during my interview. Her tone was warm, and I could almost see her smile through the phone. She asked, "How are you doing?"

I let out a nervous laugh. I thought, *I'm a nervous wreck. I'm like a sprinter on the starting block, prepped, positioned, and ready to officially start the pilot job I've dreamed of and worked toward since I was a girl too young to know how to become a pilot.* I said, "I'm not sure. That might depend on why you're calling."

She laughed. "Well, let me get right to it." I closed my eyes and held my breath. Then she said it. "I'm calling to offer you a pilot position with Atlantic Coast Airlines. Congratulations."

Glitter fireworks shot through my entire body. Kamilah was watching me, her brow furrowed. I mouthed the words, *I got the job!* Her eyes opened wide and she mimed a silent scream and a silent clap.

"Diana, may I ask you to hold on for a moment? I'm in a room full of people, and I'd like to step outside."

"Of course."

I bolted for the entrance, my footsteps making the old wooden floor creak a frenetic beat. Then I pushed open the front door and dashed outside, where the cold March air hit my face like a blessing. It was nearly impossible to keep from shouting, and I wanted to throw myself into an ecstatic dance of joy and relief, but I had to hold it together for this phone call. Out on the street, I gasped, "Thank you, Diana! Today is my birthday, and this is the best birthday present!"

"Yes, I know!" she said, her enthusiasm rising to meet mine. "I called the other applicants two days ago, but when I saw your birthday was today, I waited so you'd have an extra reason to celebrate."

How sweet of her. Chalk one up for the kind of people who work for ACA. "Oh, I'll definitely celebrate later. What a great day." I sat on the cold concrete stairs at the top of the porch, the chill pressing through my jeans. A breeze stirred, carrying the scent of damp earth and early-spring air. Spring, the wonderful season of rebirth. How perfect that we were heading out of cold winter and into the new growth of spring. "I really appreciate the phone call. What happens next? When can I expect to start? Tell me what to do."

Diana let out another soft laugh, and I knew what that meant. As an HR rep, she must have had a great interest in whether new hires were excited about the appointment, and I knew I wasn't disappointing. She said, "Training starts March thirteenth. I'll mail more information later today, but for now, enjoy celebrating, and we'll look forward to seeing you on the property soon!"

We said goodbye, and I sat still for a moment, my pulse still racing from the news. A tear rolled down my cheek, warm against the cool air, and I brushed it away. In a few minutes I'd go back inside, where I'd tell Kamilah my great news, and I knew she'd tell me we were going to properly celebrate two wonderful occasions tonight. But right then, I just wanted to pause and let it all wash over me. Sitting on those steps, I felt the possibilities for my life stretching wide like the open blue sky. I knew there were countless people around the world with infinite goals that called for discipline and determination, people who dreamed big dreams and reached for things they might never attain. I knew there were people with aspirations that appeared far off and that would call for study and practice and money and work, and more, more, more of the same for years and years. And maybe those people didn't have the opportunities I did. Maybe they didn't have the gifts. Maybe they didn't have parents to lift them, parents willing to change their own lives to help their child reach those goals. I wondered if any of those dreamers would get to experience what I was feeling in that moment, the magical buzzing, tingling joy of reaching an enormous milestone. I was a pilot this airline wanted to fly for them, to represent them.

That call symbolized a culmination of immeasurable work and staying power. That call was for my mother and father, who had been tireless in their support and encouragement. It was for Stayce Harris, who looked me in the eye, then pointed the way forward. It was a nod to my history teacher, Mrs. Marques, who was so invested in what her students wanted for themselves, she guided me to skip school and take a life-changing risk. It was for the two Kamilahs and Captains Bill Norwood and Al Glenn and the Organization of Black Airline Pilots and all the other kids at Tuskegee. I looked to the sky and thanked God, the universe, the heavens, the shared spirit, and all my ancestors. I thanked everyone who'd ever taught me something, opened a door, told me to stick with it, and cheered me on. And I let myself feel the pride of my own determination. I was the one who had done the work and studied and passed the exams and flown the hours and learned, learned, learned. And now I was going to fly jets. I took a long, deep breath, then looked down, dropped my face into my hands, and let the tears fall.

Ten days later, I walked into the ACA flight training center near Dulles Airport. The classroom looked ordinary enough, whiteboard stretched across the front wall, recessed lights humming softly overhead. There were five rows of tables on one side of the room and five on the other with an aisle down the middle. The scent of freshly brewed coffee drifted in from the break area. I slid into a seat in the front row, the closest seat to the wall, and felt the table smooth and cool beneath my palms. A couple of other women were scattered among the rows, but there wasn't another Black face in sight. That wasn't new. I'd grown used to the loneliness caused by being the only one in the room. Still, once again being "other" pressed on me with its quiet weight. A pilot one row behind me with light brown hair and a matching mustache flashed me a friendly grin. "Front row, huh? Brave choice."

I smiled. "Best seat in the room." Then I turned back and faced forward, shoulders squared. I usually sat so close to the front of classrooms I could smell the tang of the dry-erase markers. What I didn't tell the pilot was this was my answer to history. It was my way of saying I won't be pushed to the back as my ancestors were. If I belonged in a room, I belonged in the front.

I sat quietly as the room filled in. Then, at 8:00 A.M., an average-height man with neatly cut blond hair and narrow, cat-shaped eyes walked up the aisle and stepped to the front of the room holding a single piece of paper. "Good morning, I'm Captain Keith Gates, flight standards supervisor." He scanned the room, packed with twentysomethings and a few slightly older people. Some leaned forward with notebooks already open, others sat back trying to look relaxed, but under the tables, their knees bounced. Flight bags rested at their feet. Brand-new binders sat on desks. Fresh haircuts. Pressed pants and starched shirts. Polished shoes. I wore blue dress slacks, a white blouse, and a brown cardigan. We were all dressed as if we had something to prove. Captain Gates spoke with the cool calm of a pilot addressing passengers on the PA, with the vocal timbre that seemed to have been coached into them so they could make a plane full of people feel completely secure even as they bounced around in the worst of turbulence. He said, "Welcome to your first day of training at Atlantic Coast Airlines. If I read your name, grab your things and meet me in the hallway."

What could this be about? Who could be in trouble already? I wondered what kinds of violations got people kicked out of this program. Had they realized they'd made mistakes by hiring some of us? Had they rechecked test scores or watched footage that showed some of us to not be up to standard?

Captain Gates glanced at his paper and read four names, which led to shuffling and murmuring as four of the twentysomething guys stood, glanced around at other pilots, grabbed their bags, and stepped into the hallway. I looked around the room. Some people looked relieved, others confused, and others disappointed, as if they'd wanted to be chosen, as if they knew a secret the rest of us didn't. Then he said, "And Nia Gilliam, see you in the hallway. For the rest of you, your instructor will be in shortly."

This couldn't be happening. They'd made a mistake and hadn't meant to offer me the job. They'd accidentally hired too many and were cutting the list. No, no, *no.* I picked up my bag, stood up straight, walked around in front of my table, and stepped into the hall. Outside the room, the five of us stood in a staggered line along either side of the freshly painted hallway. We all threw each other curious glances. The guy standing next to me leaned over and whispered, "Any idea what this is about?"

I shook my head, my pulse ticking in my throat. "Not a clue."

While we waited, one guy tapped his foot against the speckled tile floor. Another leaned his shoulder into the wall, his eyes shifting between the floor and the white ceiling. The last two crossed their arms, one guy staring blankly down the hall, the other with his eyes closed. I pressed my back lightly to the wall, rocking my weight from side to side.

Finally, Captain Gates reappeared and gestured for us to follow him, and a few doors down the hall, we entered a classroom that looked just like the one we'd left, except this one was much emptier. Five white men, ranging in age from late twenties to late thirties in casual but professional clothes sat huddled around a table, talking easily, their voices dropping off when we entered. They glanced briefly at the four guys, then their eyes landed on me and lingered before they returned to their conversation. At first, I thought they might be new hires like the rest of us, guys who somehow already knew each other. But no, the longer I looked at them, the more I could tell they weren't brand-new. They didn't have the body language or nervous expressions of people with no clear sense of where they stood in the scheme of things.

Captain Gates gestured for us to take a seat, then he walked to the front of the room and gave us a sly smirk. "I'll bet you're wondering what's going on?"

Yeah, you might say that.

"ACA is launching something new, an all-jet subsidiary called ACJet Airlines. ACJet will be the only airline to operate the new Dornier 328 regional jets, the DoJet. And you five new hires, together with these captains"—he gestured ceremoniously toward the men at the table—"will be the very first crew members to launch the airline under the Delta Connection banner."

The captains in the room exchanged knowing looks, their smiles calm and assured. I glanced at the other new hires and saw various degrees of surprise and pride. One guy furrowed his brow, as if trying to make sense of what we'd just heard. My pulse spiked, and it was hard to tell if I was more thrilled or overwhelmed. I was going to help launch an airline? I'd been *chosen* to help launch an airline. And not one with turboprops, like those most regionals used at the time, but with jets. An all-jet regional. It felt cutting-edge. Exciting and daunting at once, but before the feeling could settle, Captain Gates's next words landed with a thud.

"The first crew base will be New York's LaGuardia, with Boston Logan opening shortly thereafter."

New York and Boston? I'd been expecting Chicago. Now I was looking at a commute, more expenses, more sacrifice. I felt excitement tangled with disappointment, proof that even dreams carried fine print. I'd be flying for a new airline brand and not out of Chicago. The reality checks were hitting me like cold water to the face. But the truth was, my career fantasies hadn't necessarily been created on much of a real-world foundation, beyond the fact that I knew being an airline pilot was a reachable goal. What thought had I given to the rest of the details that went along with a pilot's life? I'd always assumed I'd be based out of Chicago, that I'd work with people I liked, that the airline I worked for would be stable, established, and well-run. I assumed I'd be financially secure once I finally made it to the airlines. But these weren't sure things. Some of them would never be within my control. I was beginning to see that being a pilot wasn't a fairy tale without plot twists.

What would it mean to work not for ACA, the established parent company, but for ACJet, their new, untested division? Did this mean I'd have less job security? What did it mean relative to my potential salary? At what point, if ever, would I have any control—the ability to choose my base, my schedule, or the routes I'd fly? So many questions. But today wasn't the day to ask them. I'd just been handpicked for something exciting, and that was a stamp of approval by the new airline, a gesture of great confidence and faith. So I'd have to return the faith by trusting this was a good direction for me. As I'd always done, I'd learn and rise to whatever challenge came next.

The captain said, "You've all worked hard to get to this point. Over the next several weeks, we'll cover everything you need to operate the DoJet safely, professionally, and to the standards of both ACJet and the FAA. Congratulations and welcome."

After the announcements, Captain Gates directed us to introduce ourselves, so we went around the room like on the first day of any class. A couple of the other pilots came from a small airline, another flew corporate flights for wealthy clients, another one had recently been a flight instructor. Then the captain explained what we needed to know: company procedures, HR paperwork, getting work IDs, and being fitted for uniforms. For the next couple days, we underwent more orientation, and by midweek, Captain Gates announced our sim partner assignments. A sim, or simulation partner, is much more than a casual classmate. It's the person you move through every phase of training with—side by side in classrooms, shoulder to shoulder in the simulator—as you share responsibility for each other's preparation, pace, and performance. We both carried the consequences of whatever happened to us as a team. If one of us needed extra training, the timeline slowed for both of us. A missed callout, a botched checklist, a weak maneuver—things like that affected both people in the partnership. If one of us showed up ready—prepared, confident, "ahead of the airplane"—we both looked capable as a result.

Captain Gates said, "You new hires, I'm going to pair each of you with a captain. Nia, you'll be with Joel." A man sitting across the aisle in the front row waved and we smiled at each other. Shortly afterward, he got up and came over to me. "I'm Joel," he said, extending his hand, and right away I was glad we'd been paired. Years of being in training environments had taught me to brace for skepticism from other people who made me feel I had to prove myself twice over, and the skepticism always showed up fast. But Joel simply looked me in the eye and talked to me like a partner.

We started with basic "indoc," learning the airline's standards, expectations, and culture. Then came systems training, during which we memorized the specifics of the Dornier 328JET until we could picture every aircraft system—fuel, electrical, hydraulic—with our eyes closed. Procedures followed, including checklists we practiced so thoroughly we could remember their elements without effort. The recall became like instinct.

Through the six weeks of training, I genuinely enjoyed working with Joel and witnessed why he was an excellent pilot. He was consistent, prepared, and respectful. He didn't talk over me. He always showed up early, and more than once, I walked into the briefing room to find him already there, manuals open, just quietly reviewing. "Morning," he'd say, sliding a spare chair back for me.

During sims, if I missed something small, he didn't pounce on it or turn it into a power play. He just tapped the checklist and said calmly, "You want to take another look at that?" When instructors addressed us, he often waited and let me speak for myself. Joel and I were never trying to outshine each other. We were just trying to get it right, supporting each other as we worked to become the most competent jet pilots possible. And the stress of training in the simulator was so rough, I was extremely grateful to have a calm, kind training partner.

From the outside, the simulator looked like a big box on stilts, like an all-terrain walker out of *Star Wars*. On the inside it looked like the flight deck of an actual airplane. The instructor sat behind us and fed codes into the control panel to tell the simulator which scenario to throw at us, like heavy snow, strong winds, turbulence, or problems with one of the aircraft's systems. Engines failed. Fires erupted. Systems malfunctioned. Warnings chimed and lights flashed. System messages stacked on top of each other and came at us rapid-fire, sometimes before we'd finished resolving the one before. The simulator was designed to overwhelm our senses so we'd have to rely on practiced habits and teamwork to get us through any disaster. And it was so realistic, my body responded to climbs and descents just as if I were airborne in an airplane full of passengers. Joel and I followed the protocol: stay focused, trust the training, communicate clearly, and fly the airplane safely. We became like an efficient, coordinated machine. But all that had been rehearsal. Now it was time to prove ourselves during the simulator check ride. We'd be going through all that turmoil, but an evaluator would be watching our every move.

Joel adjusted his seat beside me, steady as always. "You ready?" he asked quietly.

My mouth was dry, so I didn't respond with words, I only nodded, and we lifted off into the simulated sky. The familiar rhythm of callouts between Joel and me filled the flight deck, grounding me in routine, and for a few moments, I almost forgot I was being evaluated. Then a piercing chime cut the air, and a warning message flashed on thc panel: an engine failure. My stomach lurched, but I kept my hands on the flight controls. I kept flying and reminding myself of the piloting mantra I'd learned as a student my first day at Tuskegee: aviate, navigate, communicate. I could hear my own breathing in my headset, feel the tension settling into my shoulders.

Joel's voice stayed calm. "Your airplane. Your radios. I'll run the checklist."

We worked through the engine failure together, voices low and deliberate, no rushing. No panic. When it was time to declare the emergency, I pressed the mic and spoke. "Patriot five-zero-two-six declaring an emergency. Request return to field for landing." The final minutes of the approach to landing seemed to go in slow motion, the runway drawing closer while time stretched thin. I felt the weight of the moment in my chest, in my hands, in the stillness of the flight deck. Then the wheels touched down smoothly. Silence filled the space. Behind us, the evaluator said, "Congratulations. You've passed."

The words didn't land like celebration. They landed like truth. Not just relief but recognition.

Next up was the real thing, my first flight in the DoJet with passengers, the real sign that my career was moving ahead. Five days after passing my final simulator evaluation, I would fly a DoJet from Washington Dulles to New York LaGuardia. Before this, the most passengers I'd flown professionally had been two people reporting on traffic as we flew over St. Louis, but now I'd be transporting a plane with the capacity to carry thirty-two passengers. My first time flying an actual jet plane, my first time flying into LaGuardia Airport, my first time even going to New York.

I'd been thoroughly trained in the flight sim, and now it was time to show what I knew and apply it in the real airplane with my IOE instructor, the pilot responsible for overseeing my progress during initial operating experience.

Nick was a seasoned instructor, probably in his early fifties. We'd spoken on the phone and agreed to meet at the departure gate. It was my first time walking through an airport in a pilot's uniform. During training, I'd grown used to curious looks from classmates and people at small airports I flew into as an instructor, but here I was, a uniformed pilot—young, female, and Black. Any one of those three might have drawn attention, but combined, they felt like a flashing headline.

Nick and I met at the gate, and as we boarded ahead of the passengers, I felt the weight of their eyes on me. After greeting the flight attendant, we settled into the flight deck and began our setup. "This is real-world flying now," he said evenly. "Not the sim, where everything's scripted. We'll plan for a normal flight, but you're trained. If anything abnormal comes up, we'll handle it together."

We pushed back from the gate. Nick taxied while I monitored and worked the radios, absorbing the rhythm of Ground Control and the choreography of airplanes moving all around us. When we'd reached the runway, Nick turned to me. "Your airplane. I have the radios."

"My airplane." My airplane, and this wasn't practice.

Instructions came in from the air traffic controller. "Patriot five-zero-two-six. Cleared for takeoff."

Nick repeated the instructions over the radio to the controller. I advanced the thrust levers, and the engines surged, their pitch growing louder, deeper, filling the space around me. The vibration moved up through the seat and into my chest.

Stay present.

The DoJet moved faster, and the centerline blurred beneath us as the plane's acceleration pressed me into my seat. I kept my hands steady, my breathing slow.

"Rotate," Nick called.

I eased back on the yoke and felt the nose lift. Then the ground seemed to release us, and we were in the air. The runway fell away, and the city tilted back. We were flying. The moment was enormous, and I was smiling.

The city stretched out below us. Roads threading through neighborhoods. Morning traffic was already thick. "Nice takeoff," Nick said quietly.

The airplane felt more alive than the simulator, more sensitive, more responsive. This was real air, real motion, real consequences. And the airplane felt natural, almost graceful. Now at cruise, I understood how different real-world flying was from training. The frenetic environment inside the simulator conditioned us to expect constant failures, nonstop urgency. But up there, all was calm. Just the airplane, the radios, and open sky. Flying was peaceful.

After twenty minutes at cruise, it was time to descend, and the New York City skyline emerged out of the sky. I'd always thought Chicago had the best skyline in the world, but New York was immense, sprawling, stunning. Everything I'd heard about the city now made sense. There was an energy I could feel four thousand feet up. And forevermore, New York would be the first city I flew a jet to.

The Twin Towers were magnificent. They stood proud and high above everything else, unmistakable against the sky.

Nick followed my gaze. "First time seeing them from up here?"

I nodded. "My first time seeing them, ever."

I'd seen the towers on television and read about them in magazines, but none of it prepared me for what it would be like to see the 110-story structures standing side by side like mighty sentries.

We continued north along the Hudson, and there was the Statue of Liberty. It was my first time seeing her, too, this magnificent symbol of New York and of America. She was majestic and seemed to be protecting everyone and everything around her, bridges that arched across the water, ferries that cut white trails behind them, block after block of rooftops like lids on the tops of containers full of lives stacked upward.

Then ATC called a visual checkpoint. "Patriot five-zero-two-six, report the George Washington Bridge in sight."

Nick pointed ahead. "Do you see it?"

I followed his finger. There it was, a huge band of steel stretching across the river.

"In sight," I said.

Nick pressed the mic. "New York Approach, Patriot five-zero-two-six has the George Washington Bridge in sight."

Then LaGuardia came into view, sitting along the edge of the water, hemmed in by highways, neighborhoods, and nonstop motion.

We were cleared to land, and Nick glanced over at me. "Just fly it how you were trained."

I flew the descent. I flew the turn. And I flew the final approach as the neighborhoods around the airport rose up around us. Nick monitored quietly, backing me up while giving me the space to be fully in control. The wheels touched down with a soft thump. A clean rollout.

Nick glanced over and smiled. "Well done, Nia. My airplane."

I exhaled and removed my hands from the controls as Nick took over and taxied us off the runway toward the gate.

I'd done it. I'd flown my first real jet, a jet full of passengers, in one of the most demanding airspaces in the world. Then I'd landed it smoothly. A jet. All those girlhood dreams and fantasies had now concretely and officially become realities. I sat and let the weight of that realization settle, lighthearted and joyful, innocent of the fact that in only eleven months, my industry and my country would be rocked by the stuff of the darkest nightmares.

ELEVEN

At the start of the five-hour drive from Strongsville to Chicago, I sat quietly in the back of the truck and stared out the window, picturing the plane hitting the tower. Again and again, the horrible image replayed in my mind. I closed my eyes and still saw it. Inside the truck was quiet. The radio was off, and my parents didn't ask questions, so eventually I lay across the back seat and forced myself to think about my comfortable bed and mac and cheese, my favorite comfort food, until I finally fell asleep. When I awoke, we were in Bellwood, a suburb of Chicago nine miles south of O'Hare, pulling into the driveway of the modest Cape Cod–style, one-story home my parents moved into after selling the Oak Park house, the one we'd moved to so I could attend a high school with an aviation class. The Oak Park home had served its purpose for six years, but it had never been my parents' dream home. It was simply a place they lived so I could take another step toward my dream.

For the previous eighteen months, my parents' home had served as my crash pad, the place I'd stumble into after long days of commuting back and forth to the East Coast. I came and went, never fully unpacking, but always knowing their home was my home. As they always had, my parents offered me solid ground to stand on and a safe place to go for comfort.

Now it was September 13, two days since terrorists had flown planes into the World Trade Center, and my country was no longer recognizable. The Twin Towers were gone. Both of them had collapsed, completely tumbled to the ground, creating an unthinkably massive pile of rubble. Nearly three thousand people were dead, with thousands more still listed as missing. Rescue workers continued digging through the smoking ruins in Lower Manhattan, where cars, sidewalks, and buildings were covered in ash. The air was thick with debris and toxic chemicals.

Every television channel broadcast the same images on a loop: planes crashing into glass and steel, buildings folding in on themselves and crumbling, people running through clouds of dust and smoke. Reporters spoke in subdued voices, and the word *terrorists* was now part of every conversation. Downtown Manhattan was still closed off. Military vehicles lined the streets as armed National Guard members stood watch in places that had once been crowded with tourists.

Across the country, flights were grounded. Airports were silent. The sky itself felt unfamiliar. Around the world, countries held vigils. Others sent aid. World leaders expressed solidarity, and there was comfort in all that, but national fear became more vivid every day.

The White House told Americans to stay alert, to watch for suspicious activity, to prepare for uncertainty. Color-coded threat levels became part of everyday life: yellow, orange, red—constant reminders that, as Americans, we could be targeted again at any time. More and more news spilled out about the attacks. The hijackers had used box cutters to threaten and attack crew members.

Ordinary, everyday tools, and that detail alone led to major changes at airports. Many personal items were prohibited, like mace and pepper spray, nail clippers with nail files, and little scissors. Flight deck doors were required to remain locked at all times.

For my parents, the new world order meant new worries layered onto worries they'd carried all along. They'd already spent most of my life supporting a daughter who'd chosen a career with risk baked into it. Now every news report about aviation and terrorism was filled with warnings that seemed meant for our family specifically.

The national trauma served to push people closer together. Many Americans were more inclined to stay close to and in some cases even cling to their loved ones. But I didn't know where I wanted to be or who I wanted to be close to. There was security in living with my parents, but I was more unsure than ever about what to do about the relationship I was in with Theo, an ex-boyfriend I'd known since high school and had been casually seeing for the past three months. Theo was a custodian during the day, and studied exercise science at night. Before the terrorist attacks, he and I had been getting together every time I was home from a trip, hanging out with friends and family, and going to the movies or the gym. It was easy and light. We didn't have a commitment. We didn't talk about the future. We simply spent time together when we could fit it into our busy schedules. Since I'd gotten home, I'd seen him only once, to hug and give each other the grounding of knowing we were both here, but I didn't feel like connecting more than that. I didn't want to see people or be social. I just wanted to sleep and forget.

The days blurred together. I slept late, drifted from the couch to the chair, then back to the couch. I avoided the news, but I couldn't completely shut it out. Like people in homes all around the world, my parents wanted constant updates, so the TV was on for much of the day. When the footage of the smoking, crumbling towers came on-screen, I turned away or got up and walked out of the room. On September 14, I went for a walk and looked up to see a plane flying overhead. The sight of it was a relief. It was a sign that just maybe life could one day go back to how it had been. But watching that plane also concerned me, made me worry about the psyche of the pilot. And I wondered if the sky felt different than it had just three days earlier. I hoped she or he felt safe and in control up there, but as far as I was concerned, that pilot could have the whole sky. I had no interest in going back to any of it. Who was to say whether terrorists had another attacked planned already? Who knew what their next airplane scheme was? Still, there was something about seeing a plane up where it belonged that did my heart good.

I continued my leisurely walk around the familiar streets of our neighborhood, but then a thought shot through me like a sword. It was already September 14, but I hadn't gotten my period. I was two days late. To some women, being two days late would have meant nothing, but since getting my first period back in fifth grade, I could practically set my watch by my menstrual cycle. And because I was always so organized, I made note of my cycle dates. Not to worry, I told myself. The kind of stress I'd just gone through, was still going through, would knock anybody out of balance. The effects of this trauma were psychological and physical. My sleep was interrupted throughout the night thanks to a recurring dream: I was on the runway in Boston, planes were flying low overhead, then crashing into office buildings. As debris came flying at me, I lurched and woke up. As a result, no matter how many hours I slept, I never felt rested. Stress could do extraordinary things to the body—everybody knew that. And I told myself to relax, that there really wasn't anything to worry about because I'd gotten a negative result from a doctor-administered pregnancy test only four days earlier. Theo and I had used condoms, but I wanted to go on the pill, and to get a prescription, I first had to have an exam and pregnancy test. And I had—and it was negative! So everything was going to be fine. My disturbed cycle was simply because of the stress I'd been under. Any day now, my period would return, and I'd be back on track.

Six days after the terrorist attacks, I was in my room folding laundry when I received a phone call from Rob Speaks, the director of operations who'd released me from duty on September 11. "Hello, Nia," he said with a gentle voice. "I wanted to call and check on you. How are you holding up?"

The question caught me off guard, made me feel cared for in a way I hadn't expected from my employer. "I'm okay," I said. Then, more honestly, "Not doing too well."

"I can imagine. It's unbelievable, just watching the images on the news . . ."

I wasn't going to talk about it. I didn't want to replay it, revisit it—nothing. I sat silently and started to think about whether I should hang out with Theo later.

Eventually, he said, "Nia, have you considered getting counseling?"

Hearing my name pulled me back. I said, "I'm sorry?"

"Would it help to speak with a counselor? Have you heard of the Employee Assistance Program?"

"No, I haven't."

"ACA has an Employee Assistance Program," he explained. "It's confidential counseling meant to help employees through difficult times."

I'd never heard anyone in aviation talk about seeing a therapist. I knew police officers and firefighters often met with counselors after a traumatic event, but mental health wasn't openly discussed in aviation. Nobody wanted to be seen as vulnerable or in any way not up to the job. But I said, "I'll look into it," and I meant it. I had the support of the director of ops, and I desperately wanted to feel better.

"Good." He sounded relived. Then he paused, and his voice went even softer. "Nia, I wanted to ask . . . When ATC cleared you and Shye for takeoff, why did you take off? You did nothing wrong, I just wonder. With what you saw going on across the river, what made you take off?"

Rob and everyone else in our field knew the protocol, but I could tell he wanted to understand what we'd been thinking. "We were instructed to take off. We were definitely rattled by what we saw going on in New York. But I guess we could also ask why the controllers cleared us for takeoff. The circumstances were highly unusual, but we were cleared for takeoff. The controllers did their job, and because there was nothing wrong with our airplane, we did our job."

He quickly said, "I understand. And, Nia, please take as much time off as you need."

"With pay?" I blurted. I had no idea if this kind of time off would be considered special circumstances. Would I be on a paid leave of absence?

"You'll use whatever sick time you have. After that, it wouldn't be paid time off, but if you need more time, your job will be here."

That answered that. "Thank you," I said. I had only about two weeks of sick time coming to me. But I had no intention of getting in a plane again anyway, so I was going to have to figure out what was next for me.

I hung up and began second-guessing what we'd decided on the runway that day. Should we have rejected the takeoff clearance? It was Shye's decision, but in the moment, when he asked me, "Are you okay?," should I have told him, "No. Cancel the takeoff clearance"? If we hadn't gone up, maybe the trauma in my body and mind wouldn't be so attached to flying.

Every night since the attacks, my sleep had been broken. I'd drift off only to wake up again, mind racing, body tense, never fully resting. During the day, my thoughts bounced from *I don't want to fly again* to *What happens if I don't?* I obsessed over the idea of what to do with myself now, and if I did decide to return to flying, how long would I have before going back? There was no peace, only a constant loop I couldn't shut off. Food lost its appeal, and most days I had to remind myself to take a few bites of something, anything.

My parents tried to give me space, but they'd never seen me like this. Dragging. Disconnected. Listless. Unmotivated. They didn't know how to hold what I was carrying, and I didn't know how to explain it to them. I knew then that I needed more than family. I needed a professional.

I contacted the EAP and was given the names of several therapists near me. I called a few of them and chose a woman named Glenda because she offered me an appointment for the following day, Tuesday, exactly one week after the attacks. I wondered, Was therapy anything like I'd seen in movies and TV shows? Would

Glenda just sit there nodding? Would she make me do all the talking? Was there going to be a couch? Was I going to cry? Would I leave her office feeling any better than I felt now?

Her office was in Oak Park, just eight blocks from my high school. Eight blocks from the school I'd ditched because I wanted to fly. Eight blocks from the house my parents moved to so I could chase that dream. The irony wasn't lost on me, that everything in my life had been built around becoming a pilot. Every decision. Every sacrifice. Every risk. And now I was sitting in a waiting room just down the street from the scenes of my childhood because the idea of getting back on an airplane was unbearable.

Glenda's office was simple and sparsely decorated in soothing neutral tones. A chair faced a sofa, and a coffee table with only a box of tissues on it sat between them. She was a short, white woman, probably in her mid-forties, with cropped, dark brown hair and glasses. She smiled warmly as she introduced herself and asked me to make myself comfortable on the couch.

"I need to be honest," I said right away. "I can only attend whatever sessions my insurance covers." That meant only two hours, which I suspected Glenda didn't know. Would two hours be enough?

"Okay," she said gently. "We'll be efficient with the time we have." She glanced at the clock on the wall. "How about we make today a long session," she added. "Two hours? We have a lot to talk about."

I didn't know where to begin, so I started with what I could see when I closed my eyes. The smoke. The second plane. The silence that came afterward. The way the sky looked so strange, almost confused. Wounded.

I talked and talked, words tumbling out faster than I could organize them. At one point, I looked up and saw Glenda's pen frozen above her notepad. Her brows were drawn tight, her mouth slightly open, like she was trying to take in something too big to process. "Take your time," she said quietly. Her voice was steady, but her eyes were glossy. "You're safe here."

I said, "I don't know if I can get back on an airplane. Maybe not ever."

Glenda held my gaze. "That makes sense. Your nervous system is still in shock. Your brain will keep trying to process what it went through. That means some memories may surface later. Maybe in dreams. Maybe in a sudden thought, even years from now. That's your mind doing its job. It's a normal part of healing."

I looked down at my hands. They wouldn't stop twitching.

She said, "Here's something very important for you to keep in mind: Right now is not the time to make permanent decisions. So try not to declare where you stand on the future of your career. Your wounded psyche can't be rational about such things yet. And you worked too hard for your career to let trauma take it from you."

I didn't promise, but instead said the only thing that felt true. "I just want to feel normal again."

After two hours, Glenda glanced at the clock and said, "I see we're out of time." She offered to book another appointment for the following week, and I said I'd call to schedule it, but I knew I wouldn't be back. We'd just spent my only two free therapy hours, and there was no room in my budget for more.

I stepped out of the office and walked past my old neighborhood's movie theater. How simple things had seemed during my childhood in this suburb of Chicago. My existence had been about bike rides and homework, hanging with friends and spotting planes. Now the world was a dangerous place. But oddly, the danger seemed somehow far away, and I took comfort in the way people seemed to look at each other with a knowing kind of connection. In stores and on sidewalks, I noticed more goodwill among people. Strangers seemed more patient with each other, more helpful. Kinder.

For the rest of the day after the session, Glenda's words went around and around in my mind: "Don't make any big decisions for a while." Despite how strongly I felt about not flying again, I couldn't argue with the logic of her advice. I was inside out, and unsure whether I could trust my motives, my decisions. I seemed to have lost the resolute clarity that had always been such a big part of my life. Now I was in a kind of purgatory, a confusing fog without direction.

Three days after my therapy session, my period was officially one week late, and I started to think Glenda's counsel might have been strangely prophetic and pointing toward my personal life. That did it—I couldn't just keep waiting. Late that evening, I drove to the Walgreens about five minutes from home, bought a pregnancy test, and stuffed it into my purse. When I returned home, my parents were already in their bedroom asleep. I went straight into the bathroom, locked the door, and peed on the stick. Then I waited. I stood in the tiny white bathroom my mother kept immaculate and watched the little window on the stick.

The appearance of a single line would mean the best of news, no pregnancy. No sacrifices. No shame. No explanations. No confrontations. No decisions I wasn't ready to make. No disruption to the life I was trying to hold together. One line would mean I could wrap up this little drugstore experiment and throw the whole thing in a public trash can far from our house. It would mean I could take deep, slow breaths and accept that stress was a mighty and mysterious thing, that the mind-body connection was more powerful than I'd ever known.

But what if two lines appeared? Two lines would be unbearable. It would mean my condom routine had failed me. It would mean I was pregnant by a man I was only casually involved with. It would mean making a very, very difficult decision at a time when my heart was extremely vulnerable and my psyche battered. And it would mean having to see the look in my parents' eyes when I told them.

I stared at the stick. Nothing yet.

I looked around the room at all the white—white walls, white tile, white toilet, white shelves. Then I looked down and saw something happening in the test's little window. A line was appearing.

Then a second line.

My chest boomed with a single blast, like the bright white fireworks that send one massively thudding *bang,* one big explosion you can feel right in the center of your body. There was no misreading it—there were two clear lines on the test stick. I stared at the little window, as if looking longer would change what I was seeing. Then I grabbed the box and read the instructions again. It was written clearly: Two lines meant *pregnant.*

I sat down hard on the edge of the tub, the plastic stick still in my hand. Nothing about my life pointed to a readiness to be pregnant. I didn't think I *ever* wanted to be pregnant. I wanted to cry, but no tears came. For several seconds, I felt only numb. Then came dread.

I'd always believed that if I ever faced an unplanned pregnancy, I'd choose abortion. I was careful about birth control, and I didn't think a failure of science should be allowed to dictate the rest of my life. But that was before I'd watched the second of two murderous pilots fly a plane into a skyscraper and destroy thousands of lives. The weight of all those deaths and all that loss filled every inch of me, and I couldn't bear the idea of stopping the development of the life inside me.

So now I had to tell Theo.

THEO AND I HAD MET as teenagers on a double date. The new Batman rollercoaster had just opened at the Six Flags amusement park and I couldn't wait to ride it. Once we were inside the park, our dates saw the long snake of a line and winced.

My date said, "Nope."

Theo's date said, "Pass."

I looked at Theo. "Are you up for it?"

He looked at his date, and when she smiled and nodded, he turned to me and said, "Yeah. I'll go."

We waited in line for almost an hour, talking mostly about basketball, and I thought it was really cool that we both said Kenny Anderson of Georgia Tech was our favorite college player. Finally it was our turn on the ride, which lasted a thrilling two minutes. We stepped off the roller coaster, buzzing with adrenaline, and scanned the crowd for our dates, but didn't see them anywhere. We searched for a while, checking benches, looking near the snack stands. Nothing. Eventually, we wandered over to the basketball game booth and started shooting hoops, talking, laughing, and going wherever the afternoon led us.

What started as friendship slowly grew into something more. We bonded while watching Chicago Bulls games and PBS documentaries about marine life. We dated for two years, much of it long-distance while he was away at college. When he came home for holidays, we moved easily between each other's families. Sunday dinners. Birthday cakes. Graduations. Backyard cookouts. Visits to each other in college. During the summers, I tagged along while he babysat his niece and nephews. He'd hand them juice boxes, break up arguments, lie on the floor and let them climb all over him.

"You're good at this," I teased once.

He shrugged. "They're blessings. I don't take that lightly."

To everyone else, the next steps for Theo and me were probably obvious. But after my first year of college, I had only one thing on my mind: flying. I told Theo, "I don't think I can be in a relationship and chase what I'm chasing. Not the way it deserves."

Calm as always, he said, "I want you to get where you're going."

Ending a two-year relationship was difficult. Our families had grown close, and there was sadness all around. But eventually we found our way back to friendship. Years later, after my four-year relationship with Devon ended, I looked for comfort in the familiarity of Theo and me. With us, it had always been easy, and our history made it feel natural to fall into a simple rhythm again. But there was nothing simple about the news I now had to share.

I hoped he wouldn't be angry. I hoped he wouldn't push for abortion, but at the same time, I didn't want to raise a child with him. He was a good guy, but this wasn't part of my plan for myself. I wasn't sure about much of anything anymore, but I knew the life I'd had before September 11 was gone, and the one ahead of me seemed to be taking shape without my permission.

The next evening, Theo planned to stop by my parents' house, as he'd been doing every day for the past week, quietly showing up the way good friends do. During the day, he worked as a custodian, and in the evenings he took exercise science classes to build on his degree in kinesiology. That evening after class, he pulled up in front of our house, and before he could come to the door, I hurried outside, slid into the passenger seat of his car, and gave him a quick hug. The interior smelled of clean leather and the sharp, fresh notes of Issey Miyake cologne. Theo wore a neatly pressed green T-shirt that clung to his sculpted biceps. Because of his bald head, broad shoulders, and the glint of his earring, he looked like a younger, dark-skinned Vin Diesel.

I sat with my hands folded in my lap, nails pressing into my palms. From the radio, Aaliyah's "Rock the Boat" filled the space between us.

Theo asked, "Do you want to go somewhere?"

"Let's just sit in the car for a bit."

He tapped his fingers lightly on the steering wheel, relaxed. I kept my eyes forward and let the song's gentle rhythm clash with the heaviness in my chest.

Theo said, "How did it go with the therapist the other day?"

"She told me not to make any major decisions in my current state, but now I don't have a choice."

He turned to look at me. "I don't think I unders—"

"I took a pregnancy test. It was positive." My words came out flat and heavy. Then I looked down at the floor.

The only sound was the low vibration of the engine. I braced myself for his disappointment, shock, maybe even anger. For a moment, he didn't say anything. Then he let out a slow breath, like he'd been holding it without realizing. "You're serious?"

I nodded.

"That's . . . that's good," he said. "That's actually great. Nia, this is a blessing."

His words hung in the air, a blessing. A *blessing*? How was an unwanted pregnancy a blessing? Did he not realize how serious this was? We could barely take care of ourselves, and now we were supposed to take care of a child? And I wasn't planning a life with Theo. I had no idea what I wanted for myself, but I didn't intend to marry him. What could he be thinking?

Then I realized I should give him a break. Maybe Theo was trying to do the right thing. Maybe he was just trying to be a good guy. And he didn't know if I thought this was good or bad news, so maybe he was playing it safe.

I said, "You're . . . happy?"

He smiled. "Yeah. I am. We'll figure it out. It's going to be okay."

"My parents are *not* going to be happy about this," I said. "Neither are yours. We're not even married. And people are going to judge this. They already judge everything I do."

"Let them," he said. "They're not the ones who'll be raising this kid."

I looked at him. Not a word about abortion. Theo said, *raising this kid*. I said, "You're really okay with this?"

He nodded. "I'm more than okay. We could get married."

I closed my eyes. "You just said that like you were offering to stop for gas."

He laughed softly. "I'm serious."

I didn't answer.

"I'm not saying tomorrow. I'm just saying . . . I'm here. I'm not going anywhere."

In that moment, my chest loosened a little. Not because anything had been decided but because I was no longer carrying the weight of it alone.

Now I had to tell my parents. This was going to gut me. My parents had always seen me as someone who had her footing, a daughter with a career and a plan. How was I supposed to tell them that a daughter who'd never needed prodding to do her homework, who'd plotted her professional dreams and then achieved them, had now accidentally gotten pregnant by a guy she was seeing only casually? This was going to be about ten thousand times more difficult than the day I admitted I'd lied to them and ditched school to go to a funeral. I winced at the memory of my mother back then jumping to the conclusion that I was about to announce I was pregnant. She'd been so vividly relieved when I'd told her no with shock and defiance.

I sat in the car with Theo for a little over an hour. Then I said good night and went back inside. My parents were settled in the living room sitting on the deep mahogany sofa, its fabric offering a warm pop of color against the white walls. The air still carried the aroma of the green peppers, onions, and celery Mom had blended into the seasoned chicken she was simmering in the crock pot for tomorrow's dinner. They had already eaten, and with the day winding down they were sitting slouched and cozy on the couch, waiting for the WGN evening news to come on. I walked into the living room and sat in a chair facing them. They were so content and comfortable, and I was about to launch a rocket through their lives. The world around us was falling apart, and now I wondered if my utterly disappointing news was going to break their hearts and drive a stake through my family.

"Mom, Dad. I have to tell you something."

My jaw was tight. My parents sat up straight. Then I just blurted it. "I'm pregnant."

Everything in the room seemed to freeze. The air, the television, the ticking clock. My mom's lips were pressed into a thin line, and she narrowed her eyes as if she were trying to clearly see what I'd just said.

My dad's voice sharp as he demanded, "What?"

"Um . . . Theo and I are going to be parents." My voice was small. "You're going to be grandparents."

My dad sank back into the couch and exhaled hard through his nose. The television carried on in the background, the anchor's voice like a chattering party guest who hadn't caught on that something heavy was going on just across the room. My parents looked at each other, as if silently pleading to make this news untrue, as if they were sharing magical thinking that might undo what we all knew was very much done.

Finally, my mom spoke. Her voice was sharp, edged with disappointment. "After everything you've worked for, Nia? And after all your father and I sacrificed for you to have this career?"

She didn't wait for me to answer. She stood up and marched past me to their bedroom, then closed the door behind her. She didn't exactly slam it, but she closed it with force.

Heat rushed to my cheeks. I wanted to defend myself, to explain that I hadn't planned this, that I was just as shocked as they were, but the words stuck in my throat.

My dad shook his head slowly. Then, in a voice heavy with disappointment, he said, "I'm not ready to be a grandparent." He rose from the couch and followed my mom, leaving me alone in the living room. I had hoped for the smallest ounce of support, but their reaction didn't surprise me. I knew they'd be shattered and massively disappointed, but when they both walked out of the room, I felt cut. My parents had always been my constant, the two people who had never let me feel alone. Sitting in their living room, I felt it, a heavy loneliness. I was now a problem to solve. I'd just introduced a massive life detour they didn't want to navigate.

Later, I sat on the edge of my bed and let myself cry. Not loudly, just enough to feel it move through me. How would I get through this without my parents' support? How was I going to go through it at all? My thoughts scattered everywhere. To my reputation. To the career I'd already spent years building. To a future that was about as defined as a dirt road in a snowstorm.

The following day, all three of us moved around the house like ghosts. No questions. No conversation. Just silence. Feeling unwelcome in my own home, I decided it was time to tell Kamilah, so I went across town to her place and told her everything.

"I'm pregnant," I said, and I knew I didn't have to add that the baby was Theo's. Before she could say anything, I told her about the negative pregnancy test from the doctor and the drugstore version I administered myself, then about my conversation with Theo, followed by our parents' dramatic reaction.

The first thing she did was hug me, which made me cry. It was a hug I really needed following my parents' cold shoulder. Kamilah always listened without judgment and always knew how to show empathy. She said, "This is a lot for you to deal with, Nia. So first of all, know that I'll be here to help. And Mom and Dad will come around. They're just processing it all, but I'm sorry they made you feel bad." I wiped tears from my eyes. We sat there for the next few hours talking about my options, my fears, about Theo's suggestion we get married. We didn't come up with answers, but with my sister, I could breathe.

Back home, I endured another day of silence from my parents, and their distance was so painful to me, I left the house early and stayed away all day. I was starting to feel I no longer belonged there and should consider finding another place to live. When I finally returned home that evening, both of my parents were sitting on the couch. My dad said gently, "We've been waiting for you."

My mom stood and pulled me close. The shift was confusing. One moment I'd been invisible, and now I was getting smiles and comfort. I pulled away and studied their faces. "What's going on? Yesterday you wouldn't even look at me."

My mom sat back down and patted the cushion beside her. I hesitated, then sat. "We owe you an apology," she said. "We haven't handled this well."

My dad nodded. "We were surprised. We were worried. And we let that come out the wrong way."

I looked between them. "It felt like I didn't exist."

My mother's head was down. "That was never our intention. We just . . . needed time."

I said, "What changed?"

They exchanged a glance, then my dad said, "Your sister talked to us."

My mom let out a small breath, almost a nervous laugh. "She reminded us that you're an adult, that this is your life, your decision. And that our job isn't to control you. It's to support you."

"She told us we could either be part of your life through this," my dad added, "or we could push you away. We definitely don't want to push you away."

My throat tightened. That sister of mine. What a treasure.

"We love you," my mom said. "And we're here. For whatever you need."

Their apology didn't erase the pain of the past few days. But it did soften something. It felt like a door reopening.

LIFE WENT ON. AIRPORTS REOPENED, and more and more flights were scheduled. People still had places to go, families to return to, employers who expected them back. I soon realized that I, too, had to go back to work. I was going to have to fly again, and it didn't matter that I wasn't emotionally ready. The idea of more terrorism in the sky made me tremor with fear, but my sick leave had run out, and I had a child on the way. I needed an income. I needed health benefits. I didn't have a choice.

I was senior enough to request a schedule that didn't involve flying into Newark or any of the New York City airports. I didn't know how my body would react to flying back to the scene, and I didn't want to find out, so I requested routes that took me in and out of Boston and Cincinnati; Columbia, South Carolina; and Burlington, Vermont. For my first time back in the air as a pilot, I was to fly a Boston-to-Burlington route, but before that I had to get to Boston as a passenger, and the minute I stepped into O'Hare, I could feel the change. Armed guards were positioned throughout the airport. Security lines were long and slow. People spoke in hushed voices and many didn't speak at all, just clutched their boarding passes and kept their eyes straight ahead. I was no different than the rest of the people who seemed so unsure of what to think about air travel now, and when I went through airport security, I was jolted by the way I reacted to the presence of a man in the passenger line who looked like he could have been from the Middle East. He had dark hair, dark eyes, a long beard, and some kind of wrap around his head.

I stood in the employee security line while passengers shuffled forward in the adjacent lane. Then the man stepped up to the checkpoint in front of me and was pulled aside, where a security agent patted him down. My chest tightened. My breath shortened. Panic rose up through my abdomen and shot throughout my body. I tried to stay calm and continue through to the scanner, but when the agent called, "Next," I turned around and hustled to a restroom, where I locked myself in a stall and began to hyperventilate.

What had come over me? Had I seen so many pictures of the 9/11 hijackers, those menacing, dark-eyed, dark-haired al-Qaeda members, that I didn't know better than to lump all Middle Eastern–looking men in with them? I cupped my hands over my mouth and breathed in and out slowly. I knew this reaction wasn't about that guy in the security line. It was about the terrifying images I'd seen again and again, even though I so often turned away. The endless news footage. The headlines. The incendiary language people were using. The fear that had been burned into all of us. I stood there shaking, ashamed of my own reaction. As a Black woman, I knew what it meant to be seen as a threat simply because of my appearance, to be judged before being known. And here I was, in the very mindset I had spent my life challenging. After a few minutes, I stepped out of the stall and up to the sink, where I ran cold water over my wrists, splashed my face, took slow breaths until the panic eased. Then I walked back to the security line.

When I reached the front again, the agent looked at me closely. "Why did you step out of line like that?" Her tone was firm. Suspicious.

I thought fast. "I'm pregnant. I thought I was going to be sick."

She studied my badge and compared it to my face, then nodded. "Okay. Go ahead through. Have a good flight."

I walked away feeling exposed. Humbled. Disappointed in myself. But also aware, and that mattered to me. I knew my reaction was irrational and stemming from unprocessed fear rather than hate. Recognizing that didn't excuse my reaction, but it showed me something important, that I was no longer ignoring the trauma. I was beginning to let it live at the surface. And that meant I was finally starting to learn how to manage it instead of letting it manage me.

In the crew room at Logan Airport, I waited for my flight to Burlington. All around the room, crew members asked each other, "Where were you on September eleventh?" Someone answered with a story about being mid-flight. Another described watching the second tower fall on a break room television. Heads nodded. Voices lowered. When I thought the question might be headed my way, I pulled out my cell phone and pretended to make a call.

The captain on my schedule was someone I'd flown with once before. Brett commuted from Burlington and often bid trips there so he could overnight at home. Early thirties. Reddish-brown hair. Athletic build. Calm. He approached me in the crew room and extended his hand.

"Hi, Nia. Looks like we're working the Burlington flight together. How are you?"

"I'm okay," I said. Then, after a beat, "Things around here don't seem okay."

"Yeah. It's definitely a different world these days." He shook his head. "But we'll get through it. Just one leg up to Burlington today."

"Should be an easy flight," I said.

We gathered our bags and walked out of the crew room and onto the ramp to the plane. The last time I'd been on this ramp I was being driven to meet the FBI agents. The sounds of airport machinery, and the smell of jet fuel were the same. I'd walked on this ramp hundreds of times before, but today it felt narrower. At the aircraft door, the flight attendant greeted us with a tired smile. "Good afternoon, crew," she said. "We're a half-empty flight today. I'm not surprised."

"Good afternoon," Brett said. "It may be a while before we see full flights again."

I stepped into the cabin, greeted the flight attendant, then settled in my seat. Brett settled in his. I looked around the flight deck, almost unconsciously, as if reacquainting myself with something familiar.

"Want this leg?" Brett asked.

"Sure," I replied, grateful for the normalcy of the question.

We moved through the preflight quietly, and the flight attendant said, "All set back here." Then she closed and locked the flight deck door. The sound was different now. A solid metal click. Neither of us spoke for a moment. Then Brett said, "Ready?"

"Ready."

We pushed back from the gate. The tug eased us away, and the engines began to spool, the rising whine building beneath my feet. I focused on the checklist, on the callouts, on the things that were still the same. As we taxied, I noticed how quiet the frequency was. Fewer aircraft. Longer pauses between transmissions.

The airplane ahead of us rolled onto the runway and disappeared into the afternoon sky. As we lined up on the runway, I felt something deeply comforting. It was a visceral, physical awareness of the plane and its processes. The body remembering before the mind does.

"Your airplane," Brett said.

I focused on the runway centerline that stretched out in front of me, long, straight, waiting. Today, it was just pavement.

A voice came in from the Tower. "Blueridge 2603. Cleared for takeoff."

I took a slow breath and advanced the thrust levers. The airplane surged forward, the engine roared, and the runway blurred.

"Rotate," Brett announced.

I eased back. The nose lifted. The wheels left the pavement, and the sound shifted—the hollow rush of air replacing the grind of plane against runway.

We climbed through a thin haze, and once we'd leveled at cruise altitude, Brett made the passenger announcement. He was calm, professional, steady. Then he clicked the mic off.

"I'm glad it's a short flight," he said, then glanced at the door. "Keeping this thing closed and locked the whole time feels strange. I used to leave it cracked half the time."

I nodded. I remembered kids peeking in with wide eyes. Parents snapping pictures. Curious passengers asking questions about the controls.

After a moment, he asked, "Were you flying that day?"

I hesitated, then shrugged and shook my head. That was a conversation I didn't want to have, here, now, on my first time back in the air. I said, "How do you like living in Burlington?"

Cruise lasted only twenty minutes, then we began our descent into Vermont. The trees were deep green, edged in early gold. Roads threaded clean lines between fields. Lake Champlain caught the afternoon light and flashed silver. Everything below looked pristine, unbroken.

The runway appeared ahead, straight and centered. The air was smooth, and the airplane felt balanced in my hands. As the ground rose steadily toward us, I reduced power and held the nose just slightly high. Then the wheels met the runway with a firm, honest thud, followed by a quick rush of reverse thrust and the hum of deceleration pressing us gently forward in our seats. We rolled clear of the runway and taxied to the gate to park.

The scent of warm brakes and jet fuel drifted in as we shut the engines down and the ten passengers filed off the plane. Brett gathered his things and looked over at me with a smile. "That was a good flight. Thanks for flying me home, Nia." He laughed lightly. "See you at the plane tomorrow."

When he stepped out, I stayed seated for a moment, my hands resting loosely in my lap.

It had been a good flight. Not a dramatic or redemptive return to the scene, just a regular flight that had gone as expected. Perfect.

ALONG WITH GETTING USED TO being back in the sky, I was navigating the discomfort of pregnancy on the ground. I stopped buckling my pants and instead folded them over and used a belt to hold them up. By the end of my first trimester, I could no longer tuck in my shirt, so I called human resources at ACA to order a maternity uniform.

"We don't have maternity uniforms," the woman on the phone admitted, her voice carrying a hint of embarrassment. "We've never had a pregnant pilot."

"What am I supposed to do for a uniform?"

"Maybe call the uniform manufacturer for United Airlines. They have a larger pilot group and more women. You won't be able to order a blazer, of course, but the white pilot shirt, for your epaulettes and your wings—you could get away with wearing that."

I called the M&H Uniforms store and bought four maternity pilot shirts, and for the first time in weeks, I felt comfortable when I was dressed for work. The shirt was white and collared, with button flaps on the shoulders for epaulettes, but the cut was nothing like the tailored shirt it was meant to replace. It hung loose and boxy, more like a smock than a fitted shirt. Extra fabric gathered at the sides, the front hem dipped lower, and the overall shape swallowed my frame. It met the technical requirements of the uniform, but it was unmistakably maternity. The world had crossed into a new millennium, but pregnant women in the workplace still had a very long way to go.

One day that December, I was on a United flight commuting from Chicago to Boston and wore my maternity uniform shirt and company-issued pants slightly unzipped, but held up by a belt. As I stood at the bottom of the jet bridge, just to the side of the boarding door, waiting for the last passenger to board before being assigned my seat, a white man, about mid- to late twenties wearing a polo shirt and dark slacks, walked toward me from the jet bridge. I assumed he was a passenger needing help. His expression was pinched as he said, "Are you a pilot for ACA?"

I smiled, "Yes."

"I am, too." Then, like a perturbed teacher talking to a naughty student, he added, "It's obvious you didn't read the section on uniform standards. You need to do that so you won't embarrass the rest of us." Then he turned and walked toward the boarding door.

As he stepped onto the airplane, I snapped, "I'm pregnant! This is my maternity uniform!" He looked back at me and sneered, then disappeared into the cabin.

The flight attendant at the boarding door looked at me with wide eyes. "What did he say to you?"

"It's fine," I said, though my voice wasn't convincing.

She exchanged a glance with the other flight attendant, then walked down the aisle. A few minutes later she returned to the boarding entrance and went inside the flight deck to speak with the captain, then she popped back out and gave me a sly smile. "That guy who spoke to you is a non-rev," she said. "I told the captain."

The captain stepped out of the flight deck and motioned me onto the plane. "I heard what happened," he said. "If you want, I can write it up. He could lose his pass privileges."

I shook my head. "No. I just want to go to work."

"All right. But he was out of line. And congratulations. First baby?"

"Yes."

"They grow up fast," he said with a smile, then went back to the flight deck.

I took my seat, grateful for the support. I just wanted to relax and forget all about it. But the flight attendants weren't ready to let the matter drop. For the entire two-and-a-half-hour flight, they pampered me like a VIP, bringing me warm meals from first class, slipping me extra snacks, and fussing over me with blankets and pillows. And they were nice and loud as they asked me about the baby and praised my service as a pilot, despite the challenges. The sneering pilot sat only two rows behind me and had to watch as I received first-class treatment while he sat in relative neglect. Near the end of the flight, I felt someone pause beside my aisle seat. I looked up and saw him standing there.

"Excuse me," he said quietly. "I owe you an apology. I didn't realize you were pregnant. That's not an excuse, but I need you to know I'm sorry."

I always appreciate an apology, but I had no interest in a conversation with the guy. "Okay" was all I said. He nodded and went back to his seat.

After we landed, I stayed seated while the passengers deplaned. Then I looked up and once again saw him standing beside me. He held out a folded piece of paper, and I took it from him. Then he continued down the aisle. As the last few people gathered their bags, I unfolded the note. His handwriting was tight, deliberate. *I am sorry if I offended you. I did not realize that you are pregnant. My concern was for the image of our company, which is why I brought it up privately. I'm sorry. –D.H.*

His regret was clearer on paper than it had been when he spoke, and the fact that he followed the verbal apology with a written one told me the incident might stay with him awhile. Maybe he learned something that day. By trying to make me feel small, he was the one who walked away diminished.

I was usually the only Black person or female in a classroom, and I was the first at my airline to fly pregnant. Both firsts reintroduced that familiar old feeling of standing out, and not in a good way. That kind of trailblazing rarely feels rewarding. It's isolating and sometimes deeply embarrassing, but every day I recommitted to showing up, making more space for the women who would follow.

Flying while pregnant was rough. I dealt with nausea, fatigue, and the aches that came with long duty days, but the uniform added another layer of strain. My clothes didn't fit any more than my current life fit within the dream I once had for myself. And deep within me, I carried the trauma of having witnessed a murderous attack that weaponized airplanes, the beloved vehicles of my life. Before the attacks, I was joyfully living the pilot's life I'd worked for. But after September 11, my life was not only upended by terrorism, it was hurtling toward a new chapter that for now brought only discomfort and fear. How distressing it was to discover that life didn't become more certain with age, but less calculable. My sense of direction was muddied. My desire to fly, gone.

TWELVE

I had been flying for three months since the terrorist attacks, and I told myself as long as I stayed away from New York and New Jersey airports, flying could be the gratifying experience it had always been. I was wrong. I did the job, but without joy. Flying was now work, something I simply had to do to earn a living. And I clearly wasn't the only one who'd soured on the idea of being on a plane again. Flights were often half-empty. People around the world were simply afraid to fly, and people who did fly kept an eye on those around them. When I was a passenger on flights to or from home, I watched. In security lines, people eyed each other's luggage. On flights, if a passenger stood up quickly, fidgeted too long with contents of a backpack, or went to the restroom multiple times, people noticed and continued to glance around the cabin on some kind of high alert. Most of the lighthearted banter that had once defined my experience in airports and on planes was gone. For me, it was all head down, do the job.

By the time I entered my second trimester, I was worn out. No medical restriction required me to stop flying at any specific stage of pregnancy, but my chronic exhaustion made the decision for me. When I landed in Cincinnati, it would be the end of a four-day trip. Then I'd hop on a flight home to Chicago, and put flying away indefinitely.

After stepping off the airplane, a wave of nausea hit me, and I ducked into the restroom, threw up, then braced myself at the sink until the room stopped spinning. When I looked up, I barely recognized myself. My face pale, my belly big and rounded, my hands swollen. I looked like a woman deep into pregnancy, even though I wasn't even halfway to childbirth.

A woman with microbraids, dressed in a turtleneck and a calf-length skirt, stopped me as I stepped out of the restroom and said, "Excuse me, miss, I wonder if you can help me." Her voice was smooth and low, the kind you'd expect to hear hosting a late-night radio show. I could picture people hanging on her every word.

I was used to people asking me for help in airports. Passengers see the uniform, the ID badge, and assume you have all the answers. "Yes—what do you need?"

She studied me for a beat. "Are you a pilot?"

She already knew. It was in her face, the kind of pride you see when your guess turns out to be right.

"I am."

Her face lit up. "I've never seen a Black female pilot before. I'm so proud to see you. I hope you're my pilot."

I smiled. "That would be nice, but I just finished my trip. I'm flying home now as a passenger."

"Well, I'd be happy just to walk next to you. My gate's right ahead. My name is Saniyah." She reached for my hand, not to shake it, but to hold it.

"Nice to meet you, Saniyah. I'm Nia."

"That's a beautiful name."

"Thank you. It means *purpose*."

"Well, Purpose . . ." She glanced at my maternity blouse and smiled softly. "When is the baby due?"

I pressed a hand lightly against my stomach. "In the spring."

"Your first?"

"Yes," I said, my voice catching slightly. Yes, my first. My first pregnancy. My first time going through this kind of slow-creeping physical misery. The first time I had to look my parents in the eye and see them devastated at the word *grandparents*. The first time birth control betrayed me. I'm a single woman who didn't want kids, and wasn't planning to spend my life with the father of this child, so it was also my first time figuring out how to co-parent with a man I care very much about but am not in love with.

"You and your husband must be very excited." She said it as if there could be no other storyline.

"I'm not married."

Saniyah slowed her stride and tilted her head. "Do you want to marry the father?"

Her forwardness made me a little defensive, but I kept walking with her. Theo's parents had been pressuring him about our getting married, and for the past three months he'd reminded me that he'd be ready to marry whenever I was. My parents didn't pressure me at all. They said a baby on the way shouldn't make me feel obligated to become a wife. I'd been so focused on being a good pilot and dealing with my changing body I'd thought very little about marriage. But I was thinking about it now. I said, "He wants to get married, but I don't want to walk down the aisle in a wedding dress while pregnant." I looked down at my belly. "Extremely pregnant."

Then I exhaled and looked ahead toward the gate signs glowing in the distance. I wanted to turn back time and go back to being just a pilot, not a mother-to-be. I wanted to follow my recent breakup with a lot of time on my own, taking long walks and getting to know myself again, not dating, not being comforted by the warmth of a familiar touch. And while I was back there, I wanted to warn the United States that disgusting murderous cowards were plotting terrorist attacks on September 11. I thought, *I want to go back, just to last summer so I can fix things.*

Saniyah paused just before the split between our gates. "Thank you for walking with me." Her voice had softened, but there was a firmness beneath it, and I leaned toward her without thinking. She said, "Before I leave, I'd like to offer you a visual." She looked at my ID badge then said, "Nia . . . do you mind if I ask the father's name?"

"Theo Williams."

"Okay, imagine this: You and your baby's father are in the hospital, holding your newborn. The nurse says, 'Congratulations on the birth of your son, Nia Gilliam and Theo Williams,' or 'Congratulations, Mr. and Mrs. Williams.' Which one feels better? Which one gives honor to your baby and represents family unity?" Then she smiled, turned away, and walked toward her gate.

Her words pressed into me with the force of a statement so hard-hitting, it leads to consideration instead of resistance. I knew I didn't have to marry Theo if I didn't want to, so I rarely thought about what it might mean to my child to have married or unmarried parents. My only consistent thought on the subject was that if or when we married, I didn't want to be a big, pregnant bride. But *was* I ready to marry him now? After my encounter with Saniyah, *Mr. and Mrs.* started to sound right. It was the family dynamic I'd grown up with, what both Theo and I had grown up with: two parents, one household, one last name. Was I not "honoring" my unborn child with my decision not to marry right away? Not once while wrestling with whether or not to marry Theo had I weighed whether going this way or that was honoring or dishonoring our child-to-be. But I was certainly thinking about it now.

Before the pregnancy, I'd thought Theo and I would enjoy each other for a while, then eventually move on to other phases in our lives. But when I'd found out I was pregnant and chose to keep the baby, I'd chosen a path that involved Theo, very much so. It meant that no matter what happened between us, I'd be linked to him for the rest of my life. So was I now willing to go all in and become a family unit? Was I willing to do what had to be done to offer a traditional family structure to my child? It was how my family had done it, how his family had done it, and how families everywhere I looked had done it. If it wasn't a desirable setup, why had people been doing it for centuries? Was the matter before me as simple as going forward on the path well-trodden by millions of people throughout history? I decided right then what to do. Even though the idea didn't make my heart feel light, I decided to offer my unborn child the comfort of a unified, traditional household. Before you've lived long enough to find out what's right for your own life, tradition can easily pass for wisdom.

Before boarding my flight, I called Theo. My hand trembled slightly as I listened to the phone ring and held the receiver.

"Hello?"

"Do you still want to get married?" I asked him just like that. Dove right in, no pleasantries. "We can do it before the baby arrives."

His voice was calm. "Yeah. I never wanted to wait. I'm fine just going to the courthouse."

I said I'd see him tomorrow, and we ended the call. Theo had sounded relaxed, even casual, but the finality of what we'd just said out loud hung in the air all around me. A decision had been made. It hadn't been a grand proposal, just a phone call in an airport, born out of nausea and exhaustion and prompted by the words of a stranger. Yet that small moment turned into a vow, a family, and the beginning of a story I was going to need time to learn how to fully embrace.

GETTING MARRIED QUICKLY IN A courthouse would have been easy, but I wasn't a courthouse-wedding kind of girl. A lot of aspects of my personality and life defied stereotypes, but when it came to marriage, I very much fell in line with what I'd seen in a hundred books, magazines, and movies. I wanted a traditional wedding. I wanted a white dress. A marriage was something to celebrate, for everyone involved, and I threw myself into putting together a lovely little wedding that would feel like a celebration.

The impediment was money. Our guest list topped out at three hundred, and we couldn't find our way to thinning it. But once word spread, family and friends stepped in with offers of help, and every time someone asked, "What can I do to help?" I offered them a specific task. One aunt and uncle covered the flowers, another paid for the DJ and limousine, another paid for the venue. Theo's parents took care of the cake, and my parents covered the food. As the wedding plans evolved, I felt enveloped in the arms of a village, relatives and friends so sincerely gathering around us at the start of a life we had little idea how to build. Their generosity reminded me that family wasn't defined by tradition or bloodlines but by showing up. Thanks to everyone's help, the only expenses Theo and I had to worry about were my wedding dress, a $299 special I got off the rack at David's Bridal, and our wedding bands from Kay Jewelers, which cost under $400 for both.

As the RSVPs rolled in—almost everyone replied *yes*—one response caught my eye. Stayce sent her regrets, and I nearly gasped with relief. I'd been so uncomfortable about the idea of Stayce seeing me pregnant, unwed, and, well, just not being a polished, focused pilot, I'd sent her invitation later than the others. I'd hoped by the time she received it she'd already have plans she couldn't change, and then we'd both be spared the awkwardness of having to pretend this was a very blessed event and just what I wanted for myself at twenty-five. For almost a decade, Stayce had been my mentor, and her opinions mattered to me, deeply. Although I wanted to, I couldn't cut her from the invitation list—how awful it would be if she heard I'd married and hadn't so much as told her about it, let alone hadn't invited her. I also couldn't bear the thought of her being there, seeing me, the girl who had been so flushed with ambition and joy, now a pregnant bride. Young as I was, my life already looked dramatically different from the one she'd inspired me to reach for.

As the wedding day approached, I felt heavy in every imaginable way. I was twenty weeks pregnant and miserable. But I tried to keep the misery to myself. I'd already ignored a therapist's advice not to make any big decisions; in fact, I'd gone right ahead and made a huge one, and it was done. I believed it was the right one, so what would be the point in getting into conversational tangles about it now? I needed to keep my head down, to focus on what came next, to put one swollen foot in front of the other.

I didn't have a bachelorette party. Instead, the night before the wedding, I had a quiet send-off with the women closest to me, a sleepover at Kami's mother's house, about twenty-five minutes from the ceremony venue. There was Kamilah, four of my cousins, and Kami, my longest-standing friend. I'd started college before Kami graduated high school, but I returned home to watch her crowned homecoming queen and again to see her walk across the stage in white, carrying roses at graduation. My first trip to Washington, D.C., was to visit her at Howard University, where she was an actress studying theater. She was building a magnificent life for herself.

When she graduated from college, I was in the middle of flight instructor training, but I still went with her to Europe. For two weeks, we backpacked across Italy, France, Spain, and Switzerland and slept in hostels. I wasn't the best travel companion—I brought my study guides with me and struggled to balance the pressure of training with our shared desire to fully experience our first time in Europe—but she never complained. That was Kami: steady, patient, present.

She stayed in D.C. after college, and I visited when I could. We kept choosing each other, even as life stretched us in different directions. The only time I truly struggled to understand one of her choices was right after 9/11, when she moved to New York City to further her career. I couldn't imagine such a choice, but I supported her. Kami and I knew we'd always be able to count on each other. Now she'd flown in from New York to stand beside me as my bridesmaid. To support me.

That night, surrounded by women who had known different versions of me over time, it wasn't a party. It was quieter than that. More reflective. But there was a lot of talk about the wedding, and they were all more excited about the day to come than I was. And why wouldn't they be? Weddings were fun! This was a celebration!

But to me, this night meant I was just one day away from making a massive commitment, taking vows. One day from becoming a married person. And fired up as my bridesmaids were, we all knew what nobody was saying: This wedding, this marriage wasn't happening because I'd found a dream life partner or because I was profoundly ready and well equipped to become a wife. It was happening because birth control hadn't worked. Tomorrow I'd be a wife, and four months after that a mother. But all I'd ever wanted to be was a pilot. Now it seemed my life had officially taken off running without me.

On the morning of the wedding, the weather was mild for January in Chicago. The temperature had reached almost forty degrees and the sky was a dull, white blanket of clouds. My bridesmaids, beautiful in sparkling silver dresses, helped me into my white A-line satin gown with the beaded top that sparkled in the light. I'd ordered the dress two sizes bigger than I thought I'd need on my wedding day and had it altered just two weeks earlier, but already it pressed tight against my growing belly.

I'd borrowed a vintage veil from a family friend, something old and borrowed in one. Little touches like that made me feel I was really getting married. Kami did my makeup with steady hands and a quiet focus, which comforted me. Even when we were kids, her energy had been calm, and on that morning, I leaned into it. Soon it was time to head to the Levy Senior Center banquet hall. I waddled to the limo, careful with the skirt and the squeeze of fabric across my stomach, and settled into the back seat facing forward. There were seven of us, three bridesmaids sat on the right bench, and three on the left bench, facing each other. My friends and cousins laughed, and the sound bounced around the tan leather interior, while I turned to the window. The winter sky looked so beautiful, and for a moment I thought, *What am I doing? What have I gotten myself into?*

The doubt must have been written on my face because Kami leaned toward me. Her voice was gentle. "How are you feeling?"

I wanted to say, I feel like I don't want to do this. I feel like this is a mistake. I feel like I'm watching someone else's life. Kami had always been my best collaborator, the quick-thinking creator of solutions. She'd been my masterful accomplice in crafting the day I skipped school and changed my life forever. But to help me now she'd need truth, and I wasn't about to offer it. Not now, in a limousine, on the way to the venue where soon three hundred people would be seated and smiling and waiting for me to make my way down the aisle. I forced a smile and said, "Nervous."

She rested her hand on mine. "I'm sure everyone feels nervous before getting married."

Her words, soft but certain, reminded me of how wonderfully steady she'd always been. She couldn't magically dispel the unease that had taken root inside me, but in that moment, she helped me hold it a little more quietly. I took several deep, slow breaths and convinced myself it was natural to be nervous, that countless brides for centuries before me had been nervous on their way to the altar. Reminding myself I was part of a shared experience offered a small measure of relief, and for a while, I was calm.

The limo pulled up to the venue at two o'clock, two hours before the ceremony, so the photographer, a woman from Theo's family's church who had volunteered her services, could take pictures before the ceremony. I didn't care that taking pictures first meant the groom would see the bride before the wedding—I just wanted to be efficient, which is why I chose to have the wedding and reception at the same place. And taking the photos ahead of the wedding meant we could get right to the reception after saying our vows.

The entrance of the banquet facility had a warm, rustic feel, with a fireplace glowing in the lounge area. Four steps and a ramp, lined by rails draped in tulle and artificial ivy, led down to the ballroom. At the entrance of the ballroom was a rectangular table that displayed the three-tier wedding cake surrounded by six smaller cakes, all decorated with silver and white flowers. Twenty-eight round tables draped in white linen framed a dance floor, and on the stage stood an arch decorated with the same white tulle and ivy leaves that lined the ramp and stair rails, with two paper wedding bells hanging overhead. Behind the arch sat the head table where Theo and I, along with his parents and my parents, would sit during the reception, high above the guests so we could look out across the room and take it all in. The room's floor-to-ceiling windows looked out upon a garden and pond, both blanketed in snow. The bare winter trees and still water offered a quiet, natural beauty.

Each guest table was set for ten, decorated by centerpieces of one white and one silver balloon tied to a ribbon weight and two votive candles resting on a square mirror. And at each seat lay a program with a black-and-white collage of Theo and me, pictures from childhood to the present, pieced together into the story I wanted the world to see. I had chosen the images so the picture looked whole—two lives arranged to look complete, the promise of stability and love on display. But collages were made of pieces, and to me the collage was just that, a collection of pieces, not a whole. I had no idea how to fuse pieces into a whole.

I expected to feel nervous the first time I saw Theo at the wedding venue. Instead, I felt calm. Almost neutral. He stood there in a black suit, looking more like my friend than my future husband. Familiar. Comfortable. Not the man I was about to marry, just the version of him I already knew.

He seemed excited, but not in the way a groom usually is. He moved through the room like a participant, not the center of it. Smiling. Greeting people. Blending in. I noticed the difference. Not with alarm, just awareness.

The pictures took an hour, and the first guests started arriving at 3:15 P.M. As they gathered, I stayed tucked away in the spare meeting room members of the bridal party were using to stash belongings. I was alone, both literally and figuratively. It was quiet on this side of the door, though I could hear the excitement building on the other side. Inside me, it was quiet, too.

I felt suspended in time, about to step out and perform in front of a room full of guests, many of whom I didn't even know. And even among the guests I did know, just six months earlier they'd known me as part of a long-term relationship with Devon. Many didn't even realize we'd broken up until they received a wedding invitation, my name beside another man's.

Waiting in the spare room felt lonely, but it gave me space to sit with the reality of it all. I felt alone, but I wasn't alone. I had my baby with me.

The air in the room was warm and smelled like a generic hotel lobby that had been sprayed with floral perfume. My dress was snug against my stomach when I sat on the tufted seat of the wingback chair to relieve my sore, tired back after too much standing. As I waited for word from Lena, an acquaintance who'd volunteered to act as wedding coordinator, I felt calmly disconnected from everything going on outside the door, almost as if I was floating above it all and watching a wedding day from above.

The door opened, and she stepped inside, clipboard in hand. "Nia, most of the guests are seated, and it looks like we'll be starting close to on time."

"That's good," I said, rubbing my belly. "I'm ready for the reception. This baby is hungry."

She smiled and was halfway back out the door before she added, "Oh, and I met Stayce, the pilot. I sat her at the table with your aunt Mache."

I froze. "What? No, that must be a mistake. Stayce sent her regrets. She isn't coming."

She tilted her head. "Well, she said she's a pilot for United Airlines, and I guess she's your mentor?"

"Oh God," I whispered. My throat tightened and my appetite vanished. "She's here?"

"Yes!" the coordinator said brightly. "She's really nice. So great she could make it." Then she hustled back out the door.

A rush of heat flushed my skin. My heart raced with joy and embarrassment in equal parts. I hadn't seen Stayce in more than a year, not since the last OBAP conference I'd attended. It was always joyful for me to see this woman I admired so much. But Stayce didn't know I was pregnant, so she was not only about to greet a bride, she was going to see the detour my life had taken. Beneath my excitement was deep, deep shame. My accidental pregnancy felt like a violation of everything Stayce and I had wanted for me. Now when I walked out there and saw her, I'd have to face how much I'd let her down. And not only her, but seventeen-year-old me, the girl who'd had the courage to ditch school, navigate the city, and sit in a church full of strangers on that life-changing day when I first saw Stayce in her crisp uniform, poised and certain, representing everything I longed to become. Stayce was my role model. Her eyes were the eyes of my industry, the eyes of women in aviation, the eyes of Black women in the professional world. If I disappointed Stayce Harris, could I bear it?

Twenty minutes later, Lena returned and said, "You're on, Nia. If you'll follow me to the lobby, we'll have you ready to follow the bridal party."

The bridesmaids and groomsmen walked down the aisle to the R&B song "Differences" by Ginuwine. Once everyone was in place, the DJ played, "Lovin' You" by Minnie Riperton. The birds began chirping and when the lyrics started, I walked holding on my father's arm, the wonderful man who'd supported my dreams, even when he didn't fully understand them. His steps were sure, his posture proud, as if he were handing over a daughter who had everything figured out. He'd always made me feel unstoppable. Even when I'd taken risks that would have rattled most parents, he conveyed confidence in me, always letting me know he knew I'd find my way.

As we walked, I kept my eyes straight ahead, avoiding the sea of searching eyes focused on me. "Slow down," I whispered as we moved forward. Pregnancy caused me to wobble as I walked, and speed wasn't going to make me any more sure-footed, but I was also in no hurry to get to the altar. Every step closer to the arch where the reverend and Theo stood was a step further from who I'd been before the pregnancy and before 9/11, back when life had felt so sure, when my purpose and future had been so clear.

The room was dimly lit, and I could barely make out the faces of the guests as we passed by. The stage lights pulled my eyes toward the wedding party lined up beside Theo, all waiting, their faces expressing various versions of sweet expectation. And in that moment, the shift came. It was as if I could actually feel myself stepping beyond the life I'd built. As if I were passing through a portal into an unknown universe. If I hadn't had my father to cling to, I might have stumbled or even stopped walking. But the time for second thoughts had passed. I was like a pilot with a decision to make. Like Shye on the runway, cleared for takeoff, but holding in extremely confusing circumstances. Shye had thought quickly and had made our decision. And there, only steps from my husband-to-be, I resolved to keep moving. I'd made a decision, and now I'd see it through.

I'd always heard that for a bride and groom, the wedding ceremony and reception fly past in a blur, and ours were no different. The vows, the kiss, jumping the broom, the music, the clink of glasses, the rise and fall of voices as people laughed and greeted one another, they all blended into a tapestry of the night. But the moment I saw Stayce was as vivid as my memory of her at Captain Norwood's retirement party. Theo and I stood close together in the receiving line, greeting guests eager to shake our hands, embrace, and offer blessings. Between the ceremony and all the small talk and standing, I was growing weary. But then I saw her several people back in the line, framed by strangers, but moving closer. As always, she was dressed beautifully and stood out like a star on a cloudless night.

Finally, Stayce was in front of me. Her eyes were bright and sincere as she said, "Look at the beautiful bride."

I broke into a huge smile and threw my arms around her. I hadn't realized how much I needed to see approval in her eyes. No matter what was going on in my life, Stayce's presence simply lit up the world. "Stayce! You surprised me!"

She held me for a moment, then pulled back, her gaze soft and full of pride. "You look beautiful, Nia. I'm glad I could make it."

She glanced back at the long line of guests. "Enjoy yourself, and I'll make sure I see you before I leave." It was a fleeting moment, but sweet. And just as she'd followed through on the day I met her, I knew I'd have a chance to see her again at my wedding.

Later that evening, after dinner and all the traditions, the bouquet toss, the cake cutting, and lots of dancing, my feet throbbed from walking and standing and dancing for two. I sank into a chair, letting relief wash over me as I took in the sight of my family and friends still laughing and swaying to the music, as the DJ kept the energy alive with a steady stream of R&B classics from the past four decades.

Eventually, the night wound down, and the chatter of guests began to soften. I was deeply tired, but in that moment, very content. That's when Stayce found me, with her coat already on. She said, "Nia, your wedding was fun!"

I said, "Thank you! I'm so glad you were here. I'm sorry we didn't have time to talk." If I'd had my way, I would have sat with Stayce and talked all night.

Just over her shoulder, I saw the church photographer, and I said to Stayce, "Before you leave, can we get a picture together?"

"Of course!"

We stood together, her black wool overcoat not yet buttoned, her arm slipping easily around me. The flash popped and captured a moment that to anyone watching probably looked like just another shot of a bride and a guest. But for me, Stayce had never lost her magic. She was the living embodiment of my dream, proof that what I'd imagined for myself was possible.

I turned to her. "I'm so glad you came."

"I didn't think I could at first, but I managed to rearrange my schedule. Nia, I wouldn't miss your wedding."

The words brought hot tears to my eyes, and I couldn't let her leave without admitting what I'd been carrying all night. I said, "I actually sent the invitation late, hoping you wouldn't come," I looked down at my pregnant belly. "I didn't want you to see me like this. I didn't want to disappoint you."

Her brow furrowed. "Disappoint me? How could you possib—"

"I'm not flying. I'm pregnant. These days, I'm not exactly living the life I planned."

Stayce looked at me squarely. "Nia, I'm always proud of you. Don't ever question that. That girl who approached me eight years ago—I'd never met anyone like her. You were exceptional then, and you're exceptional now."

I was grateful weddings are such emotional events. I dabbed my eyes with a tissue, not worried about who might have been watching and wondering what I was tearing up about. "Thank you for saying so. It's just that I feel kind of foolish. I had such clear plans and now . . ."

"Motherhood is just as important as flying, more important. And hey, the planes will always be there when you're ready, you know that. But you'll only get one chance to enjoy this season with your child. Don't miss it trying to live on anyone else's timeline."

"Thank you." I couldn't think of anything else to say.

She buttoned her coat and said, "I'm going to head out, but let's be in touch. And Nia, you have great instincts and solid judgment. Trust yourself."

Her words melted through all the layers of shame I'd been carrying. I'd been sure my careless pregnancy would be a disappointment to her. I was sure I'd let her down. But just then she'd been uplifting and reassuring, which was always her way. The disappointment I had to work through was coming from me, so I was the one who'd have to upright the ship, to figure out who I was supposed to be now. In my heart, I was a pilot first, always a pilot. Even when I was a child, I was a pilot. I had chosen it. It was my self-assigned identity. Going forward, it would take some real focus for me to figure out who Nia Gilliam was supposed to be in this next chapter. How was I going to balance the wife I'd just become and the mother I was about to become with the pilot I'd always been? Was I going to let other people's ideas and expectations define me now, or was I still the girl with the determination to chart her own course?

THIRTEEN

Patriotism had erupted everywhere. American flags were draped across front porches, taped to storefront windows, and clipped to car antennas. And the media hadn't moved on, not even a little. Every news broadcast still carried stories of 9/11—missing person profiles and survivor interviews that reopened my wounds again and again. People talked about the attacks constantly, as if speaking of it might help them understand it. All around the country, people hesitated before opening their mail, fearing their letters might have been laced with anthrax. It had been six months since the attacks, but nothing about life in the United States seemed to be headed back to normal.

After the wedding, I entered my third trimester. It was spring of 2002, and, like so many of my fellow Americans, I felt suspended between how to reconcile what had been lost with how to move forward. I knew I had to stay healthy for the baby; otherwise, I didn't know what moving forward meant. ACA had no policy for maternity leave for pilots, and that was a sobering reminder of the disadvantages women face in the workplace. So after flying pregnant for four months, I stepped away from the flight deck and burned through all my vacation and sick days for the year just to keep being paid, then took a medical leave of absence for the remainder of my pregnancy, knowing that once the baby was born, I'd have to rely on the Family and Medical Leave Act (FMLA), which granted me twelve weeks of unpaid leave while letting me keep my job and health insurance. That protected my position with the airline, but it did little to ease the financial strain Theo and I were under with out-of-pocket medical expenses, housing costs, and consumer debt like car loans and student loans.

The airline industry was battered. Flights were going out half-empty, and airlines were bleeding money, so they tried to compensate by charging for things that used to be included, like checked luggage and snacks. Pilots I knew were being furloughed, and every schedule cut was a reminder we had little or no job security. Security in airports changed dramatically as well. The brand-new Transportation Security Administration (TSA) took over passenger checkpoints, replacing the private contractors the airlines had used for years, and suddenly there were federal air marshals on flights, plainclothes and armed. And there was a whole new list of rules and restrictions regarding what a person could take on a plane. From outside it all, grounded and pregnant, I watched with curiosity and concern. I had no idea of what my beloved career would be like when I was ready to reenter. If I was ever ready to reenter.

While the industry around me struggled to recover, my focus shifted from the turbulence all around the world to the life growing inside me. I was still living with my parents while Theo and I looked for a place to live together. Being pregnant and still under my parents' roof meant being enveloped in their special kind of care. My mom kept saltines on my nightstand for the mornings my stomach wouldn't settle. She cooked whatever sounded tolerable to me and never complained when I pushed the plate away. Clean laundry showed up folded on my bed. My dad kept my gas tank full, carried bags in from the car without a word, and insisted on driving me to appointments when Theo wasn't available and I was too tired to take myself. Some nights he'd knock softly on my door just to ask, "How are you feeling?"

They were excited in a way that felt protective and tender, especially proud to be welcoming their first grandchild, a grandson after raising two daughters. But eventually Theo and I bought a two-bedroom, two-bath condo in Willowbrook, about twenty minutes west of our parents' homes, and we officially moved out on our own. My parents helped paint the condo, carefully brushing my chosen colors onto the walls. I picked each shade intentionally, trying to shape the energy of a home I still wasn't sure how to inhabit. We painted the master bedroom a calm, muted green—the kind of color I'd read was meant to slow breathing. The second bedroom we painted baby blue, and when it was finished, I stood in the doorway imagining the son we'd decided to name John sleeping soundly in the calming surroundings. I was deep into my nesting phase, but creating the space also offered me something solid to hold on to. It gave me hope and a sense of possibility. I was still afraid, but I could see a way forward.

Moving forward meant a baby shower, which meant Theo and I would be gifted many of the things we'd need to welcome a baby. It meant people were willing to help us, to believe in us. My sister offered to host the shower, and that alone felt like an act of love. My assignment was to create a gift registry, so with my cousin Patrice, a mother of a six-year-old boy, I roamed the aisles of Target and Babies "R" Us and pointed the scanner gun at all the items Patrice said I'd need. *Beep, beep, beep* went the gun as I shot the barcodes of baby bottles, pacifiers, changing pads, car seat, baby wipes, onesies, diapers, diaper cream, diaper bag, diaper pail. It was the most out-of-body experience I'd had in a long time—shopping for the items that would soon define my life, items I'd never used nor ever been curious about. Here they were, filling my registry, filling the cart, filling the space where my old vocabulary had once lived. For years, my conversations had been dominated by talk of altitude, airspeed, fuel flow, crosswinds, and checklists. I read instruments on a panel full of dials and understood exactly what each one meant. I knew how to manage a flight deck, how to anticipate problems before they arose, how to keep hundreds of lives safe at twenty-five thousand feet. Now my conversations would be dominated by issues of diapers, swaddles, and burp cloths as I was about to begin a mission that didn't have an official training manual.

The shower was held in the basement of my dad's parents' house. Theo walked me inside, where both our families and friends had gathered to celebrate the baby. The house was filled with the scent of pasta, garlic, and butter, and delicious fried chicken from Harold's, my favorite.

From downstairs came the steady hum of voices, laughter rising and falling, chairs scraping across the floor, and music played low in the background—old-school R&B, the kind that always found its way into family gatherings. The sound was deeply comforting, as music from the early days always was. Theo and I walked downstairs, and the room erupted. Cheers, clapping, someone yelling my name like I'd just won something.

"Here she is!"

"Look at the mama!"

"Come on in here!"

For two hours we played traditional baby shower games and opened gifts. Clothespins were clipped onto people's shirts for the Don't Say "Baby" game, and within minutes someone was shouting, "Oops—you said it! Give me that pin!" A roll of toilet paper was passed around next for Guess the Belly Size. People studied me like I was a science project, carefully unrolling the paper, then laughing when their guesses came up too long or too short. A large table was piled high with gifts in pastel bags, their white, blue, and yellow tissue paper spilling over the sides. Another large table was covered with trays of fried chicken, meatballs, lasagna, and salad. And on a smaller table covered with a light blue plastic tablecloth sprinkled with blue confetti shaped like babies and rattles was a large sheet cake with white buttercream frosting and *Congratulations on Your 1st Baby Boy* written in blue. The bar, always the hub of family parties, was covered with bowls of snack mix, and a glass punch bowl fizzed with fruit punch and ginger ale. Folding chairs filled the gaps between the sofa and recliners, while more chairs lined the walls.

All around the room, the women in my life—my mom, my grandmothers, my mother-in-law, my sister, cousins, and aunts—filled the air with chatter and laughs. On the surface, everything sparkled with joy, but the lovely shower turned out to be yet another event at which I felt strangely detached. I opened gifts, smiled for photos, laughed when someone joked that I "must be having twins," and clapped along during the silly games, but it was as if I were attending someone else's happy baby shower, as if watching it all from a distance. I knew what I was supposed to be feeling. Women at the center of baby showers were supposed to glow and gush. They always seemed overwhelmed with joy. I was just overwhelmed.

When the shower ended, Theo picked me up and loaded the gifts into the car, filling both the back seat and trunk. There were so many gifts my mom took some to her house for us to pick up another day. Back at the condo, Theo stacked the boxes and bags neatly in the nursery while I lowered myself into the rocking chair and rocked my weary body as the baby flipped and rolled inside me. Theo fell asleep in the other room, but I stayed in the rocker, listening to its faint creak against the carpet. Alone in the quiet, I told myself those elusive happy feelings would come later, that the connection would arrive in its own time.

In the days and weeks that followed, Theo and I opened and sorted the gifts and put our son's room together. John would have a perfect little boy's room, an undertaking created piece by piece by the village that continued to support us. Theo assembled an oak-colored crib that would one day convert into a toddler bed, while my dad reworked a TV armoire into a closet and storage space for tiny clothes, blankets, and bath supplies. I lined drawers with rows of onesies, socks, and gowns that smelled faintly of Dreft baby detergent, its powdery sweetness clinging to everything it touched. A changing table gifted by my aunt stood ready, stocked with diapers and wipes my grandparents gave us. A rocking chair from my parents was draped with a light blue blanket from my sister, and in one corner sat a swing given to us by Theo's parents. Along one wall was a small bookshelf lined with board books and a basket of toys given by friends and family. Below the wallpaper border, lined with images of footballs, basketballs, and soccer balls, I hung a white shelf lined with plush animals dressed in jerseys and baseball caps. It was a room ready for our little family's future.

With each passing week, my belly grew heavier, and the date circled on the calendar loomed closer. Every day, I craved cheese and sausage pizza and I ate it often, but I also ate salads and roasted vegetables. And I did my best to sleep, though rest came only in fragments, constantly broken by the baby rolling and pressing against my insides. He brushed against my abdomen in visible waves, sometimes stealing my breath and forcing me to brace myself with my hands on either side of the rocker as I tried to calm myself with breathing exercises and hope for the pressure to ease. Many times, I nodded off in that rocking chair and stayed there all night. When I woke up, I tried to rock myself back to sleep.

In the daytime, I buried myself in books about pregnancy and motherhood. I gave as much focus to the content of *What to Expect When You're Expecting* and *What to Expect the First Year* as I'd given my airplane manuals when I was in training. I dog-eared pages, underlining and highlighting passages as if knowledge could make me ready. I studied every symptom, every milestone, every warning—trying to convince myself that if I read enough, I'd be able to step into motherhood with certainty. But while the content of my aviation manuals had sent me buzzing with excitement—the explanations of terms and rules and warnings and gauges were the language of the life I craved—the pregnancy books seemed to offer an education in something that wasn't about me. It was as if I were studying the concepts of a condition affecting someone I carried, someone *over there*. These were manuals for a life I'd never wanted and couldn't make myself believe was going to be manageable.

When I was two weeks from my due date, I packed and repacked the overnight bag for the baby, a onesie, mittens, a blue cap, tiny socks, and a matching set of pastel blue top and bottoms. The car seat was strapped into the car, ready for his first ride home. I was as ready as I'd ever be, and I was profoundly ready to be done with the discomfort of pregnancy, the swelling in my ankles, the weight in my face, the constant fatigue. Motherhood was clearly coming for me. Some days, I caught my reflection in the mirror, and I saw a very tired woman with dull skin and sunken eyes. I'd gained a hundred pounds and was close to developing gestational diabetes. The weight made every minute of every day uncomfortable. For so much of my life I'd defined myself by what was above me. Most of what had mattered to me for years was up, in the sky. Now my existence seemed to be defined by gravity.

On my due date, I had a regularly scheduled doctor's appointment. Theo and I arrived at Gottlieb Memorial Hospital, where my doctor examined me, shook his head, and said, "You haven't dilated at all."

"What does that mean?" I asked.

His voice was matter-of-fact. "The baby is already very big, and he's still growing. I think it's best we induce."

I lay on the exam table with Theo standing beside me, and the doctor started doing something behind the drape covering my legs. He said, "This is going to hurt."

A sharp, scraping pain shot through me, and I gasped. "What was that?"

He stood up. "I just induced your labor. You should have the baby by tonight."

The words hit me like a jolt. *Tonight*. Not someday in the vague future whenever the baby was ready to come but tonight, when modern medicine had decided he'd come. Of course I knew the baby was coming soon. Today was his due date. But I hadn't had even the slightest warning pain. Tonight? I was going to be a mother by the end of the day?

Theo and I walked next door to Labor and Delivery without speaking much. As we stepped into the hallway, he held his arm bent so I could steady myself against him. I checked in at the desk, then a nurse led us to a room and handed me a thin gown. I changed slowly, afraid any quick movements might set off something unnatural. My delivery room was large and brightly lit. A small cross hung above the hospital bed, a rolling monitor glowed beside it, and a clear bassinet waited in the corner. The room smelled like antiseptic and clean linens, and it was quiet except for the sound of beeping machines, a steady soundtrack of waiting and worry.

Theo stood by the window calling our family and friends to let them know I was in labor and delivery. Before long, my parents, sister, and cousin Patrice trickled in, their voices low, their presence filling the corners of the room, a quiet reassurance. I lay in the hospital bed in the center of the room, while nurses moved calmly in and out. Everything was happening both too fast and too slow.

When I began having tightening in my lower back and consistent lower abdominal pain, I called the nurse and asked, "Am I able to have an epidural yet?"

She examined me and said, "Yes, you're about four centimeters, eighty percent effaced. This is usually the point when women start asking."

"I want it."

"I'll call anesthesia."

The anesthesiologist administered the epidural, and for a while I floated through contractions, numbed and disconnected. I even dozed off between contractions, drifting in and out of light sleep.

When it got late, my parents kissed me goodbye on the forehead, and Dad said, "It's getting late. We'll be back tomorrow to meet our grandson."

Not long after he left, I felt a sudden warmth beneath me. I said to the nurse, "What's happening? I feel wet."

A nurse glanced down at the sheets and paused. "Looks like your water just broke."

It wasn't the dramatic moment people describe. No explosion. No urgency. Just warmth. Wetness. A quiet shift that made everything feel more real.

"That's good," she said gently, adjusting the bedding. "That can help things move along."

Kamilah and Patrice had teased Theo about becoming a dad soon, but the hours stretched on, and I dozed off. By the time I woke again, it was after 2:00 A.M. Patrice and my sister had gone home while I slept. Only Theo was left, stretched out on the recliner, sleeping deeply.

A nurse came in to check me. She smiled.

"Ten centimeters," she said. "You're fully dilated." She gently shook Theo's shoulder. "Dad, wake up. It's time to push."

The nurse repositioned me. Explained how to bear down. Walked me through each push. Theo stayed close, his voice near my ear, though I can't remember the words. I just remember trying. Focusing. Doing exactly what they asked. I pushed. Then pushed again.

"I see the head," the nurse said.

"You're doing great," Theo said.

I pushed again.

"You're still doing great," the nurse said, but now her voice had changed. Careful. Measured.

I searched her face. "Is he okay?"

"He's okay," she said, adjusting the strap across my belly. "We're just watching him closely."

Another contraction came. Another push. My body shook with effort even through the numbness of the epidural. I wanted this to work. I needed this to work. I had followed every instruction. Every breath. Every count.

The nurse said, "I see him when you push, but he's not moving forward the way we'd expect."

I searched her eyes. "What does that mean?"

Before she could answer, the doctor came in and studied the monitor longer than I liked. Then he examined me again, quiet and focused. "You've been pushing a while," he said gently. "And you're doing everything right. But he's crowning during contractions and then slipping back. He's not making progress."

I tried not to sound alarmed. "What do we do?"

"I need to be honest with you. His heart rate is starting to dip during contractions. He's showing signs of distress."

The words blurred together. Heart rate. Distress. I looked at the monitor, but I didn't know how to read it. Theo squeezed my hand harder. I hadn't realized how tightly I'd been holding his. "We just want him safe," Theo said, his voice even and grounded. If he was scared, he didn't let it show.

The doctor nodded. "So do we."

They turned me to one side. Then the other. More pushing. Still no progress.

The room felt different now. Not panicked, but quietly serious. Focused. Everyone moving with purpose.

The doctor met my eyes again. "We need to move to a C-section. This isn't safe to continue. The baby is telling us he's struggling."

I stared at him. The words felt unreal, like they belonged to someone else's story. A moment ago, I'd been pushing to bring my son into the world. Now "it wasn't safe to continue."

"Okay," I said, even though nothing inside me felt okay. "Okay."

The bed started moving. People started moving. Wires were

unplugged. Wheels unlocked. Someone explained what was to happen next, but the words barely reached me.

Everything was happening quickly, but inside I felt frozen. I'd done everything I was supposed to do, but my body had reached its limit.

A flurry of shuffling and hustling followed. There were consent forms and anesthesia. Then I was rolled into surgery, where the sterile brightness of the operating room was blinding after the muted haze of the labor room. Theo changed into scrubs and appeared at my side, his eyes wide but steady. A tall blue drape went up between us and the surgeons. I couldn't see the lower part of my body or most of the medical staff in the room. I only felt the heavy tug and pull, the strange sensation of pressure without pain.

"What's happening?" I whispered to Theo, my eyes fluttering with exhaustion. My body felt split between presence and absence, awake but far away.

Then I heard it. "Congratulations! It's a boy!"

The doctor lifted a wriggling body with a full head of straight black hair and held him up like something out of *The Lion King*.

Theo let out a breath that sounded like a laugh and a sob at the same time. "Nia, that's our son!" Even behind his mask, I could see Theo's smile stretch across his face, deep enough to crease the corners of his eyes.

The baby's eyes opened, dark and searching, and locked on mine. For a moment, all my exhaustion fell away. The doctor carried him to a nearby table, and the room around me blurred.

"He's nine pounds, eight ounces," the doctor said.

"That's our son, Nia," Theo said again, softer now. Then he bowed his head for just a second, sitting next to me, right there in the middle of the operating room. "Thank You, God," he whispered. "Thank You." When he looked up at me, his eyes were wet. "You did that. You did that." And he squeezed my hand as if he was anchoring both of us.

My first thought about the existence of my son wasn't poetic or sentimental. It was organic and raw. I stared at him and marveled that this was a real person, a human being I was now responsible for. His health, his safety, his comfort, his happiness—all my job. Something powerful rushed through me, a force that didn't register as a thought as much as a feeling. It wasn't the kind of gentle, adoring love I'd imagined I'd feel for my newborn child. It was primal protectiveness. I felt fierce and clear about my reason for being here: This baby was mine to protect from anyone and anything. From this moment on, it was upon me to see that nothing and no one would ever do him harm. The doubts I'd carried through the pregnancy and all the distance I'd felt disappeared in that instant. This was my baby, and I knew I would do whatever it took to keep him safe. And with that clarity seeping through my consciousness, my body finally gave in to exhaustion. I closed my eyes, with images of his tiny body and little eyes imprinted on my heart.

Two days later, Theo and I left the hospital with our son strapped into his car seat. I slid into the back seat beside him, nerves raw, and asked Theo to drive slowly, as if easing down the road could protect us from the rush of cars around us. The world outside hadn't changed, as far as I could tell. The traffic lights still glowed, cars drove past, and people hurried along the sidewalks. But for me, everything was different now. I couldn't take my eyes off my baby, watching his tiny chest rise and fall, counting his breaths without meaning to, my hand staying close as if closeness itself could protect him.

At home, the quiet settled in. Family came and went during

those first days, delivering meals, folding laundry, filling the nursery with their presence. But then the visits tapered off, and it was just me, Theo, and our son. The rocking chair became my post, my body still aching from surgery, my ears tuned to every sound my baby made in the bassinet. I wasn't ready to leave him, not even for a moment. Sometimes during those quiet hours I thought about how Karen had spoken of motherhood, how she embraced the job, even seemed to live for it. And for the first time, I understood that being a stay-at-home mom was a privilege, albeit one that came with sacrifice. I couldn't imagine leaving my son for days at a time, yet I knew staying home meant giving up income and leaning on Theo to carry the financial weight. It also meant a great loss of independence, and that was an extremely painful idea for the girl who'd been taught not to depend on anyone. Without my career, without my income, I felt needy and one-dimensional. At the same time, because of 9/11, I was heavy with fear and uncertainty. Earning my way into the flight deck had offered me years of clear purpose, and once I became a pilot, I joyfully lived that purpose on flight after flight. But now the world, and specifically the skies, no longer seemed safe. All I wanted was to be with my baby, to protect him from the chaos beyond the safety of our home. He became my world.

My decision to remain grounded was made easier given ACA's financial losses, which the company tried to mitigate by offering pilots leaves of absence in the form of yearlong furloughs. For many pilots, the decision not to fly was agonizing. For me, it was much easier because of motherhood. Despite how much I hated feeling dependent, I didn't want to return to the sky. I accepted the furlough and stayed home, grateful for the option. But it wasn't long before it became clear that one income wasn't going to sustain us.

One evening, after putting the baby down, Theo and I sat at the kitchen table, bills and bottles scattered across its surface. I told him, "I want to stay home with the baby. I don't want to go back to flying. But maybe I can find something else, something where I don't have to travel."

He leaned back in his chair, his hands laced behind his head. "Okay, let's figure it out. But whatever it is, it has to be right for you and little John. I can carry the weight for now."

His confidence steadied me, but I vowed to figure this out. I had to succeed at all of it: motherhood, womanhood, career. I'd known so many women who'd handled it, who'd managed both. How different my perspective was of them now. Some of them made it look easy. *How* did they do that? My life looked so messy and disorganized. Sometimes it was overwhelming and even depressing. And that was without my having to work outside our home. I'd simply have to figure it out. I'd commit, focus, plan, and get my life back on track. If I couldn't fly, I would simply have to find another way to earn and feel balanced again. It was time to remember who I was. I wasn't a girl who sat back and moped or felt sorry for herself. And I certainly wasn't one who waited for other people to make her decisions, to set her goals. I was the girl who looked to the future, who chose a goal and made a plan to get there.

FOURTEEN

As I settled into a lonely rhythm of being a stay-at-home mom, I knew my life didn't look like the shiny kind of motherhood Karen had described as we drove across Pennsylvania. I sometimes thought about Rick and Karen down there in Tennessee, living in what I assumed was a happy, stable marriage with clear roles. I was pretty sure theirs was a marriage of choice, not one they went into because it was "the right thing to do," and that news of her pregnancies had been met with squeals of joy. Then again, that was probably true of most people who were married with kids. How strange it was for me to do what was expected of me every day feeling the decisions hadn't really been mine, that I was living someone else's life.

Most afternoons, after working his job as a custodian, Theo went to the gym, then came home around six o'clock, dropped his gym bag at the door, and headed straight to the living room, where eight-month-old John and I were usually playing with sensory toys. Even on days when work wore Theo down, his face lit up when he saw the baby, and that always warmed me. There was a rhythm to our evenings, a gentle choreography to bedtime that was familiar and tender.

One winter night, typical of our routine, Theo came home after the gym while I was standing at the window letting the baby watch snow fall. John watched with wide-eyed wonder as big white flakes fell from the sky, and, as I often did, I marveled at the idea of how many new sights and experiences my son had every day. I handed the baby to Theo, and the two of them stayed by the window, perfectly content to watch in awe until I finally said, "Let's give him his bath."

We went down the hall where Theo played with little John in the baby's room while I ran the bath, squeezing Johnson's Bedtime Baby Bath into the water, the lavender scent filling the bathroom's air with calm. On the changing table in John's room, I laid out the washcloth, lotion, powder, a fresh diaper, and one of his soft, long-sleeved onesies. Soon the shallow tub water was warm and full of bubbles, and Theo peeled off the baby's clothes, wrapped him in the hooded towel with the bear ears, carried him to the bathroom, and lowered him into the baby bath seat in the warm water, then sat at his side on a stool and talked to him in a soft, loving voice. I stood leaning against the frame of the bathroom door watching them, my boys.

Theo grinned at the baby and squeezed the squeaking rubber duck. "Look at you, my li'l man-man." Then he launched into silly faces and cartoon voices, making the bath toys come alive until John's laughter filled the bathroom. Watching them together like that, so easy and joyful, was one of the few moments in the day when I pushed distressed thoughts aside and simply enjoyed the moment I was in. After the bath, Theo dressed John for bed, then sat in the rocking chair in the nursery, while I sat on the adjacent twin bed and watched him gently rock our son back and forth. In the background, the soft strings of the *Baby Einstein: Lullaby Classics* drifted through the room, the gentle melodies wrapping around us like a musical blanket. John relaxed against his dad's chest, his eyelids growing heavy until they finally fluttered closed. Then Theo laid him gently in the crib, pausing to breathe in his baby-soft scent. We both lingered in the quiet for a moment, then Theo stood in the doorway, one hand already on the doorknob. "You good?" he asked.

I looked up, and said, "Yeah," in a voice that didn't seem to belong to me. Then, as if a switch flipped, we split apart. Our parenting moment had finished, and we went back to our separate lives. Theo headed straight to the couch to unwind by watching sports or a sitcom rerun or to talk on the phone with his friends. He had poured into the baby, and that was enough for him. But nobody poured into me.

That night, he sat at the kitchen table looking through an issue of *Sports Illustrated* while I rinsed bottles in the sink. The water ran too long. I knew that. I was lost in thoughts of a life far away.

"You tired?" he asked without looking up.

"Always," I said lightly.

He gave a small huff of a laugh. "Yeah. Same."

Then silence settled back in between us, thick and familiar.

When we did talk, it was about whether we were low on formula, about who was picking up what the next day. We didn't talk about the heaviness in my chest. We didn't talk about how small I'd begun to feel. We didn't talk about how badly I needed someone to see me. We didn't talk about those things because I didn't say them out loud. To anyone watching from the outside, we probably looked like a young family functioning just fine. But I felt myself shrinking.

Later that night we sat on the couch in front of a TV show, not cuddling, not touching. There was space between us. Theo fell asleep, and I switched off the TV and sat in the quiet, looking at the dark screen, wondering how it was possible to be in a room with someone and still feel completely alone.

I cried every day, usually while rocking John to sleep, but admitted it to no one. Silent tears fell as he breathed peacefully against me. Some days I couldn't remember when I'd last showered, and I avoided the mirror because I didn't want to see the face of the woman who looked back. That face was becoming as unfamiliar as my life. I felt passionate about nothing, in control of nothing. I loved my son deeply, and when I was near him, my heart was full, but the contentment never lasted. The moment he slept or wasn't with me, sadness oozed back in. I told myself this was just early motherhood, that it was common for women to experience strange sadness despite being given the gift of a healthy baby. I told myself it would pass. But I didn't tell anyone how bad it felt. I didn't confide in Kami or my sister. And I couldn't bear to make my parents feel even worse about the situation I'd gotten myself into, so I just kept moving through the days, trying to hold myself together as pieces seemed to be breaking off.

Right around the time the baby turned one, my emotional fog passed. But not because I had the space to fully grieve my old life or the tools to work out what I was going through. I think it passed because something deeper in me took over.

I've always had a tendency to rise to what's required. And with the weight of mounting bills and the reality that a little person depended on me, survival became my purpose. I shifted my focus from what was no longer to what needed to be and not because I felt strong, but because I had to become strong. Supporting my child became my purpose, and it's how I endured that very dark season. I wasn't healed, nor was I whole, but I vowed to get back in motion. One day at a time. One choice at a time.

Theo was still working, but had recently gone back to school to earn an associate degree in exercise science, which meant even more bills. He already had a degree in kinesiology and wanted to become a personal trainer to earn more money, but it would be a year before he'd complete the exercise science program. White envelopes covered the kitchen table, and I sorted them into three piles: *pay now, pay later, can't pay*—stacking them neatly to one side so Theo would have space to study. It wouldn't be long before we'd be chased by collection agencies, so one day after I put the baby down for a nap, I sat at our desktop computer and stripped my résumé to a document so lean it barely reflected my life. I decided I'd start looking for work in bookstores. I loved to read, and I loved being surrounded by books, so why not work in a bookstore? And bookstores were generally quiet places. Maybe I could make a little money and find a little peace. I listed my associate degree and my enlisted experience in the Air National Guard, but deleted everything I'd done relative to becoming or being a pilot. I couldn't bear the thought of a hiring manager asking why someone who'd been trusted to fly airplanes for a living was now applying to shelve books. The truth was, while I needed to help pay the bills, I also needed to do something for myself. I needed a place where, even for a few hours, I could step outside the house and remember who I was before my life became about changing diapers and living the same day over and over.

When Theo got home from work that night, I handed him our son and drove fifteen minutes down Kingery Highway to fill out job applications at both Borders and Barnes & Noble, both locations only a short drive from our condo. I dropped off my abridged résumé, then drove home with the contentment of knowing I'd at least taken a step.

The next morning, a manager from Barnes & Noble called. "Evenings and weekends?" he asked.

"That works!"

ON A SATURDAY MORNING, three days later, I pulled into the Barnes & Noble parking lot at eight forty-five, fifteen minutes earlier than the manager had requested, and at nine o'clock, when the automatic doors slid open, I stepped inside and inhaled the scent of books. A woman behind the register looked up.

I said, "I'm Nia. I'm meeting Travis. This is my first day."

She smiled. "He told me you were coming. Welcome." She handed me a lanyard with a temporary name tag and pointed me toward the back office, where the manager, Travis, shook my hand and showed me the break room, the schedule board, the employee lockers. Ordinary things. Small things. Each one felt like a door reopening.

Travis showed me how to alphabetize the shelves, how to check the computer for inventory, how to straighten displays without overthinking it. "Don't worry," he said with a smile. "Everyone's first day feels awkward."

None of it felt awkward. It felt grounding. I nodded, sliding a book into place. It fit perfectly between two others. Order. Simple. Manageable.

A customer approached me. "Excuse me, do you know where I can find Toni Morrison books?"

"Yes," I said, surprising myself with how comfortable I felt already in this huge store, directing customers. "Right this way." I led her down the aisle, and by the time I returned to my section, I realized I was standing differently. I felt looser, lighter, and my breathing came more easily. The sense memories flooded back to me, all my childhood trips to the mall with my mom when she took me to a bookstore, then parked me in a corner and said, "I'll be back in thirty minutes. Stay right here." I sat cross-legged on the floor reading book jackets—fantasy/adventure, suspense, fiction—to decide which one I'd take home. After each visit, I left the store, joyfully clutching at least one new book, and I was almost as excited about the free bookmark that came with every purchase.

Now an employee of a bookstore, I found joy in simple tasks, like chatting with customers about their selections, placing books on hold, and arranging and tidying bookmarks and endcaps with care. Working in Barnes & Noble made me smile again, inside and out. I looked forward to coming to work. It was the first time since the attacks I felt truly at ease, in an atmosphere that made sense.

One evening at the end of my second week at the store, my mother walked in. I was working the register, and I smiled at the familiar sight of her surrounded by walls of new books. She paused to take in the space, then smiled as she approached me.

"Hey, Mom." Standing there with a bookstore counter separating me from my mother felt both odd and comfortable.

"Hi, love." She glanced at my name tag, the neat stack of receipts, and the line of bookmarks I'd straightened earlier. "You look good here."

"*Thank* you," I said with theatrical exaggeration as I gestured across the store like a game show hostess. "What can I help you find?"

She laughed. "Do you have James Patterson's new book, *The Big Bad Wolf*? You know I like a page-turner."

"Oh, I know you do. Let me check." I typed in the title, and we walked together toward the thrillers, past tables stacked with best-sellers.

She ran her hand along a row of spines like she was petting a row of friendly cats. We found the section with a wall dominated by James Patterson books, and I pulled down a copy. She turned it over in her hands and said, "So, how's work?"

I straightened books while I talked. "It's nice. Peaceful, actually."

"I can see that." We both looked around the store, so orderly and tidy. Clean, new books in stacks, standing in rows on shelves. Soothing, neutral wall and carpet colors and calm lighting overhead. People speaking in low tones, as if expected to behave with the quiet politeness they showed in libraries. Then she said, "What about your career? Are you thinking about going back to flying?"

It was as if she'd pressed her thumb into a tender bruise on my arm. I kept my gaze on a table display, adjusting books by half an inch here, flicking off a speck of dust there. "I don't plan to. Everything changed after 9/11. I don't . . ." My words trailed off.

She was quiet in that way she'd always been so good at. Her kind of quiet seemed to say, *I'm listening and I'll wait.*

After several seconds, I said, "I don't know if I want to go back."

There was more silence. None of her responses in this conversation came quickly. It was as if she was intentionally following her words and mine with enough silent beats to let them truly sink in. Then she gently said, "You miss it," as if she were stating a fact as obvious as the coming rain.

"I miss the joy flying always gave me," I said, surprised at my own honesty. "But that day took it from me. Or I let it go. I don't know. Anyway, I'm fine here." I glanced around the store again, as if I wanted my mother to understand that everything in this building was contributing to my wellbeing. "It feels so calm and safe here."

She held my look, her eyes softening. "Safe can be a place to heal. But it's nowhere to live. Not for someone like you, Nia."

I stood stunned. My mother's use of my name made very clear how serious she was. I opened my mouth to protest, then closed it.

She leaned toward me. "I heard something on the radio the other day. Do you remember the Columbine school shooting a couple years ago?"

"Yes." Of course. Everybody remembered Columbine. Two high school students planned to bomb their school, and when their bombs didn't go off, they opened fire and killed a bunch of other kids and a teacher, injured several others, then killed themselves. It was a horrific example of gun violence in a country already riddled by gun violence. And it started a national discussion about mental health in teenagers.

My mother said, "I heard an interview with a survivor. She talked about how taking a writing class helped her heal. She said after going through that trauma, putting the words on paper helped her work through it—somehow eased the psychic burden. I thought something like that might help you, too."

I stared at her. "Writing?"

She shrugged. "Why not? You journal all the time. That's writing. This woman talked about a memoir-writing class she took." She paused and watched me think, then added, "Maybe the community college has one of those continuing education classes. Or maybe the library."

Right away I thought of a list of why nots: Money was tight, I didn't have time, I had a baby, writing wasn't going to change what happened. But I felt the suggestion settle in, somewhere deep and undeniable. I wanted to stop dreaming of planes crashing into buildings. I wanted to stop picturing hijackers attacking flight crew. I did want to heal. But what if time and therapy and writing and distractions and more writing and family support and even a sweet little job in a bookstore couldn't guide me back to being joyful? And an even more frightening idea haunted me: What if the joy of flying was over for me forever? What if the terrorists had stolen it from me? "I don't know," I said, softer now. "Maybe."

She smiled as if I'd just blurted an enthusiastic, "Yes!" Then she rested her hand on my arm. "Just think about it."

At the checkout, she placed her book on the counter. "Your father and I will be over this weekend to see our grandson."

"That'll be nice," I said. "Maybe Theo and I will go to a movie."

She smiled. "Have you talked to your sister? She got a cat. Your dad says he doesn't want to visit her now."

"I give him three days."

Mom laughed. I placed her new book in a bag, dropped in two new bookmarks, then tilted my head and said, "Thank you for shopping at Barnes & Noble."

When she left, the bell over the door chimed, and I stood at the register, the air around me heavy with truth. I wasn't flying, and I wasn't working toward flying. I hadn't even come close to healing from the gutting caused by the events on 9/11. But why would I have? I'd spent only two hours with a therapist before life had raced ahead, sending me back to work as a pregnant, uncomfortable pilot, then into a marriage. And the world around me had shown little sign of returning to normal. The events of 9/11 had stirred up fear, uncertainty, and even chaos. It seemed the United States wasn't healing, and neither was I.

Me. Writing? Healing? Could I share my pain and fears with strangers when I couldn't even share them with the people who loved me? I didn't want to be vulnerable. As a Black woman and pilot, I already felt scrutinized, judged. Would people in a memoir class be allowed to read my writing? If I told a classroom full of people how close I'd been to falling apart on 9/11, it would only confirm what some already assumed, that I didn't belong. Wouldn't it?

But I did belong. And I was tough, really tough. Even while I carried shock and grief, I'd shown up again. I showed up and did the job. But was I tough enough to write and maybe read aloud deep, dark fears? Was I brave enough to go back to the morning of September 11 and re-create the events for a memoir class? Could I admit to strangers how much it had knocked me around and how rattled I felt even two years later? I didn't know. But I knew this much: I wasn't going to let fear keep me from finding my way back to myself.

That night when I returned home from the bookstore, I sat down at the computer and searched the College of DuPage website, where I found a continuing education course called "Creative Writing—Memoir." It was held one night a week, and it was affordable. I hovered over the REGISTER button for a long minute as I barraged my brain with all the why nots. Then I took one big step over my pile of reservations and clicked.

On the first night of class, I walked down a dimly lit hallway in the college's older wing. It was the kind of space that seemed to echo even the quietest sounds. Light spilled into the hallway from a room all the way at the end of the building, and I walked toward it. The room felt like a time capsule with adult-size desks arranged in rows, a chalkboard on one wall and a whiteboard on the other. Written in neat cursive across the chalkboard was *Writing the Memoir*. How strange it felt to walk into a classroom about writing, to take a course that wasn't about aviation, wasn't about making my way to the sky. Then again, wasn't that at the core of why my mother had directed me here? I chose an empty desk at the back of the room, hoping I wouldn't fall apart, and hoping, just as much, that I might finally start to put myself back together.

A slim woman with red hair cut in a bob stood at the front of the room and smiled.

"Hi, everyone. I'm Carie. I'm really glad you're here." She tucked a strand of hair behind her ear. "I've been teaching writing for a few years, and what I love most about this class is that everyone walks in with a story, even if you don't think you have one yet."

A few people nodded.

"This is a workshop, not a performance. You don't need to be polished. You just need to be honest."

I counted fifteen students, and I appeared to be the youngest. The others seemed to range from forties to sixties. And as had been the norm in so many rooms I'd entered all my life, I was the only Black person present. One by one, people offered their reasons for being there. Some wanted to preserve family stories, one wanted to explore the summer in Europe that changed her life, another wanted to make sense of a divorce.

When it was my turn to speak, I tried to keep my voice steady. "Just over a year ago, I went through some trauma I'm not ready to share." The room was still, not so much as a rustle of paper or clearing of a throat. "My mom suggested I take this course to process it."

Carie nodded. "Thank you for your honesty." She looked across the room at all of us. "Thank you all for being here. People write memoirs for all kinds of reasons, and quite often they discover that their reason for writing about an experience changes as they go. In this way, it's a mysterious and sometimes miraculous practice. It's arguably the most personal genre of writing, but memoir isn't therapy and shouldn't be used to try to replace therapy. But there's no denying the therapeutic benefits it can have. You should also be ready for a very common experience memoirists have: It can be gutting and painful. To recount the stories you're here to develop, you'll have to revisit them, relive them, immerse yourselves back in the experience. So don't be surprised if your emotions swing." She looked at me, then at the woman who'd spoken of divorce. "That especially applies to those of you writing about pain, trauma, and loss. But one wonderful thing that comes from writing about our lives is that we often reach a kind of clarity we hadn't expected. When you sit with your memories and put them into words, you're forced to reflect, to be honest with yourself, and to make sense of what you've lived through. Sometimes, without meaning to, the writing itself can offer a measure of healing."

Her words gave me hope. Maybe this class was the right place for me.

Carie walked back and forth across the front of the room as she spoke. "This class includes six meetings, and by the end, each of you will have read a short excerpt of your work aloud. I'll pass around a sign-up sheet, and you can decide if you'd like to read sooner than later. It's best if we have three readers per night."

When the sign-up sheet reached me, I wrote my name in a space under the date of the last day of class. I was in no hurry to stand in front of these people and tell them about the worst experience of my life.

Most of that evening was spent on introductions and an overview of what to expect, plus some in-class writing. Carie said each class session would include lecture, in-class writing, discussion, and some people reading their work. The two hours went by quickly, and as we packed up, Carie offered a final thought. "You may not all be here to heal from something. You may have joined the class to preserve some memories or to develop your writing skills. Or both. But whatever brought you here, my hope is that you'll leave with a little more peace than you came in with."

Peace. When had I last felt genuine peace? And as much as I appreciated Carie's good intentions, did she really think we'd find peace through writing?

Over the next five weeks, we spent thirty minutes in class writing. We were given prompts and wrote in ten-minute bursts. We read excerpts from Frank McCourt's *Angela's Ashes* and Mary Karr's *The Liars' Club* and took note of how small details make a scene vivid and how emotional honesty creates a kind of intimate connection between reader and writer. I read the work of memoirists who shared deeply private secrets, embarrassing moments, and painful family memoirs. I'd never realized how powerful a genre memoir is, and it fascinated me how immersed I could be in the stories of people I'd never heard of. The class helped turn us into both informed writers and active readers. In the last several minutes of every class session, three students read a couple pages from the memoir they were working on. I didn't speak much, but I listened hard as they read their stories of grief, embarrassment, doubt, and courage. Hearing others say personal things out loud made me feel connected to them, just as Carie had said would happen. I witnessed how the intimacy of sharing something you feel vulnerable or guilty or regretful about is a way of letting people in, and the trust involved is powerful. I felt emboldened by their readings and grateful that like me, they were just trying to sort things out. I wasn't the only one who didn't have tidy solutions for what haunted her.

As the final class approached, I was nearer to having to face something I very much feared. My journal sat at the back of one of my drawers, buried under clothes I hadn't worn since before pregnancy, the ones I hoped I'd fit again someday. Late one night, after Theo and our son were asleep, I sat at the kitchen table under the dim light and with paper and pen wrote about that morning in Newark and the day that followed. My hand shook as I wrote, but I kept going.

On the last night of class, as I drove onto DuPage's campus, my body trembled with awareness that this was the night I'd read my story aloud. The last person I'd spoken with about the experience on September 11 had been my therapist. She was trained to hold the weight of it, to help me process it. My classmates were not. I didn't know how they'd receive what I was about to share. I wasn't even sure I was ready to hear it myself.

As the students ahead of me read their work, I tried to listen, but my mind kept drifting back to my own story. One woman shared how she met her husband of forty years. Another student wrote about building his family home. Both spoke about wanting to leave their stories behind for their grandchildren. When they finished, everyone sat in a brief, thoughtful silence, the kind of pause that follows something tender. I could feel my throat tighten. Their stories were soft and full of love, and what I was holding had neither. My heart thudded. I was next.

Carie looked at me. "Nia, you're our last one. Whenever you're ready."

I was sitting in the back of the class, and a soft rustle moved through the room as chairs shifted and bodies turned to face me. Despite the revealing nature of memoir, I'd been quiet for much of the six-week class, before, during, and after each session. People in the class probably thought of me as the woman who worked at Barnes & Noble and kept to herself. I stood up, cleared my throat and took a steadying breath. "I am a pilot for a regional airline based on the East Coast." My voice sounded thinner than usual, and already I could feel the words clogging in my throat. "I am on a leave of absence, and for now, I'm working at Barnes & Noble. I'm a new mother with a one-year-old, and he's a big reason I'm not flying anymore. But it's also because I had a traumatic experience at work."

Everyone in the room was looking at me. Most of them had kind, expectant expressions on their faces. I cleared my throat again, clutched my folded writing excerpt in my hand, and looked at the many faces in the room as I spoke. "On the morning of Tuesday, September eleventh, 2001, I was at work waiting on the runway at Newark Airport to fly to Boston. My captain and I watched smoke engulf the North Tower of the World Trade Center, and we wondered what awful thing was happening across the river. Then I watched in horror as United Flight 175 flew straight into the South Tower."

A collective gasp filled the room.

"Shortly afterward, ATC cleared us for takeoff anyway, so we did as instructed. We lifted the plane into the air and flew back toward Boston, passing not far from the smoking towers as we did."

Carie's hand moved to her heart, her eyes wide. Some of the students closed their eyes and shook their heads.

"I wrote in my journal that day, in real time, while I was living it," I said quietly. "What I'm about to read is the first attempt at taking that experience and shaping it into a story."

I swallowed hard and read what I'd written, all those fresh impressions I'd scribbled in the back of Rick and Karen's rental van. I read to the class my words about Shye's and my confusion, about how we debated what could have been happening over there but stayed focused and followed protocol, how we heard the mysterious transmissions from the other flight, which I'd since learned was Flight 93, the flight that crashed in a Pennsylvania field after extraordinarily brave passengers organized and fought back. I shared my recollections of the experience from taxi to touchdown in Boston. I kept my eyes down, wiping away tears as I read. My voice trembled, but I didn't stop. When I finished reading and looked up, everyone was wiping or dabbing their eyes.

"Sorry, I didn't mean to make everyone cry." I let out a nervous giggle. The class applauded louder than I'd ever heard them clap. Then I took my seat, still shaking, but relieved. I felt I'd just done something very important.

Carie stood and thanked everyone for sharing. "Your stories matter," she said, her voice thick with emotion as her eyes swept the room, then paused on me. "I hope you continue writing yours." Her warm smile seemed more like a blessing than a goodbye.

Almost everyone stayed after class to talk about what I'd read. Some people wanted to share their 9/11 stories, and others simply said they loved my piece. A few even suggested I turn my story into a book. I shook my head, almost embarrassed by the idea. I hadn't come to start a book. I'd come to start finding my footing again.

For the first time, I didn't feel in a hurry to leave class and rush home, and I thought about what this was, this relief I was feeling. Then it came to me: For the first time, I didn't feel I was carrying the memory alone. There was something about letting those people in on my experience that served to disseminate the weight of it, to spread it around so others could help carry the burden. Sharing the experience out loud hadn't necessarily healed me, but in the process of letting all those listeners see what I'd seen, something inside me eased, and on that night it was as if at least a piece of me shifted back into place.

FIFTEEN

After the night I read my story to the class, it was easier to open my eyes to the effect the events of 9/11 had on my life. Something about sharing my excerpt with those people and hearing their kind feedback gave me new perspective. It was as if I'd opened up to a support group and broken out of emotional limbo. For a long time, a 9/11 reel had run quietly in the background of my mind. If a show about the attacks came on television, I left the room. When people wanted to talk about that day, I changed the subject. I told myself I was tired of hearing about it, but in truth, I just didn't trust what might surface if I dug into it. But after reading about my experience for the class, I started to have a sense of control over it all, as if I could decide how much power the experience should hold over my life. If all that had come from a writing class, then my mother and Carie had been right: The potential result of letting a story out, of declaring fear and pain out loud was enormous. For the first time in almost two years, I had the feeling I might not stay broken.

But, of course, my life was still very complicated. In 2003, the economy was still shaky. Jobs were scarce everywhere, not just in aviation. Shortly after the class ended, Theo lost his job. Even with our savings, there was no way my part-time work at the bookstore was going to cover our expenses. The only thing that made any sense was that I return to the sky. But it had already been eighteen months since I'd taken my last flight, when I'd flown from Boston to Cincinnati. At the time I was pregnant, weary, and sad, and since that flight, the idea of getting back in the air only made me feel sad once again. The reality was, although aviation had brought me immeasurable joy prior to 9/11, when I stepped away from flying, I was so battered and distracted, I hadn't thought much about it since. And I didn't even question my giving almost no attention to the thing that had once been my greatest passion, probably because I had plenty of other things filling my thoughts. I was overwhelmed by the trauma brought on by 9/11, surprised by a pregnancy that pushed me to rethink my relationship with Theo, and needed to prepare for a baby to enter our lives. Then we married and moved into a new home. During all that, I was tired, depressed, and generally lost. Who had time to look up and watch for planes to go overhead?

But after Theo lost his job, I didn't have the luxury of "to fly or not to fly." I had a child depending on me, and flying planes was the only lucrative skill I had. Theo and I had the same kinds of bills as anyone else: mortgage, utilities, cars, food, and education/student loans, but we also had all the expenses that came with having a baby, and the extent of those expenses never failed to surprise me. I'd always heard "It costs a lot to have a kid," but it wasn't until I paid bills for baby food, diapers, baby clothes, healthcare, and developmental toys and classes that I understood. It was time to grow up and view my being a pilot in a new way. For years, I'd dreamed of taking to the air, talked about it nonstop, even romanticized it.

And when I finally earned my license, I was elated to have achieved the dreams of that ten-year-old girl who used to lie in the grass and watch the sky. But life had moved on, and now being a pilot was about earning a living. Plenty of people did work they weren't in the mood for, didn't feel inspired by, or simply despised—all in the interest of adulting. Who was I to think I should be able to skip out on the best income source available to me just because I didn't have the spirit for it anymore? The needs of the little boy in the next room weren't interested in my fatigue or my fearful heart.

In two months, my ACA leave of absence was going to expire, which meant I had the next eight weeks to get my mind right. This was the longest I'd gone without flying, and I needed to reacclimate before stepping back into my career, so I decided to re-certify as a flight instructor. That meant I had to retrain, then pass another flight evaluation in a small plane, the same kind of aircraft I'd been in when I'd first learned to trust myself in the air. Back to the beginning.

In the economic aftermath of 9/11, government workforce assistance programs were expanded, and I qualified for a program designed to help people retrain and return to work. It covered the $3,000 I needed to reinstate my license. I chose the flight school at DuPage Airport, forty minutes from our home. On days when Theo had classes, my dad—now retired and fully embracing his role as grandfather—came over and watched fifteen-month-old John. Otherwise, Theo stayed home with our son, who was pure giggling motion with fast feet and a trail of toys behind him.

On the first day of my retraining at DuPage, I stepped into the quiet classroom and looked around at the walls covered in faded training posters of lift diagrams and weather charts, and whiteboards with weight-and-balance calculations scribbled in dry-erase marker. There were only a few students. One sat at a table with his instructor, their heads close together over a sectional chart. Another sat inside the non-motion training simulator, his headset on, face serious. For a moment, I stood still just inside the doorway and let the familiarity settle through me. The smell of old coffee. The faint electrical hum of the stationary simulator. A printer whirring in the back office. It was like standing on the edge of something I thought I'd lost for good, like finding a beloved childhood toy at the bottom of a long-forgotten box.

I heard a voice. "You must be Nia." I turned to see a man standing at the front desk, mid-forties, ball cap pulled low, pen tucked behind his ear. He stepped forward and offered his hand. "I'm your instructor, Matt. We spoke on the phone."

His handshake was easy. No performance. Just calm. "Nice to meet you," I said.

He looked around the space. "Does any of this look familiar?" he asked with a warm laugh. "When we spoke, you said you fly for the airlines, but you haven't been in a small plane for about . . . three years?"

"That's right."

"And the last time you flew at all was over a year ago."

"Almost two years," I corrected him.

He nodded, then smiled. "That's okay. We'll shake the rust off." The steady, unbothered way he said it made my shoulders drop a bit.

We started with ground review. Airspace. Weather. Procedures. The things I used to know cold but that were now layered over with lullabies, feeding schedules, pediatric appointments. Some of it came back quickly. Other parts I had to reach for.

"That was a solid knowledge review," Matt said finally. "Let's go fly."

Out on the ramp, the air smelled like hot pavement and avgas. The Cessna 172 sat waiting—simple, familiar, just like the airplanes I'd flown in college. I walked slowly around the plane during preflight, my hand tracing the back of the wing, and I checked control surfaces, fuel caps, tires. It felt less like inspection and more like recognition.

We climbed inside. The seats were worn. The headset smelled faintly of warm plastic. I started the engine, and the plane vibrated beneath us. Taxiing felt awkward at first. The rudder pedals were incredibly responsive, forcing me to go lighter. We lined up on the runway, and I eased the throttle forward. The airplane gathered speed, the controls settling into my hands. When we lifted off, something inside me seemed to take off as well. The airplane responded to my touch with a lightness and honesty that reminded me why I fell in love with flying. The horizon leveled and my breathing did, too. We practiced stalls, turns, and landings, and the muscle memory came back slowly, then more surely. When we landed that first day, I sat there for a moment longer than necessary, hands still resting on the yoke. It felt like being reunited with a love I thought I'd put behind me.

For the next ten days, I drove to the airport every day for two hours of ground review and an hour in the air with Matt. After our final flight, we sat at the table inside, and he flipped open my logbook, signed his name, and slid the book to me. "You're ready."

Next came my check ride. Five days after my last flight with Matt, I drove to DuPage to meet with my examiner. And then, as if some wondrous force in the universe wanted to send me a message, after I'd settled into the classroom, I looked up to see Bob Flynn, the FAA examiner and my "faux grandfather" who'd been my flight evaluator on that magnificent day when I was eighteen and earned my pilot's license. Bob walked into the classroom and looked the same except that his curly hair was now all white. Nearly a decade had passed since our day together, and since then my life had changed with the momentum of stampeding horses, but seeing him took me right back to that wonderful time in my life when things weren't so complicated. Bob had the soothing nature of a loving grandfather. When our eyes met, I could have cried. He held his arms open and said, "Granddaughter!"

I welcomed his embrace. "Bob, it's so good to see you!" He felt like an old friend, and for a moment, I forgot he was there to evaluate me.

He asked, "How have you been?"

I told him about my son and that I'd taken time off work, but was now headed back into the pilot's seat. I didn't tell him I'd witnessed the attacks on the World Trade Center. I didn't talk about the fear I carried about returning to work. We talked about how the industry had changed, how everything felt tighter, more procedural, less forgiving. Fewer jobs. A sense that no one moved through aviation the same way anymore. Bob said, "It's not the same world it was."

"No," I agreed. "But it's still the same sky."

Most of our ground review was spent catching up on old times, and then he asked me to explain how I'd teach a stall. Before I'd even finished, he said, "I've seen enough. Great job. Let's fly."

Bob and I walked out to the Cessna 172, and I welcomed the cool morning air. I took in long, deep breaths to center myself and help prepare for what felt like a kind of maiden voyage. The last time I'd flown with Bob in this same type of plane, it had felt so daunting. Now compared to the DoJet, the Cessna felt small and simple.

The routine of the preflight inspection came back with ease, then we taxied and took off. When we were in the air, even though Bob tested me on things like stalls and steep turns, being with him up there felt like taking a buddy for a Sunday ride. We landed and taxied back to the ramp, then I shut down and secured the plane, while talking through each step, explaining the proper techniques and procedures. Inside the office, Bob reached for my logbook, clicked his pen, and smiled. "You step into the airplane like you never left it. That's not something you can teach." Joy and pride rushed through my entire body.

He signed the logbook, and when he handed it to me, it was as if he'd just awarded me a diploma, like he'd returned a missing piece of myself. I looked at the book and smiled at the sight of his signature with its special flourish. And at the bottom of the page, he'd written, *Congratulations, Granddaughter.* He smiled. "You're ready."

I knew I was ready. I left the airport with a fullness I hadn't felt in two years. I was on my way to coming back to life, and the sensation was so dramatic, I paused to consider what the lightness meant. The truth was, when I'd run full steam toward the dream of becoming a pilot, that was a sign of how well I knew myself and what could fill my heart. At a very young age, I thought of myself as a pilot-to-be, and I was clear about the life I wanted. But I'd never imagined myself a parent. Motherhood had never once factored into my daydreams for my future. Yet now that John was in my life, I experienced the magic of motherhood every day. I was learning about a new kind of love and seeing what it felt to be truly needed. I was watching myself make parental decisions I was proud of, and I willingly sacrificed in the best interests of my child. My son delighted me every day with his laughter, his grasping of new skills, his sweet way of communicating with hand gestures and facial expressions. All those life changes had enriched my life and matured me. But something had been missing. There was no denying the hunger that had set in and lingered since that last work trip I'd flown before my maternity leave back in 2001. And now, after the flight with Bob, there was no denying that the hunger had been eased.

I drove home from the airport with the logbook on the seat beside me, like a treasured passenger I was honored to transport. When I pulled into the parking lot of our condo, I sat for a moment, letting the day settle over me. Then I reached for my phone and called my mom. She answered right away. "Hi, Nia!"

"Mom, I did it. I reinstated my CFI today."

"I'm not surprised." I could hear the smile in her voice. "You were born to fly. I'm so glad you remember that."

I reached for the logbook and placed it on my lap. "It felt really good. Better than I expected."

Then she said something so simple and clear, it hit me like a slap on the back. "You might have lost sight of it in the past couple years, but flying was never just a job for you. It's your purpose. And purpose doesn't disappear just because life gets hard."

I let her words sink in as I ran my finger over Bob's signature in my logbook.

Then she said, "And listen, you have little John watching you now. Make sure he sees his mom get back up."

My throat tightened. "He will."

"I know. That's why I'm not worried. Whatever you put your mind to, you do."

My mother's perspective on just about everything had always been important to me, but on the subject of navigating parenting and career, I took her especially seriously. She was my first role model. She loved being a mother and did an extraordinary job of it, all the while being a passionate teacher who cared about her students and her school. And she'd made it look so easy. Only now I realized what an accomplishment it had been. When we hung up, I sat for a while in the quiet of the car and let my mother's words linger as the significance of the day sank in. I felt steadier than I had in a long time.

RETURNING TO DULLES TO RETRAIN with ACA felt both familiar and foreign. I moved through training quietly, more observant than talkative, happy to be back, but not with the enthusiasm I'd had when I was a new-hire pilot. A few of the other pilots were returning from leaves of absence, others were there to qualify in a new airplane. I was there to requalify in the plane I hadn't flown in two years.

I listened as the other pilots swapped stories in the classroom and between simulator sessions. They compared checklists and talked about commuting. They debated which base had the best routes and talked about landings, schedules, instructors, and flying. Their energy was bright. Mine was steadier. Quieter. I wasn't much older than most of the pilots there, but I carried a different kind of experience now. I'd lived through trauma, and thanks to time, therapy, and writing, I'd restored what had been shaken. I'd also given birth and was now raising a child. Coming back as a mother made flying feel different, more sacred, and more purposeful. Now there was a person in the world who would grow up watching how I handled responsibility, risk, and return. Flying was now part of the legacy I was shaping.

Early in the retraining, I realized something else: It was a relief to sit in a room where the conversation wasn't about where you were on 9/11. Nobody asked. The only thing that came close was when I saw Shye again. I ran into him as he was walking out of a classroom, and we greeted each other with an embrace full of everything: history, joy, relief, memories. We walked back into the classroom and caught up on the past couple years. Then he said something I hadn't seen coming: "I'm not flying anymore. I'm full time in the training department." He paused and said, "On the ground."

I didn't ask questions, and I could see in his eyes he knew he didn't have to explain it to me.

After training, I was in a hotel at the Washington Dulles Airport awaiting an assignment. The phone rang. It was Crew Scheduling.

"We've got a trip for you. A Newark turn and Charleston overnight. Report time 1300."

"Newark." I repeated. The word landed hard.

"Yes. You're flying with Captain Roscoe Edwards," the scheduler replied. "I'll acknowledge the trip for you."

I swallowed. "Okay. Thanks. I'll be there."

I hung up. I sat down on the edge of the bed. Newark. Of all the cities. Of all the first legs back, Newark. It felt less like coincidence than a confrontation.

I picked the phone back up and called my mom. "My first trip back is to Newark."

She didn't gasp or rush to reassure me. She let the silence breathe. "Well," she said finally, her voice steady, "maybe that's exactly where you're supposed to go."

I hadn't thought of it that way.

"You know," she continued, "I'm already listed as a standby passenger to Newark on Sunday. Your aunt will be in New York for the week, and I was going to stay with her. No hotel, no airfare." She paused. "I could just go a day early and take your flight."

I smiled despite myself.

"That would be fun," she added. "It's been a long time since you've been my pilot."

There was something gentle about the way she said it, like this was just logistics, just timing. But I knew better. She wasn't rearranging her plans for convenience. She was getting on that airplane for me.

"You don't have to, Mom."

"I know."

The next day, I arrived at the airport an hour earlier than necessary to see my mom before the flight. Her flight had landed from Chicago, and here at Dulles she'd connect on my flight. I was at my departure gate when she walked up to meet me. She looked like any other passenger, with a small carry-on in hand, and boarding pass tucked neatly into her purse. She was dressed in black slacks and loafers, a white blouse, a black cardigan—simple, composed, like she was attending something important. I smiled proudly at her, feeling pretty important in my uniform.

She pulled me into a strong, steady hug, then stepped back and looked at me. "You ready?"

"I am." And I was. "The flight isn't full, so you should get a seat, Mom. I'm going on the plane. I'll see you when you board."

She squeezed my hand once, as if sealing the moment. "I'll be back there cheering you on."

When my mother stepped in the cabin, she stopped at the flight deck, and I introduced her to the captain. Then she smiled and said, "I'll be in seat 12A."

After all twenty passengers were on board, the flight attendant closed the cabin door and we pushed back, started the engines, and taxied to the runway. As we lined up on the centerline, something shifted inside me. Not fear. Not panic. Just the memory of another runway at an airport I had intentionally avoided for the last three years, not because I couldn't fly, but because I wasn't sure I was ready to return.

The nose wheel settled on the painted stripe. The runway stretched long and open ahead of us. And the steady hum of engines waiting for release.

"Blueridge 2630, cleared for takeoff."

I advanced the thrust levers. The airplane surged forward, gathering speed with quiet certainty. The runway markings blurred beneath us. The vibration through the pedals felt alive, grounding.

"Rotate," the captain said.

I smoothly pulled back on the yoke and lifted the nose. As we climbed into the clear blue sky, with only a few scattered clouds above us, I felt my breathing settle into an easy rhythm. It felt good to be up there again, steady and present, but as we began our descent into Newark, something flickered in me. It was a familiar tightening, the kind you feel when you think you've healed from a heartbreak, then months later come face-to-face with the person who broke your heart. But I stayed focused and flew the approach with a steady hand, calling out the checklist items with clarity. When the wheels touched the runway, the landing was smooth.

After we parked at the gate and the passengers began to deplane, my mom stepped into the flight deck. Captain Edwards said, "I'm going inside to get the flight plan for our next leg." He waved her into his seat, then got off the plane with the passengers. She lowered herself into the seat carefully, almost reverently, and for a moment, she didn't speak. She just looked. Her eyes moved slowly across the instrument panel at the rows of gauges, the switches, the thrust levers, and then out through the wide windshield to the ramp below. She reached out and lightly touched one of the knobs, as if confirming it was real.

Watching her there, I thought about some of what she and my dad had done to get me here. The model rockets with my dad. The weeks at Space Camp. The decision to sell her beloved home so I could attend a high school with an aviation program. The cross-country drives chasing flight hours. The tuition payments. The quiet reassurances when the path felt uncertain. My mother and father had supported my dream before there was any evidence it would amount to anything.

She leaned back in the seat and took a slow breath, looking out at the sky through my windshield. "That was a great flight," she said softly. "The takeoff felt like we were in a rocket, like the ones you and your dad launched." She laughed and touched her heart. "And the landing was so smooth. You did a wonderful job." Then she shook her head, almost in disbelief. "I'm so proud of you."

I smiled, and what I felt was deeper than pride. Sitting there, surrounded by the instruments that once felt impossibly complex, I realized this wasn't just my seat. It was the outcome of every sacrifice she'd made without asking for recognition. And now she was seeing it all for herself. In that moment, I felt both like her daughter and the woman she'd raised me to be.

"I just love all this for you, Nia. And I'm so excited that your son gets to see what strength looks like." She touched my arm. "Keep living your purpose, and he'll find his." Then she got up and said, "I'd better get off this plane before they start boarding your next flight." We leaned into each other for a loving squeeze, then she stepped off the plane and walked up the jet bridge.

I looked out the flight deck window and marveled at how strange the Manhattan skyline looked without the Twin Towers standing tall and mighty. I said a silent prayer for all the innocent people who died that day and for those who made it out of the towers but would never be the same again. And for all the first responders and the search and rescue teams and all the health care workers. I thought about the legacy my mother had poured into me, starting with that newspaper clipping of Bessie Coleman. I thought about the little boy at home who would one day learn how his mother kept going when life got hard. And I thought about the words my mother had just left me with. "Keep living your purpose and he'll find his."

As it turned out, my becoming a pilot had been so much more than a girl's fanciful dream. It was more than a pursuit or goal or passion. Like a pianist born to play or a track star born to run, I was born to fly. All those years ago, I'd realized it and had gone after it with head-down focus. From the time I was ten years old, I was as sure of it as I was of my parents' love. But on 9/11, that certainty was so jolted it was no longer clear to me if "pilot" was who I was intended to be or simply someone I'd once been, someone who'd flown with a light heart because she'd never been through the kind of trauma that could dim or even extinguish that light. Up until the autumn of 2001, my commitment and resolve hadn't been tested. But now I was a pilot who'd been knocked around and had her faith upended, but also one who'd worked her way back into a seat that fit her like a tailored suit.

We weren't on the ground long before our new passengers boarded. Once the cabin door closed and the ramp agent signaled us to push, I settled back into my seat. We taxied to the runway and waited for our departure clearance. Then came a voice from Newark Tower. "Blueridge 2504, cleared for takeoff."

As we rolled down the runway, I thought about the last time I'd felt this sensation beneath my feet at Newark. The rumble of acceleration. The forward pull. On that day, the sky had been fractured—smoke billowing from the towers, the air thick with disbelief and fear. How peaceful this flight felt by comparison. The same physical rhythm—the roll, the speed, the lift—but none of the chaos. Just a clear horizon and an undisturbed sky. We took off, and the DoJet rose the way it always had.

I could see how far I'd come. The woman who'd once rumbled down a runway unsure of what the sky would demand of her had returned with steady hands and a deep trust in herself. As the ground fell away beneath us, I understood this wasn't a return to who I'd been before. It was something fuller. I'd come full circle, carrying the past with me but no longer letting it set the course. All around, the air was calm, and above, the sky was a clear, brilliant blue. It was a beautiful day to fly.

EPILOGUE

It's been twenty-five years since I sat on the runway at Newark Airport and watched a terrorist crash United Airlines Flight 175, a Boeing 767, into the South Tower of the World Trade Center.

In the years that followed, I trained on and earned my type rating on that very aircraft, and ten years after 9/11, I pushed the thrust levers forward and flew a 767 full of passengers to Hawaii as a United Airlines pilot. The 767 used in the attacks had been a kind of innocent victim in the whole horror show, but it bore the stain of that day. As I sat in the right seat of a 767 years later, I understood the duality of such things, how something painful and dark must be overcome as we pick up the pieces left intact and reclaim our rights to what was ours, what we won't allow to be taken from us. Now, every time I take off in a jet, it's like a quiet act of reclamation. Every landing, proof that evil didn't get the final word.

In 2005, I left Atlantic Coast Airlines and joined United Airlines, formerly Continental. Over time, I earned type ratings in the Boeing 737, 757, 767, 777, and 787, and in the Airbus A320. I've flown long domestic routes. I've flown across oceans. I became a captain. The girl who once stared up at contrails became the one leaving them in her path.

When my son was three years old, I watched a spark ignite a flame, just like the one I'd experienced decades earlier. He fell in love with the idea of flying. His favorite toys were planes. He filled pages, and occasionally bedroom walls, with drawings of airplane wings and windows and contrails. When an airplane passed overhead, he'd stop mid-sentence, point skyward, and shout, "Plane!" And sometimes, "Mommy!" Maybe it started with his seeing me walk through the door in uniform. Or maybe it had always been in his blood. But it was unmistakable. He wasn't just watching airplanes, he was studying them. At four years old, he began launching model rockets with my dad, and I often stood nearby, clapping as their creations shot into the sky. Sometimes I'd glance at my father and he'd glance back and flash the same knowing smile I'd seen decades earlier when I launched rockets with him.

In 2010, I welcomed my daughter, Stayce, into the world—named for the first Black female pilot I ever met. I wanted my daughter's name to honor Stayce Harris's legacy. To carry strength. To carry possibility. Stayce hasn't been bitten by the flying bug, and that's fine. Her runway will lead to different destinations. Although still a teenager, she already understands independence but doesn't wear it as armor. Her strength isn't performative; she doesn't seem to need to prove her worth. She simply knows who she is.

After eighteen years of marriage, my husband and I divorced, and through it all, we've been clear that our children remain our priority. The structure of our family changed. The foundation did not. When I make decisions for my children, I often lean on the examples set by Alma and John Gilliam. They raised Kamilah and me with structure, accountability, and unwavering love, always love.

For my son, toy airplanes gave way to flight training and eventually a pilot's license. Today, although we fly for different airlines, I share the sky with John, an airline pilot at twenty-four. It brings me quiet joy to know he's found work that feels like a calling. And I trust my daughter will find hers in her own time.

In 2016, my passion expanded into deeper purpose after I made a connection that changed my life, much as meeting Stayce Harris had. I received a message from UPS pilot Angel Jean-Charles, then flying for the Coast Guard. She wrote that she'd never seen a Black woman flying wide-body international aircraft and that discovering me had turned her into a "fangirl." Her words hit me hard. Seeing someone who looks like you in a space you aspire to occupy can shift what feels possible. Her energy was infectious, and her sheer delight over connecting with me took me right back to the day I'd gushed over Stayce. And once again, I was struck by how momentous it can be for someone to find inspiration and even possibility and hope in the form of another. Seeing me, a Black woman, piloting enormous jets on international flights, told Angel that she, too, could reach for that goal. Representation isn't simply symbolic; it can be transformative.

As I read and reread Angel's message, I confronted a truth I'd long known: Black women were still unlikely to see themselves represented in professional flight decks. And I realized I no longer wanted to sit back and hope for more representation for people like Angel, so I turned purpose into action when that year, alongside Angel Jean-Charles, I co-founded Sisters of the Skies, an organization built to create access, provide mentorship, and fund flight training for women who might otherwise never reach the runway. Then, at the end of 2017, I approached Ret. United Airlines Captain Theresa Claiborne, the first Black woman in the Air Force, to help establish Sisters of the Skies as a 501(c)(3). Captain Claiborne's involvement added depth and credibility to our efforts, and in many ways, her presence affirmed that the work extended beyond any one founder; it was a collective commitment to widening the runway. Thanks to Sisters of the Skies, scholarships are awarded, mentorship circles are formed, doors are opened.

What I've learned in the past twenty-five years is that purpose doesn't necessarily appear like a beacon or savior. Sometimes it waits quietly until dust settles. After witnessing terrorism on September 11, I nearly walked away from aviation. And when I returned to my beloved career with an open heart, that felt like victory. What I didn't know at the time was that staying with it would lead me to ways to honor pioneers like Bessie Coleman, Janet Harmon Bragg, and Stayce Harris. And had I quit, Sisters of the Skies wouldn't exist to open doors for countless pilots to come.

I now fully understand the difference between dreaming and doing, between imagining and achieving. A pilot must be cleared before departure. She waits for timing, coordination, and readiness. Aviation is bound by protocols, procedures, and very important rules to ensure flights will take off, fly, and land safely. But the dreamer has no such guard rails. For the dreamer of any age, there are no boundaries to what might be. If her dreams are fueled by passion and purpose, they can become lifelong realities. She needs no approval to begin, no permission to believe she belongs. The dream, the path, the milestones—they're hers alone to pursue. She must consider herself, at all times, cleared for takeoff.

ACKNOWLEDGMENTS

This book, like my life, has been guided by a higher power. I acknowledge God, for the grace, protection, and countless lessons that have shaped my journey. Every chapter of my life has unfolded with purpose, and for that, I give thanks.

To Tamira Chapman, Porscha Burke, Jennifer Baker, and the team at Storehouse Voices: It is an honor to be published by you. Thank you for recognizing the importance of this story and for making it possible for me to share it with the world. I am deeply grateful for your faith in me as a debut author.

To my writing coach, Brooke Warner: Thank you for your belief, your advocacy, and the meaningful work you do to help aspiring authors bring their books into the world. Your support and guidance made this journey possible.

To Regina Brooks, my dream agent: I'm deeply grateful that what once felt aspirational became reality. Thank you for believing in this story and in me and for making it so clear you're always in my corner.

To my collaborator, Jodi Fodor: You have been a steady light throughout this process, and I could not have completed this journey without you. Thank you for the laughter when the work felt heavy, for your expertise, and your patience. Your being so good at what you do made the process that much smoother for me. I'm grateful the book is finished and even more grateful to have gained a friend.

To my parents: Thank you for showing me what unwavering support and genuine sacrifice look like. Your acts of service, both seen and unseen, created the foundation that allowed me to dream boldly and move forward with confidence. Because of you, I learned what love in action looks like, and that lesson continues to guide everything I do.

To my sister: Thank you for your patience, your grace, and your quiet strength. I know that sharing a childhood with someone whose path required so much attention wasn't always easy. I recognize the sacrifice you made, often without acknowledgment, and I will never forget it.

To my son and daughter: It is truly an honor to be the vessel through which you came into this world. Thank you for giving me a purpose beyond flying. And thank you for enduring the many days I was away, then offering patience and grace when I returned home depleted.

To Ken Rapier: Thank you for taking me under your wings and believing in me, guiding me, encouraging me, and supporting me. You are the best AvDad a pilot could have.

To Nicole "Nikki" Hayes: Thank you for your forty years of friendship, support, and encouragement, and for being my first partner in this writing journey.

To Carole Smith: Thank you for inspiring me and encouraging me to return to writing and to the story I was meant to tell.

To Glenn Turner: Thank you for coming into my life just when

I needed a wing woman to help me navigate the ups and downs of this writing journey. Your emotional support, words of affirmation, and nonstop laughter got me through to the end.

To the Organization of Black Aerospace Professionals (OBAP): You were established the same year I was born, and our growth has, in many ways, run in parallel. I'm grateful for your presence in my life and within this industry. The support you gave me wasn't only financial, but foundational. Through OBAP, I gained mentors and a community that expanded what I believed was possible and challenged me to rise higher. You modeled the responsibility of reaching back and creating lasting pathways for others.

To my aviation community and mentors: Thank you for your guidance in moments both large and small. You may never fully know the weight your words, your time, and your example have carried. I'm grateful for the role each of you played in shaping my journey.

To Sisters of the Skies (SOS): Bringing you into existence has been one of the most meaningful experiences of my life. As a co-founder, I carry both pride and responsibility for what we've built. I'm grateful for the opportunity to give back and to help create the space I once needed.

ABOUT THE AUTHOR

CAPTAIN NIA GILLIAM is an accomplished airline pilot with over twenty-five years of experience. A trailblazer in aviation, she co-founded Sisters of the Skies, a nonprofit dedicated to increasing the number of Black female pilots. Her contributions have earned her numerous prestigious awards and media recognition. And her story has captured the attention of major media such as CBS News, the *Essence* Disruptors Series, and *Marie Claire*. A Chicago native now living in Houston, she is a breast cancer survivor, champion for representation in aviation, and proud mother of two.

ABOUT STOREHOUSE VOICES

STOREHOUSE VOICES celebrates culturally rich narratives that reflect the dynamic influence of communities across the globe. Our imprint is dedicated to amplifying underrepresented and overworthy voices in fiction and nonfiction, with a focus on accessible and engaging content that honors the past, disrupts the present, and imagines new futures.

LEARN MORE ABOUT US AT STOREHOUSEVOICES.COM.